HOUSE OF ABRAHAM

House *of* Abraham

LINCOLN AND THE TODDS,
A FAMILY
DIVIDED BY WAR

Stephen Berry

HOUGHTON MIFFLIN COMPANY
BOSTON · NEW YORK
2007

For information about permission to reproduce selections
from this book, write to Permissions, Houghton Mifflin Company,
215 Park Avenue South, New York, New York 10003.

www.houghtonmifflinbooks.com

Library of Congress Cataloging-in-Publication Data
Berry, Stephen William.
House of Abraham / Stephen Berry.
p. cm.
Includes bibliographical references and index.
ISBN-13: 978-0-618-42005-6
ISBN-10: 0-618-42005-3
1. Lincoln, Mary Todd, 1818–1882 — Family. 2. Lincoln,
Abraham, 1809–1865 — Family. 3. United States — History —
Civil War, 1861–1865 — Biography. 4. Todd family. I. Title.
E457.25.B47 2007
973.7092'2 — dc22
[B]   2007013992

Book design by Melissa Lotfy

PRINTED IN THE UNITED STATES OF AMERICA

QUM 10 9 8 7 6 5 4 3 2 1

Photo credits appear on page 256.

Contents

The Todd Family

ROBERT SMITH TODD (1791–1849) married ELIZA PARKER in 1812. They had six children:

ELIZABETH PORTER TODD (1813–1888) married Ninian Wirt Edwards in 1832 and moved with him from Lexington, Kentucky, to Springfield, Illinois. A "second mother" to her younger sisters, she invited Frances, Mary, and then Ann to stay with her — all of whom married Springfield men. Elizabeth attended Lincoln's inaugural, returned to Washington in 1862 to console Mary on the loss of her son, helped Mary during her confinement for insanity, and cared for her during her final days.

FRANCES JANE TODD (1815–1899) moved to Springfield shortly after the Edwards's arrival. She married William Smith Wallace, a local doctor who owned the drugstore below Lincoln's law office. The Lincolns' third son, Willie, was named for him, and Lincoln appointed Wallace a paymaster in the Union army, saying "he is needy . . . and I personally owe him much."

LEVI OWEN TODD (1817–1864) began in business with his father, but floundered after the older man died. In 1859 his wife, Louisa Ann Searles, divorced him for cruelty. Though a Union man, he did not serve in the Civil War, and died in 1864 of "utter want and destitution."

MARY ANN TODD (1818–1882) moved permanently to Springfield shortly after the Wallaces were married. She and Abraham Lincoln met, became engaged, and became spectacularly disengaged in the winter of 1840–41. A strange reconciliation followed, and they were hurriedly married in 1842. The Lincolns had four sons: Robert, Eddie, Willie, and Tad. Only Robert survived to adulthood.

ANN MARIE TODD (1824–1891) was the fourth Todd sister to make the move from Lexington to Springfield. She married Clark Moulton Smith, a leading Springfield merchant, in 1846. She was a gifted seamstress but also "the most quick tempered and vituperative . . . of all the Todd sisters."

GEORGE ROGERS CLARK TODD (1825–1902?) was just a day old when his mother died of childbed fever. He graduated from medical school in 1850 and became a gifted surgeon. Like his brother Levi, he had an irascible temper and a heavy thirst. And like his brother, his first wife (Ann Curry) divorced him for cruelty. He served as a surgeon in the Confederate army and after the war was charged with the abuse of federal prisoners.

ROBERT SMITH TODD next married ELIZABETH "BETSEY" HUMPHREYS. They had eight children:

MARGARET TODD (1828–1904) married Charles Henry Kellogg, a Cincinnati merchant, in 1847. Both attended Lincoln's inaugural, but both had strong ties to the Confederacy, and Charles committed actual treason.

SAMUEL BROWN TODD (1830–1862) attended Centre College and then moved to New Orleans after his father's death. There he married Clelie Cecile Royer and clerked for her father, a French gardener. Sam served as a private in the Confederate army and was killed at the battle of Shiloh in 1862.

DAVID HUMPHREYS TODD (1832–1871) ran away from home at fourteen to fight in the Mexican War. He participated in the California gold rush in 1850 and in a Chilean revolution in 1851. In July 1861 he was in charge of the Richmond prisons, but was relieved of duty amid allegations of prisoner abuse. He commanded an artillery company with distinction during the siege of Vicksburg.

MARTHA K. TODD (1833–1868) married Clement White in 1852 and moved with him to Selma, Alabama. She attended Jefferson Davis's inauguration in 1861. In 1864 she was (erroneously) exposed as a smuggler and a spy, much to the embarrassment of the Lincoln administration.

EMILIE PARET TODD (1836–1930), called "Little Sister" by the Lincolns, spent six months living with them and the Edwardses in 1855. The next year she married a Kentuckian, Benjamin Hardin Helm, who rose to the rank of brigadier general in the Confederate army before he was killed at Chickamauga. Despite being a Confederate widow, Emilie stayed at the White House for a week in December 1863.

ALEXANDER HUMPHREYS TODD (1839–1862) was the youngest of the Todd boys and the one all the sisters united to coddle. While serving as Helm's aide-de-camp, he was killed in a friendly-fire incident outside Baton Rouge. Although Mary Lincoln claimed not to care about her Confederate brothers, she admitted that Aleck's ghost occasionally comforted her at night.

ELODIE BRECK TODD (1840–1877) was on a visit from Kentucky when she met her future husband, Nathaniel Henry Rhodes Dawson, at Jefferson Davis's inauguration. Stranded in Selma, she was cut off from her home and her mother, and though she supported her husband and the Confederacy, she would not allow the Lincolns to be abused in her presence.

CATHERINE "KITTY" BODLEY TODD (1841–1875) visited Springfield after Lincoln's election and became infatuated with his friend Elmer Ellsworth, a dashing Union captain. As the war progressed, however, she became more staunchly Confederate and ultimately married William Wallace Herr, the man who had helped carry Hardin Helm's body from the field at Chickamauga.

Introduction

The division of "house against house" foretold by
our Lord was never more complete and utter.

— UNION ARMY RECRUITER, 1861

B Y SEPTEMBER 1861, the Todd family, once "united and happy,"
was a wreck. Like the nation itself, they had come apart at the
seams, leaving sister Elodie to marvel at the political world's de-
structive power. "Sometimes it seems hard to realize all that has trans-
pired in the last five months," she noted. "It appears more like a painful
dream." Elodie was a member of the Kentucky Todds. Her sister was
Mary Todd Lincoln. Two of their brothers had joined the Confederate army. Elodie had made her choice when she had rashly become
engaged to a Confederate captain she barely knew. Now, with Kentucky standing by the Union, she was trapped in the Deep South, cut
off from her home and her mother. Her sister Mary seemed inclined
to cut her off entirely. Stretched between the federal White House and
the Confederate trenches, the Todds were a national catastrophe, and
Elodie worried that worse was yet to come. "Surely there is no other
family in the land placed in the exact situation of ours," she lamented,
"and I hope [there] will never be [another] so unfortunate as to be
surrounded by trials so numerous."

Of the fourteen children born to Robert Smith Todd, six sided with
the Union and eight sided with the Confederacy. Four of them were either casualties of the Civil War or had husbands who were, if we count
Lincoln in that number. And certainly Lincoln should be counted a
casualty of the war. Less obviously, but no less certainly, he should be
counted a Todd. His contact with his wife's family was far more sustained than his contact with his own. His entire adult life had been

awash in a sea of Todds. Not including his wife, he dated a Todd, loafed with Todds, confided in Todds politically and personally, benefited from Todds, and benefited Todds in turn. For all the important moments of his adult life — the births and deaths of his children, the successes and failures of his career — there was always a Todd around to slap his back or squeeze his hand. And it was a presence he counted on. From the house on Eighth and Jackson in Springfield, and later from the White House, the call to "Come" continually rang out from the Lincolns, and Todds came. Extending the survey to cousins, Todds introduced Lincoln to his wife and to the law; they plucked him from obscurity, marveled at his rise, and then followed his body to its deathbed and its grave. In short, the Todds were a critical part of the matrix in which Lincoln was formed.

He was not unappreciative. "In the scramble for jobs presidential relatives did well," reported the *New York World* in 1861. "In an unparalleled display of nepotism, [President Lincoln] has appointed his whole family to government posts." Mary Lincoln objected vehemently to such characterizations. These are "villainous aspersion[s]," she wrote of a later case. "Mr. L. has neither brother nor sister, aunt or uncle, and only a few third cousins, no nearer ones; that clears him entirely as to any connection." Technically, she was right. With no brothers or sisters, with a mother who had died early and a father with whom he was never close, Mr. L. was unusually alone in the world. But in pointing all this out, Mary had only cinched the *World*'s case. If the Todds weren't Lincoln's family, then who was?

And Lincoln was good to his family. Worried that the war would divide them, he had offered political and military positions to many of the Todd males, some of whom had rejected the offers and instead joined the Confederacy. Even then, he did not turn his back on them; over the course of the war he wrote multiple passes for various rebel Todds to come north, and on one occasion allowed Emilie Todd, the wife of a slain Confederate general, to stay in the White House, despite the ensuing scandal. The Todds became for Lincoln the emblematic family of the war: his attempt to keep them together paralleled his larger struggle to keep the national family together. From the Todds, he learned much of what he knew about family; through the Todds, he experienced many of the agonies of a family divided by war and shattered by grief.

In their grief, the Todds were not always as good to Lincoln. Even before the Civil War he was sued and slandered by Todds. Some of them disliked him because they thought he would never amount to anything, and then disliked him even more when he did. During the Civil War, things got progressively worse. Sometimes innocently, often on purpose, a few members of the Southern wing of the family waged psychological war on the White House and used their connection to assail and scandalize its occupants. For the entirety of his presidency, Lincoln had to live down one after another humiliation at Todd hands.

Taken as a clan, then, the Todds were not always very nice. They could be pampered and prideful. They could be quick-tempered and vain. They made grudges easily, and they held them long. They were often preoccupied with the surfaces of things and insensitive to the substance. Mary Lincoln once described her sister Ann as malicious, miserable, false, wrathful, and vindictive. Glancing over the list, Ann recognized the traits instantly: "Mary was writing about herself," she responded coolly. Sister Elodie was more self-aware, though no less critical. Above all, she warned her fiancé, "I am a *Todd*, and some of these days you may be unfortunate enough to find out what they are." Of course, with his gift for language, it was Lincoln himself who most pithily lampooned the pretensions of his wife's family. "One 'd' was good enough for God," he quipped, "but not for the Todds."

The Todds suffered for their sins, however. Before the war, as North drifted from South, the Todds drifted from one another. The older sisters moved one by one to Springfield. The younger brothers moved one by one to New Orleans. The rest of the siblings remained in a Kentucky that began its career as a western state and ended it as a Southern one. Thus, by the time Lincoln was elected, the Todds found themselves strung across the nation's great divide; their experience of the war would be an emotional mess. But it was a mess on a grand scale. The Todds were everywhere in the war. They were present at Lincoln's inaugural. They were present at Jefferson Davis's inaugural. They were present at most of the war's major engagements, from Bull Run and Shiloh to Gettysburg, Vicksburg, and more. And they paid the price for their participation. Brother Sam was shot through the gut and died at Shiloh. Brother Aleck was killed in a friendly fire incident outside Baton Rouge. Hardin Helm, Emilie Todd's husband, was shot off his horse and died at Chickamauga. Abraham Lincoln, Mary Todd's husband, was shot in the back of the head at Ford's Theatre. As a family, the Todds lived the war — in all its drama, division, confusion, exhaustion, and trauma — more completely than any other. Indeed, if one wanted to write the history of Civil War misery *on both sides* from the perspective of a single family, one could scarcely do better than the Todds, who belonged, after all, to the first family of the United States.

The Todds, then, were a miserable family in both senses of the word. They were occasionally hard to like. They were not merely divided by the Civil War but shattered by it, left broken down, hollowed out, and haunted by ghosts. But this is the war as it really was: damage heaped upon damaged people. And all this partly deserved, totally self-inflicted suffering was all but irredeemable, except perhaps by Lincoln. In this respect, the Todds' misery was critical. Though it achieved nothing lasting for themselves and only embarrassed the nation, it moved the nation's president. Despite and sometimes because of their disreputable conduct, the Todds helped to constitute Lincoln's understanding of family and, most important, his understanding of a family at war. In the trials of the Todds, Lincoln saw all the fractured families, and he took their collective grief and fashioned it into words that gave the war whatever redemptive meaning it has. When Lincoln delivered his second inaugural address, calling on Americans to "bind up the nation's wounds, to care for him who shall have borne the battle and for his widow and his orphan," he was talking, in part, about his own family. Two Todd brothers had been killed in the war; one Todd sister had lost her husband. There were two widows and seven orphans in the Todd family alone. In prescribing "malice toward none" and "charity for all," Lincoln was addressing a nation of Todds, united by blood and divided by bloodshed.

This book is not a complete biography of the Todds, nor could it be. The historical record, especially for the early years, is too thin. Besides, following fourteen "principal characters" — and their spouses, and their children — over the course of a lifetime would be unwieldy. Of necessity and by design, this book focuses on the fates and movements of the handful of Todds about whom the most is known and with whom Lincoln had the closest association. And of necessity and by design it focuses on the war years, when the Todds' tragedy played before a national audience.

Of the Northern wing of the family, particular attention is paid to two sisters: Elizabeth and Mary. Elizabeth was the eldest Todd and was like a mother to her younger sisters. It was she who first moved from Lexington, Kentucky, to Springfield, Illinois, and there established the seat of the Northern Todds. In the 1830s, Lincoln and Elizabeth's hus-

band, Ninian Edwards, were up-and-coming Whigs together. Their relationship soured, but Lincoln and Elizabeth remained close all their
lives.

The Southern wing of the family has never been studied. Most biographies of Mary mention the irony of her Confederate connections
but nothing more. Here particular attention is paid to two sisters, Emilie and Elodie, and one brother, David. Emilie was called "Little Sister" by the Lincolns. She was their favorite and remained so even after she married a fellow Kentuckian, Hardin Helm, who rose to the
level of brigadier general in the Confederate army. Elodie — "Dedee" to
the Lincolns — was not as dear to them. She married her Confederate
captain, Nathaniel Dawson, and managed to love the Lincolns personally even as she loathed them politically. Brother David was not close
to the Lincolns at all. During the war he often said that he wanted to
cut his brother-in-law's heart out. Together these Todds represent the
full range of Confederate relations with the Lincolns. They are given
the most attention, however, not because they are the most informa-
tive but because the most information has survived about them. Other
Todds will be introduced, sink, and resurface as the limits of the historical record, and of narrative, permit.

What emerges is a portrait not of a family but a nation. Perhaps
the Todds *weren't* always likable. Neither was America. But America
punished the Todds for being representative of itself. The siblings who
sided with the North were suspected of Confederate leanings. The
siblings who sided with the South were suspected of Union leanings.
It didn't matter how many of them fought or bled or died for their
respective sections; still they could not do enough to prove their patriotism. To their contemporaries, the Todds' division was not tragic
or heart-rending but pathetic and disturbing. The family embodied
something the nation wanted to forget — that the war wasn't "us vs.
them" but "us vs. us." And yet precisely because the Todds' experience
was so relevant, the nation could not avert its eyes. The family received
inordinate press coverage. They were the wound into which America
couldn't help sticking its finger. And so the Todds lived the war in a
fishbowl, as a constant source of speculation and scandal, even as their
numbers dwindled, even as brother after brother sacrificed his "last
full measure."

No family could have survived such a test. The war was an emotional amplifier. Whatever dynamics a family had going in only became more pronounced as the conflict dragged on. Thus fault lines be-

came rifts and rifts became chasms under the remorseless weight of suffering. By war's end, there was little familial feeling left between the two halves of the Todd family. Emilie Todd, the Southern sister closest to the Lincolns, was the last to pour hate into the spaces love had filled. In 1864, she wrote a blistering letter to Lincoln, blaming him for all her family's misery. Her husband and two brothers lay buried in hasty graves, some of them in places she had never heard of. At twenty-eight, she was threatened with becoming a brotherless, fatherless, husband-less mother of three. The man who had made her so, the commander in chief of the Union army, was her own brother-in-law and, perhaps most painfully, the only man left who could help her. What could she do with such grief except to lay it at his door? And when, shortly af-ter she wrote this letter, she learned that Lincoln himself had been as-sassinated, what could she do with those feelings but write to his son Robert to ask if he needed her to come comfort him?

The Civil War was a vast mosaic of such family crises. Across the country, husbands, brothers, and fathers left their homes to kill or be killed; wives, sisters, and daughters were left to tend to the dying, the newborn, and the fields. No family had ever experienced such disloca-tion; many would never be the same afterward. But the Civil War was a family crisis in a larger, more symbolic, sense too. In the nineteenth century, the language of politics was infused with familial meaning. Today, we rarely call George Washington the "father" of our country. Senators don't call each other "brothers" (and not merely because the brothers now have sisters). We don't talk about "fraternal feelings" or "sister states." We don't talk about our "national family." But once we did. In a still young country almost without history, these tropes grounded our nascent patriotism in the sturdier soil of family love. At every barbecue and picnic, ruddy politicians tight with whiskey and bloated with rhetoric reminded every man in earshot that he owed two great and reinforcing debts: one to his father for giving him a roof, an education, and a name and another to the Founding Fathers because he breathed free air in a world everywhere else ruled by tyrants and kings.

But by drawing familial meaning into civic life, such tropes made the Civil War all the more disturbing. A Union was breaking up. A House was dividing against itself. Siblings were seething with fratricidal rage. The familial metaphor no longer underlined national affection but national dysfunction. As Elijah Babbit warned his fellow Americans in 1860: "Feuds which exist between members of the same families, where they do exist, are the most bitter of all feuds. Wars [between] the same people . . . are the most bloody, the most savage, and the longest continued, of any wars that take place in this world." And so it was with the Civil War. Americans hated Americans with an intensity that can only come from the perversion of former affection. Capturing the prevailing mood, Mary Chesnut penned in her famous diary: "We are divorced, North from South, because we hated each other so."

As with many divorces, the separation was protracted and painful; as with many, hate, like love, proved too cramped a category to capture the feelings of people who had lived together so long. And this is what makes the Todds so emblematic. They lived all the untenable emotions of a nation at war with itself. They were our nation in miniature — a maddened family in a house divided, struggling vainly to hate its own blood.

1

Bluegrass Beginnings

D ANIEL BOONE CROUCHED uneasily over a set of footprints that meandered toward the horizon. These tracks are *too* easy to follow, he thought. There's too much debris along the trail, too many fresh blazings on the trees. These Indians aren't concealing their path; they're advertising it. They want to be followed.

The whole expedition was beginning to seem like a bad idea. The Indians had attacked Bryan's Station the day before, slaughtering livestock, torching cabins and crops. They had tried to take the fort, but, lacking siege equipment, they'd been turned away. They had seemed like a small raiding party. Colonel Todd's decision to go after them had seemed sensible. Now Boone wasn't so sure. Examining the tracks more closely, he saw that the Indians were walking in one another's footprints, disguising their numbers. The more he thought about it, the worse he felt about whatever lay ahead.

Boone couldn't have known how right his feeling was. He couldn't have known that in less than a day, his son would be gurgling up blood in one of the most lopsided Indian victories of the frontier wars. The Indians' feint against the fort at Bryan's Station had worked perfectly, just as Simon Girty had promised. An American adopted by the Shawnee and allied to the British, Girty had assembled an army of Indians from various tribes. He had inflamed their desire for revenge by calling for a massive slaughter of the "Long Knive[d]" white men who had "destroyed the cane, trodden down the clover, [and] killed the deer and the buffalo, the bear and the raccoon." But most important, he had given them a plan. They would send most of their force to lie in wait in the ravines around the Blue Lick. A smaller party would then lay siege to the fort near Bryan's Station, wreaking the proper amount of havoc, raising the appropriate level of alarm. But they would allow some of the settlers to escape to Lexington, Boonesborough, Harrodsburg, and other surrounding communities. The Kentucky militia would be mustered; it would pursue; and it would be slaughtered.

Boone didn't know this, of course. But when Colonel Todd called for a council on the south bank of the Licking River, he voiced his concerns. "Colonel, they intend to fight us," Boone announced, and he proceeded point by point through what he had seen. The blazings, the debris, the doubled prints—it all pointed to an ambush. Todd had been the most vocal proponent of a hurried pursuit. He had even urged the party forward when a suggestion was made to wait for reinforcements. But he knew enough to trust Boone. No one knew the area better than Boone.

Central Kentucky is a region of undulating limestone plateaus. The grass that flourishes there, while not exactly blue, sprouts purple buds in springtime and gives the open acreage a bluish tint. Boone had little regard for the purple buds. But the limestone bedrock of the region had another benefit: the waters that traveled through it picked up a high concentration of calciferous salts. At certain bends in certain rivers, animals would congregate in the thousands to slake their thirst and their appetite for salt. For hunters like Boone, such places were the equivalent of a modern deli, a smorgasbord, an exhibition of God's bounty. The Licking River had two such places, the Upper and Lower Blue Licks, and Boone knew them both intimately. He had hunted there, of course. But he had camped there for long periods as well. In the winter of 1778, Indians had so devastated the food supplies of surrounding Kentucky settlements that Boone had taken a detachment of thirty men to the Blue Licks to distill salt. In some ways, the salt at the lick was more precious than the game—without it communities couldn't cure enough meat to make it through the winter. Boone and his men had been boiling salt at the Blue Licks for a month when they were captured by the Shawnee. Boone had eventually escaped, but some of his men were not as lucky.

It was with understandable trepidation, then, that Boone approached the scene of his capture four years earlier. The Americans were at a terrible disadvantage on this terrain. Before they could even engage the Indian war party, they would need to cross the river bend at the Lower Blue Lick and scramble up and over a hill, all before they could see what waited for them in the ravines beyond. Boone considered himself as brave as any man walking, but he was no fool, and when Colonel Todd asked him his opinion, he gave it: the militia should wait.

Now it was Todd's turn to make a definitive judgment. He could listen to Boone and back down from his earlier decision to pursue the Indians, or he could further commit his militia to precipitate action. He hadn't grappled with the dilemma for long when Hugh McGary, the notoriously unstable leader of the Harrodsburg men, began whipping up sentiment for an immediate engagement. Plunging into the river, he wheeled his horse and, raising his rifle above his head, bellowed: "Them that ain't cowards follow me, and I'll show [you] where the yellow dogs are." The imputation of cowardice shot through the Kentuckians like a high voltage. First the Harrodsburg men, then the rest of the assembly began to follow McGary into the river.

Historians of the resulting battle of the Blue Licks have unanimously agreed that at this point there was nothing Todd could do. The Indians' trap was too clever. The Americans' blood was too hot. The Licking River had become Todd's Rubicon: he could only commit himself to the battle or be left behind to be consumed by his own cowardice. This assumption is untrue. Todd knew the volatility of McGary's character. He knew the depth of Boone's knowledge. His militiamen were undisciplined, but they understood the basic workings of military rank. McGary was an emotionally erratic major. Todd was a colonel and the ranking officer present. If he had asserted his authority and stood firm against McGary and his own earlier judgment, he might have forced his men to stand down. Instead, he too led his horse into the river and onto the hillside beyond.

With the Licking forded, the 182 men fell into three loose formations. Boone, with his son Israel, commanded the Boonesborough men on the left. Todd, with his brother Levi, commanded the Lexington men in the center. Stephen A. Trigg, with McGary, commanded the Lincoln and Harrodsburg men on the right. Some of the officers, including Todd and Trigg, remained mounted, but most of the men chose to leave their horses at the river. With guns loaded, the three columns started up the hill, preceded by an advance guard of twenty-five men — Boone, Trigg, McGary, and Todd among them. The men had crested the ridge and were all but on top of the ravines when the Indian war cry rang out on all sides.

The Indians' initial volley devastated the Kentucky force. Twenty-two of the twenty-five members of the advance guard fell almost instantly. Boone and McGary were two of the lucky ones. Trigg and Todd were not. Trigg was knocked from his horse and lay bleeding in the dust and confusion. Todd took a bullet in the chest, and though he remained upright, he seemed senseless, blood "gushing out before and behind him." Simon Girty's plan now began to unfold like a nightmare for the Kentuckians. Withering enfilade poured in from the ravines at the right while Indians rose out of the ravines at the front to grapple with the white men hand to hand. Armed with their rifles, the Kentuckians were ill prepared to fight at close quarters with tomahawks and knives. And none of them could get a good bead on the murderous rifle fire pouring into their flank from the ravine.

Only Boone's boys kept their wits. Positioned on the left, they hadn't been as exposed to the flanking fire, and they still had their commander. Rallying them, Boone plunged forward into the melee. When the Indians fell back, he was elated. His charge was working. Just at that moment, McGary rode up. "Why are you not retreating?" he asked Boone. "The Indians are all around you." Looking back, Boone realized with horror that the Indians had one final surprise. The force that had ambushed them from the ravines was only part of the war party. The rest was filling in behind the Kentuckians, taking control of their horses and blocking their retreat.

Any semblance of order now fell away. Trigg's and Todd's lines had already collapsed. Their men ran pell-mell and panic-stricken for the Licking, where they made easy marks. Some were picked off as they came down the slope. Others were stabbed or tomahawked as they crossed the river. Neither option appealed to Boone. If he and his men could make it to the woods at the left, he figured, they could find a crossing downriver from the massacre. Securing a riderless horse for his son Israel, he told the boy to go on ahead. Boone had turned to search for another mount when he heard a bullet find its soft mark behind him. Whirling, he was staggered to discover that his son had waited. Israel was on his back, writhing slowly in the dirt. His eyes were dim and his heart pumped blood in strong pulses from his mouth. Throwing Israel over his shoulder, Boone made it to the woods, but he could hear the footfall of three Indians in pursuit, all of them gaining. As well as he knew the terrain, he also knew he couldn't escape, not carrying so much weight. Boone let the boy go and sprinted for the river.

For the Indians, the battle of the Blue Licks was a sweet victory.

They lost only four men. They avenged a whole series of spring massacres in which white men had descended on their villages, slaughtering women and children. They beat back the encroachment of white settlers onto lands occupied by their forefathers' forefathers. And they did it all on a portentous and sacred site. The buffalo and the elk had congregated at the Blue Licks in numbers too high to count before the white men had decimated them. The Indians had avenged their losses too, and they fell to scalping the dying and the dead with a sense of justice long delayed.

For the Americans, the Blue Licks was a devastating defeat. They lost 40 percent of their force — more than sixty men. News of the bloodbath spread quickly throughout central Kentucky and prompted many families to abandon their homesteads and slink back over the mountains. When it was safe to return to the battlefield, settlers found the bodies of their loved ones scalped, blackened and bloated in the summer sun, and picked at by flies and fishes, pigs and panthers, wolves and vultures, and who knew what else. It was an irony no one appreciated: the smorgasbord at the Blue Licks now went the other way — white men were being served up at God's natural deli.

Recriminations followed directly upon grief. Boone blamed himself. He had led his son into an ambush and then abandoned the body afterward. Colonel Benjamin Logan, the officer who might have reinforced Todd, blamed another colonel, George Rogers Clark, for posting too many men to the west and leaving central Kentucky unprotected. Colonel Clark, in turn, blamed Colonel Todd. With a man like Todd leading them, Clark figured, reinforcements would only have added to the number of bodies bobbing in the shallow water of the Licking.

Such finger-pointing did not last long. It was bad for morale. Kentucky's settlers were shaken and grieving. Hearing that their militia was incompetent and conflicted didn't make them feel any more secure. Instead, in what amounted to a collective case of amnesia, everyone involved decided that it would be best to misremember the pitiable rout at the Blue Licks as a doomed but heroic stand. The dead men's families didn't want to know the truth. Few survivors wanted to tell it. And no American wanted to admit that Indians could so completely get the best of them. It was more comforting to think that Todd and his men had, by simple ill luck and the treachery of a white savage, walked into an ambush where despite overwhelming odds they had beaten back wave after wave of bloodthirsty red heathens.

Thus, by the good grace and willfully bad memories of his countrymen, John Todd was not ridiculed as a man who had marched into a massacre, gotten shot in the first volley, and been dragged off by his horse to be stripped and butchered and scalped beyond recognition. Instead, he was held up as an indefatigable Indian-fighter and frontier war hero. This worked to the primary benefit of his brother, Levi, who had survived the engagement at the Blue Licks and was thereby the rightful repository of his brother's legend. Kentucky's governor made Levi the clerk of the Fayette County Court, a position that proved lucrative and influential. Levi made money on every document, deed, and deposition, every mortgage and marriage license that was processed in the court; and he was in the thick of every land deal, public auction, and construction project in the county. By the time he died, the Todds were one of the wealthiest, most landed families in central Kentucky.

Ironically, then, John Todd's massacre at the Blue Licks was a great legacy to his family. With their one pathetic sacrifice, the Todds grew in stature and esteem. From a single act of folly descended a whole line of aristocrats. Unfortunately, the Todds descended in both senses of the term. After Levi's death, they settled into a languid but perpetual decline. The land got divided; the money got spent. Each generation seemed a little less prominent, a little less promising, than the one that had come before.

II.

BY THE TIME Robert Smith Todd was old enough to notice, his father, Levi, was positively corpulent. Even so, the boy knew from his bedtime stories that the fat man had once been an Indian-fighter, a patriot, and a pioneer. Indeed, as he understood it, his father had led the perfect male life. He had survived the heroic bloodbath at the Blue Licks. He had carved a vast estate out of Indian country. He had risen to prominence as one of the founding fathers of Lexington. In short, he epitomized all that an American man should be. With the best of a generation of giants, he had vanquished redcoats and savages and erected with his bare hands a civilization free from tyranny in the Edenic forests of the New World. His father had earned his comfort — and his corpulence — and Robert wanted to be just like him.

The Todd family now lived at Ellerslie, a twenty-room country manor house outside Lexington. The compound was named for a sixteenth-century Scottish village from which the Todds had supposedly hailed. Such pretensions were not unique to the Todd family. America was a proud new nation, and, then as now, proud new money sought comfort in tradition. The income that built, furnished, and compulsively expanded Ellerslie came from lawful but not always savory sources. Though he was a member of the bar, Levi found the practice of law disagreeable. Though he was a large slaveholder and landowner, he had little taste for farming. His capital came mostly from his position as county clerk and from land speculation. During and after the Revolution, the government often paid its servicemen in land rather than money because it had plenty of the former and precious little of the latter. In the financially volatile years of the early republic, Levi would buy up this land scrip from distressed veterans at deflated prices, eventually accumulating seven thousand acres. Such habits, coupled with his clerkship, made him the occasional object of resentment. In 1803 a group of debtors descended on Ellerslie and threatened to burn it down, partly to get at the land records and partly to get back at a system that promised freedom but delivered penury. No one was hurt in the incident, and for the Todds it was a perverse symbol of their success. A family isn't truly landed gentry until an enraged mob threatens to burn down its "ancestral" estate.

Like his father, Robert Todd studied law — and like his father, he didn't have much interest in practicing it. Admitted to the bar in 1811 at the age of twenty, he was more enthusiastic about the impending war with Britain. Once again redcoats were threatening American liberty, and Robert was thrilled to have the opportunity to rise and be counted. Most of Kentucky's young men felt the same way. Since 1776, an entire generation of sons had grown up in the occasionally cold shadow of their Founding Fathers. The War of 1812 gave this second generation of American patriots a chance to prove themselves worthy of the first. They would secure — and they would thereby deserve — their Revolutionary heritage.

Robert Todd had, if possible, a sorrier war record than his uncle John. After enlisting as a private, he barely made it across the Kentucky border before coming down with pneumonia and returning home. There he found something more diverting than law or army service — a rich young cousin named Eliza Parker. The Parkers were, like the Todds, one of the first families of Kentucky. A marriage between the clans had the sort of dynastic aptness that looks good on an invitation and assures attendees that the family stock is up and their emotional investments are secure. Eliza brought more than her social standing to the marriage, however. She was by all accounts attractive, with a happy talent for contentment. Some might have gone so far as to call her actually placid, but in that day and age, placidity was considered a good quality in a wife. What Eliza saw in Robert is unknown. He came from an elite family, certainly, and he was not unattractive himself: six feet tall, with practiced graces and large brown eyes that had just a little sadness in them. His hair was brown and thick where it wasn't thinning. His face was strong, though perhaps too ruddy and full in the jowls to be called handsome. Temperamentally, he was, like all the Todds, high-strung and thin-skinned. But Eliza was disposed to be sunny, and her fiancé's fits of temper or pique would have floated through her life like occasional summer storms. The couple was married on November 13, 1812, in the home of Eliza's mother, the formidable widow Parker. To keep her son-in-law on a short leash, the widow gave Robert a lot adjoining her own house on Short Street, where the couple built their new residence. Supposedly, Robert rejoined his regiment after the wedding, but there are no records to support the claim and the timing of his children's births suggests that he spent the war years close to home.

Robert and Eliza had six children who survived infancy: Elizabeth (1813), Frances (1815), Levi (1817), Mary (1818), Ann (1824), and George (1825). After George was born Eliza developed what was probably childbed fever. Physicians had noted a connection between delivering babies and developing fevers as far back as 1500 B.C. Aside from giving the condition a name, however — puerperal sepsis — they hadn't made much progress since. Some thought that birthing generated a miasma that sickened the mother. Others thought the rigors of delivery overwhelmed the female mind. Regardless, most doctors prescribed purgatives and bloodletting, which allowed their patients to puke and bleed while they died. Without antibiotics or painkillers, delivery in Eliza's day was like being shot from the inside out by a very large, awkwardly shaped, painfully slow-moving cannonball that left a woman with massive exit wounds in tissues peculiarly susceptible to infection. All too often, the source of infection was the doctors and midwives themselves. Not until 1843 did Oliver Wendell Holmes suggest that obstetricians wash their hands and their instruments, especially after autopsies, before using them to deliver babies. (Even then, Holmes's suggestion was greeted with skepticism: "Doctors are gentlemen," snorted a leading physician upon reading Holmes's paper, "and a gentleman's hands are clean.")

Regardless of the source of the infection, it was clear within hours of delivery that Eliza was in trouble. Robert rounded up all available doctors, including the leading authorities from the nearby medical school at Transylvania College. The physicians consulted and conferred. Most likely, Eliza was cupped, bled, and liberally dosed with emetics and laudanum. If so, she spent her last hours deliriously vomiting and then, at the age of thirty-one, joined the millions of women who had left the world the same way.

Eliza's children were spared such scenes. They had been sent across the street to their grandmother's at the first sign of trouble. There they sat on her porch and stared at their mother's drawn curtains. At ages eleven and ten, Elizabeth and Frances had some sense of what was going on. At eight and six, Levi and Mary had only that odd combination of unspecified dread and hyperspecific images: doctors pulling up in hurried gigs; slaves raising little dust devils as they ran to and from the drugstore; pained expressions on the faces of adults who until then had seemed to know everything. On July 6 the Todd children returned to their home, put on their best clothes, and sat as still as possible while the reverend prayed for their mother's soul. Then they followed her body to the churchyard and began their motherless lives.

Robert's wifeless life did not last long. Within weeks he began secretly courting Elizabeth "Betsey" Humphreys. The Humphreyses were a socially prominent Frankfort family. Two of Betsey's uncles were professors at Transylvania and two were United States senators — one from Kentucky and the other from Louisiana. As Robert figured it, an alliance with the Humphreyses would be, if anything, more advantageous than his alliance with the Parkers had been. But the timing of his suit was scandalous. Custom required that when a relatively young man lost a wife in childbirth, he should give his community time enough to pity his situation and eulogize the self-sacrificing mother who had gone so gracefully to God's Kingdom. By pursuing Betsey so early, Robert had breached a public trust.

He had breached a private trust too. His children needed him. They needed to know that he had loved their mother and loved them still. But he had laid his grief aside. He was already pursuing a second family. He had not even told them of his new romance. They learned of it secondhand — from a friend of firstborn Elizabeth's who lived in

Frankfort. They were left to whisper among themselves as he got on with his life. Their mother was dead; their father was cold comfort and keeping secrets.

The widow Parker was apparently livid. Her son-in-law, with whom she had had her occasional difficulties, was now committing the *most* grievous crime — insulting her dead daughter's memory. Though she might have been tempted, she could do nothing to poison the children's mind against him. As with most nineteenth-century fathers who drank reasonably, Robert was blindly respected by his children. They loved him the way they loved their last name; they were *of* him, and to think less of him was simply to think less of themselves. But while the widow Parker could not disparage Robert's conduct, she could disparage his choice of wife. She could poison the children against any woman who might seek to replace her daughter in their hearts. Thus, even before Betsey had joined the family, a fault line was forming that would trouble the Todds the rest of their lives.

In spite of the domestic turmoil, or maybe because of it, Robert pressed his suit discreetly but firmly. He faced a paradoxical problem. Without a wife, he was dependent on his sisters and the widow Parker to take care of the children. But in trying to get a wife, he had alienated them all. Now his house was full of disapproving women and moping children, which made it impossible to travel and difficult to concentrate on business. What he needed was to win Betsey's hand as soon as possible. Then the disapproving women would leave and he could return to his routine. During the Christmas holidays, five months after his wife's death, he proposed.

Betsey was in an unenviable position. At twenty-six, she was in danger of becoming a spinster. The man who offered to save her from such a label was a widower with six children who lived a stone's throw from his dead wife's notoriously difficult mother. Even if she could overlook that, there was the tackiness of his timing. Already people were beginning to talk, and while Robert could afford to be cavalier about gossip, Betsey knew a woman's reputation was more fragile. Thus, when Robert proposed, she said yes — and then bustled off to New Orleans without saying when she intended to return. If he would not respect his wife's memory, she would. If he would not wait the appropriate amount of time, she would make him.

Robert wrote her faithfully, but even by Victorian standards, his "love" letters were stilted and staid: "To have the promise of your hand

and to possess your affections is to me so highly desirable that I cannot for a moment doubt that as I have been assured that I possess the latter I shall also in due time possess the former." Betsey must have read that sentence several times before she could parse its meaning. And she probably spent even more time on sentences like this: "My ideas of the felicity and duties of a matrimonial relation may perhaps be of a sublimated character, but if so, I would imagine would not the less enable me to enjoy or dispense them or to discharge those duties incident to that relation." All of Robert's letters have this strange and obfuscating legal cadence. Perhaps not knowing any better he had used a business letter as his model for romantic correspondence. Or perhaps he was subconsciously signaling to Betsey that they were negotiating a contract, not making a love match.

Regardless, one emotion emerges with abundant clarity from Robert's correspondence — desperation. "I must beg leave to remind you of the promise made in your last letter to name a short day for our marriage," he pleaded in one missive. "I am sure if you knew my situation, you would not hesitate to comply with my wishes in fixing on a day for our [wedding] in this or the early part of the ensuing week," he hectored in another. "I am anxious for that period to arrive when I can in the face of heaven and the world with pride & pleasure call you mine irrevocable," he entreated ominously in a third. In the face of such pestering, Betsey grew even more distant. His tortured prose and peevish prodding, his "sublimated" affection and six children, were hardly calculated to win a girl's heart. At the same time, she was tired of thinking of new ways to put him off. Occasionally it seemed easier not to write at all, but that only made things worse. "I think I have some little cause to complain [of] your *total silence*," Robert grumbled on one occasion. "I fully expected to have heard from you during the last week," he lectured on another. Ultimately, Betsey acquiesced. But by the time she did, Eliza had been in the ground a respectable year and a half. Whatever else she might face as Mrs. Todd, Betsey would not suffer the stigma of impropriety. Though she might yet lose the campaign, she had won the first skirmish of her marriage.

Betsey gave birth nine times in the next fifteen years. Her first child, a boy named Robert, lived only a few days. He marked the second (and last) time Robert Todd would attempt to pass on his name. After that, in rough two-year increments, baby piled upon baby: Margaret, born 1828, was followed by Samuel (1830), David (1832), Martha (1833),

Emilie (1836), Alexander (1839), Elodie (1840), and Catherine (1841). After that, Betsey slipped mercifully into menopause. The number of Todd children would be frozen at fourteen: six from the first marriage and eight from the second.

III.

THE DYNAMICS of large families are different from those of small ones. The webs of affection and intrigue are more complicated. The parents are more splintered and exhausted. Full of crying babies and slamming doors, stomping feet and petty disputes, their home is a bedlam of colliding minidramas. There is always an infant to be changed, rocked to sleep, or buried; there is always a child to be scolded, congratulated, or married. Everyone is always getting ready — for school, for church, for bed — and rarely at rest. Peace is fleeting; privacy is nonexistent; emotional turbulence is constant. Their house is not a home but a hive.

This was certainly true for the Todds. Mary said it was like living in a boarding house. She and her siblings, she implied, were but guests in a common building, always on their way out, preoccupied by their own lives, own friends, own destinies. But she made this uncharitable assessment later in life, while bitter and looking back. In truth, the Todds were like any big family. They loved and hated one another at the same time. They hugged or they throttled one another, depending on the emotional needs of the moment. They were, remembered one observer, "a large family of boys and girls who jested much and seized on the slightest pretext to tease each other unmercifully." In the Todd family, there was no quarter given or sought. No one cried "uncle." They all gave as good as they got, and if they didn't, they licked their wounds and plotted their revenge. Sharp tongues and quick tempers were not resented; they were required. Volatility and lashing wits were part of a common bond. Thus, whatever they might later say, the Todds were, always and inevitably, a family. They shared a common parent, common experiences, common memories. They knew the same people, went to the same schools, told the same stories. And, most important, they formed genuine attachments, as children always do with the playmates of their youth. However they ended it, the Todds did not begin their lives as a bitter or a divided family. They were simply a big one, teeming and tempestuous.

In day-to-day control of the tempest was Mammy Sally, the Todds' slave nurse. Certainly, she was the most constant presence in the children's early lives. With most patriarchs of the period, Robert Todd believed child rearing, like childbearing, was natural only to women. What he wanted from his progeny was pleasant episodic contact. They should be presentable in public, peaceable in private, and a delightfully rare diversion from civic affairs. Betsey too was a distracted parent. She had inherited six children — and one cantankerous "mother-in-law" — from her predecessor, and she was for all her fertile life beset by babies, at her breast or in her belly. Three years and two pregnancies into her marriage, she was already looking "very thin & badly," according to a cousin. Eleven years and seven babies later, she was simply a husk. No one knew exactly when, but at some point the children had o'erstormed her mental ramparts. Betsey had withdrawn irritably into a shadow-world of vague maladies her family referred to simply as her "frailty." Whether physiological or psychological in origin, her partial retreat left her little engaged in the moral development of her children, even the ones who were fully hers.

By default, then, Mammy Sally was the children's day-to-day "authority" figure. They collectively remembered, "Sally was a jewel of a black mammy. She alternately spoiled and scolded [us] ... but [we] loved her and never rebelled against her." Undoubtedly they did love her, and she probably loved them back. But the idea that they never crossed her is ridiculous. Stories abound of the Todd children testing Sally's patience. Indeed, she seems to have been the butt of every joke they didn't play on one another. Tellingly, the children's claim that they "never rebelled" was made after the Civil War, when many Southern families were writing happy fictions about the softer side of slavery. The Todd children knew that Mammy Sally was a slave. This may not have affected their love for her, but it certainly affected their obedience to her. They were numerous and white. She was singular and black — and she was the only thing standing in their way. Of course they rebelled — and not occasionally but daily.

Needing help to control her many charges, Sally borrowed the notion from African tradition that the jaybird was the devil's snitch. The jay, she told her wide-eyed wards, took note of all their misbehaviors. When Mary hid Mammy's slippers, Jay was watching. When Ann protested the curling of her hair, Jay made a note of it. Then down to Satan each week went the jaybird with all the black marks to be made against the Todd children in the devil's dark book. Failing with such stories to scare the children into obedience, Sally appealed to an even higher power, promising a misery everlasting to those who tried her patience. "[Sally] preach[ed] the gospel to us with impassioned oratory and great dramatic effect," one of the girls remembered, "and our youthful escapades called down upon our devoted heads such dire punishments in the future that we shivered with half-believing fear and stopped our ears with our fingers." But Sally had no authority of her own. She had only what she could borrow from God or the devil, and by their own admission the children only half believed her. "Mammy," Mary once asked. "Do you think you could have dreamed about the old bad man [the devil]? I am sure I saw you nod [off] in church." Such teasing would have been "merciless" with the Todds, and Mammy was not exempt. She was a comedic figure in the family, not an authority figure. The children laughed with and sometimes at her more than they obeyed her. Certainly they loved their Mammy Sally — they loved the role she played, but it's harder to know whether they loved Sally herself.

This combination of an absent father, a frail mother, an enslaved nurse, and a large family meant that the Todd children grew up just a little wild. They never fully learned a child's most important lesson: self-restraint. The authorities in their lives were all too remote: Father was someone to aspire to; Mother was someone to appeal to; Sally was someone to laugh at. But it fell to their wider society to teach them what proper men and women should do and be.

IV.

THE TOWN of Lexington is nestled in a soft and undulating valley. The land around it rises and falls like a gentle green ocean frozen in time. While the Todds lived there, the town's pretenses were at their zenith. Lexington was the self-declared "Athens of the West," an "oasis of civilization" west of the Mississippi. Like many preposterous claims, this one had some basis in fact. The town itself was gorgeous. The roads were wide and well kept; the sidewalks were accommodating; the brick homes that lined them were ample and well appointed. The appearance of sophistication, which is in some measure sophistication itself, was nurtured at every turn. The town had the requisite number of churches (three) and newspapers (three) to show that it supported a diversity of views without encouraging eccentrics or extremists. There was a theater and a waxwork museum. There was a candy shop and a public library. While most of the West was listening to campfire songs, tom-toms, or crickets, Lexingtonians gathered by the hundreds to listen to Beethoven and Mozart. On July 14, 1819, an Italian harpist gave a concert in Lexington. For the first time west of the Alleghenies, the sweet strains of the angels' instrument wafted out over the frozenocean of green. Some intimation of the town's refinement may be gleaned from its renown for its hats. Any town that makes a living at something so fashionable and yet so expendable as haberdashery must be civilized — and must be doing all right for itself.

The town had substance as well as sophistication. The local college, Transylvania, had a law school and a prestigious medical school. The sons of governors, senators, and congressmen were among its students. Then too Lexington was the seat of western Whiggery, being the home of Henry Clay, a three-time presidential candidate (if a three-time loser). Clay was a great favorite with the Todds. He was often a guest in their home. Robert campaigned for him, threw receptions for him, and never stopped believing that he would one day be president. Clay's vision for the West was different from that of his main Democratic rival, Andrew Jackson. Jackson spoke for the common man, the rifle-happy dirt farmers who dreamed of fat women, fat vegetables, and taking potshots at the census man. Clay spoke for the common man on the make, the progress-happy hat merchants who gushed over new postal routes and macadamized roads. Clay's popularity in Lexington, while in no way universal, made the town more respectable. His bids for the presidency put the town on the political map. And most important, his speeches on internal improvements fed the dreams of men like Robert Todd who believed that with positive press, positive thinking, and a plank road or two, their town might rival Philadelphia or Boston.

But Lexington's veneer of respectability was as thin as muslin. The local piano merchant was also an undertaker. The local bookstore sold violins and pistols on the same shelf. The town's various boosters and boards could buff out its rough edges, but Lexington remained rough somewhere near its heart. Whatever its pretensions, the city was essentially western. From the age of fourteen, many of its males carried concealed weapons, pocket pistols, dirks, knives, or cane swords. Like their watch fobs, these discreet death-dealers were essential accoutrements for the discriminating gentleman. Unfortunately, they were not mere fashion accessories. Lexington's homicide rate was approximately four times those of the eastern cities it sought to emulate. "If you go into the Northern states," remarked Kentucky lawyer Ben Hardin, "it is a rare thing if you can find a man in ten thousand with a deadly weapon on his person. . . . In these states you may arm yourself to the teeth, and track your steps in blood with impunity." The town's leaders lamented the problem, but they were at a loss to explain it. Had their Scottish forbears left a "homicidal humor" in their blood? Had the Indian wars brutalized their impulses?

The answers are more prosaic, less flattering. For starters, they drank too much. Alcohol flowed like a river through the town. The bourbon that would one day make Kentucky famous then made it infamous. Kentucky was, and remains, ideal bourbon country. The salt in the soil ensures that the corn and the water have very low concentrations of iron, which tend to blacken and sour the mash. Then too the Bluegrass's hot summers and cold winters are ideal for distilling. Following the dictates of their land, then, nine-tenths of Lexington's antebellum farmers operated stills. Four taverns and 139 local distilleries served Lexington itself. The purest whiskey was ten dollars a barrel, and it was so good, slobbered a witness, that "A Man might Get Drunk on [it] Evry Day in the year for a Life time & never have the Delerium Tremens nor Sick Stomack or nerverous Head achake." Virtually every male drank to occasional excess, and if he didn't, he made a spectacle of himself. No home, with the possible exception of the reverend's, hosted a dry party without risking its reputation, and no public man could make it in politics if he couldn't hold his liquor. "Them days the Bank officers and welthy men woold Come down and Fish, up the Creek a week at a time" remembered one local, and they "Came prepaird to Engoy the Sport. They Brot the Best provisions and always The Best of old Burbon . . . to Make one Feel Renewed after the toils of Fishing." Lexington's men didn't just drink after the "toils" of fishing, however. Then as now, alcohol served as a social lubricant, making cotillions more convivial and conversations more interesting. But, then as now, alcohol served as a social irritant too. Coupled with the concealed arsenals, bar brawls became murder scenes and misunderstandings ended at the morgue. In 1824, the governor's own son killed the man he had been drinking with, and no one, including him, could remember exactly why.

Lexington's "refinement" aggravated the problem. The town's shallow sophistication gave its sons more pride than humility. What they best understood about manhood was that cowardice was its opposite; they dreamed of opportunities to prove their courage, not their decency. They were what observers called "bowie-knife gentry" — toughs in tailored suits spoiling for a fight. "I think I never saw a place more strongly tinged with presumptuous, self-confident vulgarity," noted one visitor. Like most Southerners, Lexingtonians subscribed to the code duello. Honor was a man's most prized possession, and he defended it with his life. But dueling in Kentucky had little of the esprit de corps that marked affairs of honor elsewhere. Antagonists chose deadlier weapons at closer ranges, and they were rarely "satisfied" until their opponent was bleeding. The code was supposed to contain violence, but in Kentucky it merely justified it. In 1829, the Todds' cousin Charles Wickliffe shot the editor of Lexington's local paper because he had published a letter "uncomplimentary" to his father. The editor was unarmed, fleeing the building, and shot in the back, but the jury deliberated for only seven minutes before concluding that the boy had done right. His family's honor had been insulted, and an insult was something "no man in Kentucky could submit to without loss of character." Inevitably, such violence fed upon itself. Shortly after his acquittal, Wickliffe was called out by one of the editor's friends, who shot him through the heart at the ridiculously close dueling range of eight paces. This editorial avenger was then himself hounded into a sanitarium by the relentless persecution of Wickliffe partisans. In Lexington, the traditions of the duel were commingled with the traditions of the feud. Violence was bloody, clannish, and committed in a self-justifying cycle.

Slavery too played a role in desensitizing Lexington's residents to violence. In keeping with its self-image, the town strove to appear moderate on the issue. Colonization schemes were soberly discussed. Antislavery proponents were heard out. Lexington even had its own homegrown abolitionist, Cassius Clay, who printed and posted his broadsides with relative impunity. The town's essential moderation was captured by a local paper when it claimed that no family should hold more than ten slaves. At higher numbers, the author reasoned, slavery lost its personal touch. Masters were forced to hire abusive overseers, and slaves became faceless drones in far-off fields rather than integral members in a close-knit household. This was the happy fiction many elite Lexington families loved to believe, that slaves were simply domestic servants who worked for room and board and the ultimate job security — a hereditary position.

But it was the personal touch that made the institution so foul. Behind the lace curtains adorning Lexington's prettiest homes, slavery could be just as brutal as it was in the malarial rice fields a world away. Robert Todd's friend Fielding Turner, for example, appeared to be a model master. He was a retired judge and a leading citizen of the town. His wife, Caroline, was a Boston-born daughter of a wealthy and well-placed family. Their house was the finest in the city, their bank account was ample, and their servants numerous. But Caroline Turner had a dark cast of mind. Large and muscular, she discovered something at the heart of slavery that she loved and perhaps became addicted to — an outlet for her sadistic urges. Her neighbors whispered about what went on: she beat her slaves too often, too viciously, too happily. But they only whispered and did nothing. Then in the spring of 1837, Caroline threw a young slave boy out a second-story window. He landed awkwardly on the Turner's prim flagstone courtyard; the fall broke his arm and leg, injured his spine, and left him crippled for life. In the wake of the incident, Fielding revealed what the town must already have guessed: Caroline had a psychotic temper that fell most savagely on her slaves. "She has been the immediate [cause of] death of six of my servants by her severities," Fielding admitted sadly. The only way to protect the ones who remained, he decided, was to have her committed. Robert was one a handful of men called in to review the case, but despite Fielding's revelations, nothing could be done. Caroline might have been vindictive and cruel, but she was perfectly sane. And so she went back to beating her slaves behind lacy curtains. A few years later, Fielding Turner died, but he tried one last time to quiet his wife's rages. "None of [my slaves] are to go to . . . Caroline," he noted in his will, "for it would . . . doom them to misery in life & a speedy death." Somehow Caroline again thwarted her husband. She contested the will, retained possession of some of the slaves, and even bought some more. On August 22, 1844, her reign of terror came to an end. She chained a young slave to a wall and had begun flogging him when he broke free. In a frenzied instant, he grabbed her by the throat and broke her neck.

Caroline Turner was an unusually cruel mistress. Most Lexingtonians didn't beat their slaves — they sent them down to the slave jail to be beaten publicly by a professional. But this is a distinction without a difference. The institution of slavery rested on a kind of violence that brutalized the tastes and impulses of the entire town. When word of an insurrection in Tennessee reached them, Bluegrass masters set to torturing the truth out of their servants with an abandon that shocked even a longtime resident. The insurrection proved nothing but a wild rumor, but that didn't stop whites from indulging in "unwarrantable cruelties to the negroes, reviving in many instances the exploded tortures of the Middle Ages and of the Inquisition." And just down the street from the Todds' front door lay Lewis Robards's infamous slave pens. The center of a shadowy kidnapping ring, Robards's operatives swooped down on Ohio's free black families and snatched as many children as they could find. Some were broken in Robards's dungeon and sold to points further south. Others joined his "select stock" of "yellow girls" who lived in a sumptuous upstairs apartment where their favors could be bought for a night or a lifetime.

Even in the most radical households, families discussed eventual manumission over a dinner cooked and served by slaves. Growing up amid their enslaved servants, white children gained an inflated estimate of their own power. Thomas Jefferson himself remarked on this effect of slavery: "The parent storms [while] the child looks on, catches the lineaments of wrath, puts on the same airs in the circle of smaller slaves, *gives loose to his worst passions;* and, thus, *nursed, educated, and daily exercised in tyranny,* cannot but be stamped by it with odious peculiarities."

The town's final problem was that it was dying, and the Todds were partly to blame. Together with the rest of Lexington's founders, John and Levi had located their "Athens of the West" fifteen miles from the nearest navigable stream. Henry Clay could say all he wanted about plank roads, but waterways provided the biggest economic boost in the years before railroads. As the steamboat revolutionized transportation, Louisville and Cincinnati became bustling centers of commerce while Lexington's significance shrank to the point where it was *only* making hats. Businesses drifted away, as did Transylvania's medical school, as did many new migrants. "I don't like the idea of living in a finished or decaying place," noted one, "[nor] of raising our children where they cannot find employment." And so, ultimately, the town was left in the care of those founding families whose pedigree made them too stubborn to leave. They spent their lives polishing their ancestors and bickering about the past, never admitting that the future had passed them by.

V.

WHAT DID the Todd children learn growing up in a dying town amid slavery, arms, honor, and alcohol? First, it should be noted that there is no evidence that Robert Todd was an alcoholic or anything like it.

In an era when even the bank president kept a jug cooling in the local creek, Robert was unusually snobbish about his refreshments. He had his spirits, like his best furniture, shipped upriver from New Orleans. His supply of wine was ample but also select; his mint juleps were legendary but always served in cut crystal. Robert's watchword was moderation. He kept his liquor cabinet well provisioned because it was expected of a successful host. His guests may have swayed a little when they rose from his table, but they never fell down. In short, Robert drank the way he walked or practiced politics — decorously — ever mindful of the ladies, his reputation, and his name.

Three of his sons proved less discriminating. As they grew up, Levi, George, and David all developed a dependence on alcohol. For them, the availability of booze, coupled with the town's declining fortunes, created a problem. There was no work to do that slaves weren't already doing. There was no profession that appealed to them more than that of a gentleman, which they understood to include gambling, drinking, and puffing one's chest.

This should not be held against them. Henry Clay's sons fared little better in Lexington. Clay was the "Star of the West," the leading light of his political party and a genius rightly acclaimed for his decency. And yet his sons were, according to a sympathetic witness, "all a disgrace to his name." The first was driven to a lunatic asylum by "the violence of his passions," the second was a "sot," the third was "so jealous & irritable in his temper that there is no living with him," and the last two gave "no great promise of steadiness" either. The temptations held out by Lexington were legion; opportunities were scant. Lexington's sons were left to indulge themselves with bright dreams of their coming greatness while they availed themselves of the town's cheap liquor and cheaper women. Of the Todd boys, only the youngest, Aleck, escaped the cycle fully, and he had an unusual advantage. By the time he was born Betsey was so exhausted from child rearing that she hired an extra nurse from New Orleans. To get back at a system that enslaved her, the nurse made a habit of holding Aleck's infant body upside down against a wall until his face turned almost black. His parents suspected that he was being abused but they never found a mark on him, so the practice continued unabated for a year. Perversely, it may have been one of the reasons that he developed such an unusually clingy disposition.

The Todd girls had problems living in Lexington too. As one member of the household noted, "[We] had few privileges & led very dull lives. We had no amusements to vary the monotony, no parties to bring us in contact with girls beyond our homes, and worse than all no books with charming little stories to excite noble impulses and stimulate us to acts of kindness and courtesy." Instead, the girls dreamed mostly of joining the world they could see beyond their windows: a town bustling with women so preoccupied with not looking western that they tended to overachieve. As one visitor from Boston noted: "The ladies of Lexington pay their respects properly and promptly according to the town's social custom of forenoon [but I] was astonished to see callers arrive in satin and silk as if they were going to an evening function. No Boston lady would ever be so conspicuous. 'How is Dr. Holley,' they would ask and would adjust their flounces, scarcely touching their backs to the parlor chair lest they form a wrinkle or disturb a hair." Given their environment, it was quite natural for the Todd girls to mistake raiment for refinement. With no one to tell them different, they came to understand that if they could only display themselves properly, the world would embrace them. Certainly this is what prompted Mary at the age of twelve to stay up all night sewing willow branches into her hemline. So far as she knew, looking like a lady was the most important part of being one.

Another story from Mary's childhood offers similar insights. The most authoritative version begins, "A small white pony galloped down the shady street, on his back a slender thirteen-year-old girl. . . ." The particulars of the story are straightforward. Robert, the indulgent father, buys Mary a small white pony from an itinerant theater troupe. Seizing the opportunity for display, Mary rides the pony over to Ashland, the home of the revered statesman Henry Clay. Galloping up to the door, she is informed by a servant, "Mr. Clay is entertaining five or six fine gentlemens." (The servant's grammar, we must understand, was part of the story's "charm.") Mary, being a "vivid, little person," will not be put off. Her business is every bit as urgent as any gentlemens'. "I've come all the way out to Ashland to show Mr. Clay my new pony," she says peevishly. "You go right back and tell him that *Mary Todd* would like him to step out here for a moment." Amused by the message, Clay emerges with his guests. "My father says you are the best judge of horse-flesh in Fayette County," Mary informs him. "What do you think about this pony?" Happy to be complimented in front of guests, Clay responds that the horse "is as spirited as [its] jockey" and, whisking Mary from the saddle, escorts her in to dinner. There, amid a lull in the adult conversation, Mary blurts out, "Mr. Clay, my father says you will be the next President of the United States. I wish I could go to Washington and live in the White House. I begged my father to be President but he only laughed and said he would rather see you there than to be President himself. He must like you more than he does himself. My father is a very, very peculiar man, Mr. Clay. I don't think he really wants to be President." Charmed in equal parts by her verve and her artlessness, Clay responds, "Well, if I am ever President I shall expect Mary Todd to be one of my first guests. Will you come?" Overwhelmed by his offer, Mary's crush on the great man bursts its bounds. "If you were not already married," she offers demurely, "I would wait for you." At this, the room erupts with laughter. Mary can feel that some of the amusement comes at her expense, but she's unsure how much. "I've been gone a long time," she says, slipping off her chair. "Mammy will be wild! When I put salt in her coffee this morning she called me a limb of Satan and said I was loping down the broad road . . . to destruction." Mary curtsies grandly. She mounts her little pony and off she rides, all ribbons and curls bouncing on the breeze.

In this story, the Todds saw their sister and their sister saw herself; this was the Mary they all knew: bold, bright, and, by whatever twist of fortune, headed for the White House. But the story captures other features the family was blind to, possibly because they shared them. Mary could not imagine a man who both loved himself and didn't want to be president — not because the president could do the most good but because he lived in the nicest house and was the most distinguished, the most prominent, the most envied man in the country. Only someone "very, very peculiar" would want less than that for themselves. Mary, like the rest of the Todd children, prayed for prominence, not contentment. She craved the world's envy, not its love. Any other way of thinking was as odd to her as a man who didn't want to be president.

The Todds, it should be said, were not so different from their neighbors. In a materialistic culture, they indulged; in a litigious society, they sued; in an age of individualists, they looked out for themselves; in a region renowned for quick tempers, their tongues fell like lashes; in a society where men drank to excess, several of the Todd boys outdid themselves; in a region of ambivalent slaveholders who tut-tutted and did nothing, the Todds tut-tutted and did nothing; in a brutal world, they had a high tolerance for other people's pain. None of this made them a bad family; it made them a typical one. The Todds' faults as a family were, by and large, America's faults as a country. America was itself then materialistic, litigious, individualistic, quick-tempered, hard-drinking, ambivalent (or worse) about slavery, and possessing a high tolerance for other people's pain. And, like the Todds, Americans were a family drifting apart. They had forged a bond in infancy, in the crucible of revolution, but in the years after 1776 they drifted, scattered. In this sense, the Todd children's very representativeness would become their most pressing problem.

2

Scattered

A S THE TODD CHILDREN came of age, centrifugal forces spun many of them out of their Lexington center: They were a large family, even by the standards of the day, which was an economic strain. They did not all have the same mother, which was an occasional social strain. Twenty-eight years separated the oldest from the youngest, so they did not all know each other well. And Lexington offered few opportunities, especially in comparison to points farther west or south. For all these reasons, the Todds had a center that could not hold.

But as they spun off in their separate directions, centripetal forces were at work too. Today we are apt to say (if we talk of the Todds at all) that they were only half siblings. *We* say that. *They* didn't. Such terms were not used much in an era when the early loss of a parent and a subsequent remarriage were so common. To themselves and their society the Todds were just brothers and sisters.

Then too the sibling relationship was different in the nineteenth century. Growing up, brothers and sisters were often the whole of one another's early worlds. There was no compulsory public education, no play dates, no stable peer groups. Sisters, especially, spent most of their days and (if they slept together) all of their nights with one another. Reflecting this, the sibling relation was deeply sentimentalized in Victorian culture. Brothers and sisters were expected to love and rely on one another. They were expected to find in one another the idealized qualities they would later look for in their mates. All of this was no less true in cases in which siblings barely knew each other. In a sister you had a sister, even if you'd never met her, and not only *could* you impose on her, but you'd be *expected* to; indeed, you'd be expected to love her the instant you met her because it was only right and natural that you should. This intimacy, even where it was false, operated in families as large and unwieldy as the Todds. Mary Todd, for instance, may not have grown up with her youngest brothers and sisters. Nevertheless, she knew Elodie as "Dee," Catherine as "Kitty," Alexander as "Aleck," and so on. Such nicknames are a passable index to the family's affection or at least to its sentimentality. The Todds would scatter in the years before the Civil War, but they would remain attached to one another by ties of contrived sentiment and genuine affection.

I.

THE FIRST TODD to emigrate from Lexington was firstborn Elizabeth. At nineteen, she left the nest before her youngest siblings were even hatchlings. Though her mother had died when she was twelve and her father had remarried a woman she never entirely took to, Elizabeth was the best adjusted of the senior Todds. She alone had lived in the Lexington of her father's dreams, when the city was at its zenith: when Henry Clay might still become president, when local Transylvania College still attracted the finest sons from the finest families. By all accounts, Elizabeth favored her mother in appearance and deportment. An acquaintance described her succinctly as "a very — very pretty woman," and though no one said she was placid, people did use the sort of words they had applied to her mother: sweet, gentle, subtle, and charming.

Given her nature and attributes, Elizabeth did exactly what her father hoped she would do: attract one of those finest sons. His name was Ninian Wirt Edwards, a Transylvania law student whose father was the governor of Illinois. With easy manners and correct opinions, Ninian was described by his aunt as "one of the loveliest youth I have ever known. Never did I meet with more purity of sentiment and amiability of feeling in any *female*." Ninian met Elizabeth when both were teenagers. He escorted her and her sisters to dances and concerts and quickly became a constant in the Todds' lives. So inevitable was the couple's eventual engagement that it seemed as if it had already taken place.

But there was a small problem. Ninian's father (like Elizabeth's) was a highly placed large landowner with all the appurtenances of wealth but little of the actual money. When Ninian wrote him that he wanted to marry and set up housekeeping, his father urged delay. "The next year [will] push me so hard," he wrote his son, "that I shall not have one cent to spare you." Instead, he suggested that Ninian wait until he could support himself or, failing that, that he and his new wife come to live with him when Ninian's course work ended. It was an appealing offer. Ninian's father was the governor of Illinois and a widower. Moving in with him, Elizabeth would become the ranking hostess in the state, and Ninian might become a sort of political heir apparent. Accepting the offer, the couple married on Valentine's Day, February 14, 1832, and, as instructed, they remained in Lexington while Ninian finished up at Transylvania. Unfortunately, while he did so, his father broke his end of the bargain — first by losing the governorship and then by dying. From a purely financial perspective, this was even better for Ninian than the original plan. His father's house was now available, and his inheritance would come early. The couple moved first to Kaskaskia, where Ninian set up a law practice, but, after liquidating some of his father's estate, he decided to become a merchant and move to Springfield instead.

Today we tend to think of a move from Kentucky (a former slave state) to Illinois (a former free state) as a move from south to north. When Elizabeth made it in 1834, it was a move from east to west, or, more precisely, from west to west-er. In this sense, she was only going with the demographic flow. America was on the move in these years — and many Americans were moving to places that hadn't been on the map when they were born. In 1818, while Elizabeth's parents were listening to that Italian harpist, Springfield was five lonely cabins that looked like they'd been half-digested by the prairie. The town hadn't existed at all until 1817, when Robert Pulliam and a bedraggled crew of cattle herders erected a temporary structure to shield them from the snow. Pulliam had abandoned the camp when winter broke, but he had returned the following year to find that families had occupied his cabin and built others beside it. The vast prairies had intimidated the newcomers at first. By their reckoning if the soil was any good there would be trees growing on it. When their first crop of corn shot up fifteen feet as fast as Jack's beanstalk, they began to spread the gospel: here was a farmer's paradise. By the 1820s, streams of settlers were flowing into Illinois, most of them Kentuckians. The state was like a tall glass of water filling up from the bottom.

Elizabeth found Springfield a good deal rougher than Lexington, at least in terms of exteriors. For starters, the city had a mud problem. When wet, the soil of central Illinois becomes a sticky black loam that has all the consistency, and some of the adhesive properties, of a paste. In the rainy season, the mud puddles became so vast that an observer half-jokingly suggested that the city's thoroughfares, as they were impassable anyway, could turn a tidy profit as rice paddies. The mud problem was amplified by the "hog nuisance." At home in the city's myriad marshes, itinerant swine congregated in unsettling numbers to gorge themselves on the garbage citizens had thrown into the streets and gutters.

All the mud in the world couldn't obscure the fact that antebellum Springfield seemed to have one thing Lexington didn't — a bright future. Ninian, among others, thought that the state capital should move to Springfield from its temporary home in Vandalia. Partly to effect such a change, he ran for state legislator in 1836. On the campaign trail, he met a fellow nominee on the Sangamon Whig ticket, Abraham Lincoln. Edwards was not impressed with the man's exterior, which he described as "mighty Rough." But after hearing Lincoln speak, Edwards felt lucky to have such an ally.

The 1836 election was an unusually nasty one. Candidates exchanged barbs and occasional blows day after day in town after town until tempers were worn to a frazzle. At a rally in Springfield, Edwards grew so incensed that he jumped up on a table and pulled a gun. Lincoln's mouth was the more devastating weapon, however. He had a tenor voice, slightly shrill, that rang out over an assembly like a bell. He had a talent for "pour[ing] oil over troubled waters" and a bottomless supply of anecdote that could humor (and focus) an unruly crowd. And when he wanted to, Lincoln could cut a man to ribbons, even reduce him to tears. Hectored by an opponent, George Forquer, for his youth and inexperience, Lincoln waited patiently until the older man had said his piece. Forquer was widely respected, but he had recently changed his affiliation from Whig to Democrat and taken a lucrative appointed post. He was also something of a curiosity about town for having installed a lightning rod on his house (the first Lincoln had ever seen). Putting it all together, Lincoln gave the man a dressing-down so devastating it became the stuff of Illinois legend. "The gentleman has alluded to my being a young man," he told the crowd. "But I would rather die now . . . than, like the gentleman, change my politics and simultaneous with the change receive an office worth $3000 per year, and then have to erect a lightning-rod over my house to protect a guilty conscience from an offended God."

Lincoln and Edwards were both elected. With the other seven members of the Sangamon delegation that term, they formed the Long Nine, so known for their unusual height. Lincoln was the longest of them all in both physical proportion and political skill. Though second youngest, he became the floor leader and point man on most Whig legislation that term. The most critical success of the session, especially from Ninian's perspective, was the naming of Springfield as the new state capital. Overjoyed, Ninian invited the entire legislature out to celebrate. Between the cigars, the oysters, and the eighty-one bottles of champagne, he was left with a tab of $223.50 (almost $4,000 today). But he was consoled by what he had achieved for his town. Almost overnight, Springfield's air crackled with the sound of saws, chisels, and carriage wheels, not to mention an infectious sense of self-congratulation. As the new seat of state government, the town would host not only the legislature (and all who had business before it) but the state supreme court and the federal district court (and all who had business before them). Inns were booked, property values soared, and the city was aflood with lawyers and laborers, lobbyists and land agents.

Lincoln washed in with the flood. After the adjournment, he went home to New Salem, said goodbye to a few friends, and moved to the town he had helped make a capital. He arrived with two saddlebags and almost no money. Inquiring at the general store about the cost of a mattress, he seemed so obviously crushed by his own penury that the proprietor, a fellow Kentuckian named Joshua Speed, offered to share his bed above the store. In the version the two would later tell, Lincoln vaulted the stairs, dropped his bags, and declared, "Well, Speed, I'm moved!" They would share the bed for four years; Speed would become the only man to whom Lincoln unburdened his whole heart.

Lincoln adapted rather quickly to his new surroundings. At first the flourishing of carriages and relative refinement of the residents made him long for the little river towns he knew best. But he was fairly well connected for a stranger. His mentor, John Todd Stuart, had moved to Springfield, and together they opened a law practice. The townspeople were predisposed to like Lincoln because he had done so much to realize their dreams. And of course he knew Ninian, whose house on the hill was the social center of the town. The two men did have a basic problem: Ninian thought he would have the brighter future. He was a governor's son who had been quickly elected to the legislature and become the toastmaster of a new capital. But here his rise ended. Plain and unpedigreed, Lincoln would go on without him, lurching down high roads and low, all the way to the presidency. Why? What didn't Ninian have? In 1840, Lincoln won renomination and Ninian didn't. Trying to console his friend, Lincoln said that the only reason he won his race was because the party needed him to make speeches to the rubes.

He was partly right, but he was also too modest. Asked to put his finger on what made Lincoln a success in this period, an acquaintance noted: "Well it is hard to say just why. It was because of the standing he had got in the country . . . because he was a good fellow — because he told good stories, and remembered good jokes — because he was genial, kind, sympathetic, open-hearted — because when he was asked a question and gave an answer it was always characteristic, brief, pointed, apropos, out of the common way and manner, and yet exactly suited to the time, place and thing — because of a thousand things." Ninian Edwards would serve the state legislature off and on in one capacity or another for more than twenty years. But he was a "thousand things" short of Lincoln. Like Salieri to Lincoln's Mozart, he would occasionally resent Lincoln's success, but he would always, if grudgingly, recognize his superiority. Within the first year, he had talked so much of Lincoln that his wife and her sister Frances, who was visiting, demanded that he bring the man by.

Frances wasn't impressed. The second born of the Todd girls, she had come to Springfield shortly after the Edwardses' arrival. Her father had given her $150 to compensate Elizabeth for her room and board. The message was clear. By the time the money ran out, Frances should have found herself a husband. Lincoln was not the man for the job. "Yes, he took me out once or twice," Frances remembered, "but he was not much for society. He would go where [we] took him, but he was never very much for company." She did appreciate the way he appreciated her at the piano. "He liked music . . . he liked to hear us sing," she remembered, "although in all my life I never heard him [even] whistle." The biggest strike against him, though, was the fact that he was "the plainest man in Springfield."

More attractive was a local doctor named William Smith Wallace. Unlike Lincoln, Wallace was all amiability. He had graduated from the University of Pennsylvania School of Medicine in 1824. Disliking the

practice, he had traveled west to speculate in land but almost immediately he abandoned the scheme. Perhaps from the vantage of Philadelphia he had overestimated his skills, his bankroll, or his opportunities. Perhaps, as lore has it, he was prevailed upon by Springfield's
merchants to return to the practice of medicine. Regardless, on July
27, 1837, he announced in the local paper that he would offer his services from his new drugstore, the Golden Mortar, which would also
carry "paints, oils, dye stuffs, fancy articles, cigars and other forms of
tobacco." As it happens Wallace's store was just downstairs from Lincoln's law office. Lincoln, of course, did not smoke or use tobacco,
but he often hung around those who did, while they did, to ply them
with the "good stories" and "good jokes" he would become famous for.
Wallace was a captive audience for such things. A comfortable chair
could never buck him. He dipped liberally from his own tobacco stock
and laughed at everything Lincoln said, though he could never get
the punch lines right when he told the jokes himself. He and Lincoln
would be great loafing buddies for the rest of their lives.

After keeping "company quite a while," Frances and William were
married on May 21, 1839. Elizabeth gave them a big wedding and did
all the catering herself. She loved the role of hostess, loved her house,
and loved Ninian in part because he had made such things possible.
The Edwardses were "quite prosperous and lived in a very good style,"
Frances remembered. "My sister liked society, and gave a good many
parties. . . . I was married in a white satin dress . . . the invitations were
printed, and it was quite an affair." Elizabeth's motivations went deeper
than a flair for hosting, however, and deeper than her sister allowed.
At the core of her self-conception, she saw herself as a second mother
to her siblings. The strain of the role would eventually hollow her out,
but in the early years she was happy to provide for her sisters. When
Frances moved in with William, it created, Elizabeth said, "a vacancy
in [their] family." She immediately asked her sister Mary if she would
like to come and fill it.

II.

MARY ARRIVED in Springfield in June of 1840. She considered herself a sort of refugee from her mother's house, meaning she had come
to the Edwardses' to find a way never to return. In the nineteenth century, this meant that she needed to find a man, a fact she accepted too

fully to resent. Fortunately, the house on the hill was an auspicious place to trawl for such things. Her sister was an acclaimed hostess, especially during the legislative assemblies that dominated the winter season. These parties were attended by most of the town's "society people" and virtually all of the legislators. Typically, the supper was an overwhelming spectacle. It was "spread on a long table, the principal decoration of which was a centerpiece or pyramid made of jellies and creams and sponge cakes and macaroons, and the viands were abundant and of delicious quality." Women arrived in their best dresses; they checked their coats and their husband's hats, and if they had an infant, they checked it too and hoped to get the same one back at the end of the night. It was at just such a dinner that Mary met her future husband.

In the nineteenth century, courtship relied on what was called "sparking." The male and female world, embodied in one man and one woman, were brought together, like the antipodes of a battery, to see if they sparked. The potential for lifelong friendship or sexual compatibility were not much talked or thought of. These things could be negotiated after marriage. All that was required was the passing of three basic compatibility tests: how you looked, what you liked, and whether your temperament would complement or clash with your intended's. Abraham and Mary passed the first two tests and foundered spectacularly on the third.

Neither Abraham nor Mary was, in a superficial sense, attractive. Mary had pretty skin, pretty eyes, and soft brown hair like her father's. Unfortunately, she had also inherited his tendency to portliness. A self-described "ruddy pine knot," Mary was fatter than her sisters and fleshy in ways that even a floor-length hemline couldn't hide. Compared to Abraham, however, she was gorgeous. Frances, charitably, had called Lincoln plain, but that apparently didn't begin to cover it. Lincoln's ugliness was and is the stuff of legend. No man is as ugly as Lincoln was supposed to have been. According to witnesses, Lincoln's every feature was independently unattractive, and yet all were somehow out of place on his ungainly frame. It was as if God had, for sport, put together something as unnatural as a hippogriff or a hydra. Arms too long, hands too big, chest too narrow, head too misshapen, hair too unruly, face too cragged: Lincoln was a composite of discrete ugliness that achieved not even a consistent final effect. "To say that he is ugly," noted one eyewitness, "is nothing. To say that his figure is grotesque is to convey no adequate impression."

Of course, no one contributed more to the legend of Lincoln's ugliness than he did himself. Early in life he had made a decision. Too many men were blind to their faults or tender about their appearance. He would go the other way, embracing, even exaggerating, his defects and disarming his critics. Thus, when his longtime rival Stephen A. Douglas called him two-faced in front of a crowd, Lincoln corrected him: "I leave it to you," he told the audience. "If I had another face, do you think I would be wearing this one?" There were a dozen such lines in his repertoire. By far his favorite was an anecdote about a woman on a train. Lincoln claimed that he had been riding in a car when he became aware that a woman was staring at him. "Sir," she noted when she had completed a close study, "you are the most unattractive man I have ever seen." Sensing that she wanted either an apology or an explanation, Lincoln shrugged and said, "Well, I can't help it." "Yes," replied the lady, "but you could stay home." Lincoln loved to tell this story. Like many of his best anecdotes, it addressed and dismissed a subject all at once, and left light laughter in its wake.

Humor could leaven and deflect, but it could not change an essential fact: Lincoln's unattractiveness shaped his life and occasionally hurt his feelings. He didn't look in a mirror any longer than he had to (and, judging by his infamously unkempt hair, probably not that long). Instead, he gathered around him, as all do, the surfaces that reflect only the most likable self-image. Children, animals, and the men who loitered about a potbellied stove couldn't notice or didn't care that Lincoln was ugly; they loved him blind, and he loved them blind in return. They would forever be his preferred company. Women were different, especially the belles. Interactions with them turned on banter and breeding — not anecdote and feats of strength — and attractiveness mattered. Stepping into the Edwardses' parlor, Lincoln had to lead with his face, the one he couldn't help, the only one he could wear, the one written all over with "the plain and simple annals of the poor." Any woman in the room could read its lines; here surely was a man whose grandmother had been charged with fornication, whose mother had been marked by a "want of teeth [and a] weather-beaten appearance," whose father was "plain [and] plodding" and perhaps not even his own, whose childhood involved hoeing under a heavy sun, living in a succession of dirt-floor cabins, and cozying up to a local slattern who left him fearing he had contracted syphilis. And sure enough, just as Lincoln entered, one of the belles let out a peal of laughter.

"What were you laughing at just as I came in?" Lincoln asked Mary

Todd after being introduced. "You," Mary replied directly. "You're so tall." It wasn't much of a compliment — more a statement of fact — but it carried a coy appreciation too. Lanky as well as homely, Lincoln was built just like Henry Clay, Mary's beau ideal of a man. As it happened, Clay was Lincoln's beau ideal of a statesman. Over the next month, chatting at a half-dozen such soirees, they would discover many such superficial points of accord. Both loved Kentucky, Shakespeare, poetry, and the Whig Party. This last was particularly important in 1840, an election year like no other. "One who witnessed the Presidential campaign of that ever memorable year would have supposed that the whole world had run mad, and rushed into the wild contest on the sublime issues, that log cabins are the best of all buildings, hard-cider the most delicious of all drinks, and coon-skins the finest of all furs." Thus, Abraham and Mary quickly passed not only the first but the second test of courtship. Liking the same things, they found it easier to imagine that they liked each other.

By the time they reached the third phase — what the two parties *are* like — Lincoln was on the road campaigning. Thus, this most critical stage of their courtship would proceed almost entirely by mail — and as witty writers riding a wave of Whiggish success, they were borne inexorably toward an understanding that they would marry. Within days of his return to Springfield, however, Lincoln thought better of it. In truth, it is a wonder the couple made it as far as they did. Their engagement, if that's what it was, was sustainable only because they'd spent so little time together (almost none of it alone) and because they had written themselves into love in a political reverie. The intoxicating effects of the election now over, Lincoln, particularly, had an eye-opening morning after. Meeting Mary for the first time in months, he managed to be shocked by her bad qualities, most of which had been apparent from the beginning and all of which she would have readily owned. She had, it's true, "improve[d] astonishingly" in Lincoln's absence, which in the parlance of the day meant that she had gotten truly fat. Perhaps she was not yet "a fair match for Falstaff," as Lincoln's last disastrous love interest had been, but she was in the class of "Mrs. Glenn [and] old Father Lambert," the reigning local heavyweights. Having grown up amid a prairie-hardened people, with a mother and stepmother as lean as jerked beef, Lincoln found exuberances of female flesh disconcerting, not only in themselves but in all they symbolized. Mary, he seemed the last to discover, was self-indulgent in all kinds of ways. She loved "glitter Show & pomp & power." She could be imperious and prone to

tantrums. Most disturbing, she had a tongue like a "Damascus blade," and Lincoln pitied the man who would be on its business end. With a rising sense of panic, he realized he was in danger of becoming exactly that man.

Compounding his collapse of affection and amplifying his sense of dread, he found himself falling in love with someone else. A recent arrival from Alton, Illinois, Ninian Edwards's niece Matilda was the kind of beautiful that immediately warps the social dynamics of a small town. Men bustled into the Edwardses' parlor to stare at her in artless wonder, and Mary was thrown into shadows colder and darker for the fact that, unlike herself, Matilda had a faultless personality and did almost nothing to put herself forward. That Lincoln should have been impressed by the contrast is not surprising. What is surprising is that his friends had to point out the impropriety of falling in love with a woman who was staying under the same roof and perhaps sleeping in the same bed as Mary, who thought of herself, at least, as his fiancée. Compounding all *this*, Lincoln's best friend, Joshua Speed, the man with whom *he'd* slept peaceably for four years, was also smitten with Matilda and was quite possibly in love with her too. The whole situation was romance-novel ridiculous, but it turned the winter of 1840 into one of those magical seasons that occasionally happen in the lives of young people. They can't know at the time, of course, that the assembled persons will never be assembled again, that they all complement one another uniquely, that the weird electricity that arcs between them completes a strange circuit of sexual energy that will build in power until it shorts out rather spectacularly.

Lincoln's wiring was the first to go. He tried to break it off with Mary by letter, but Speed called him a coward and threw the letter into the fire. He next tried to break it off in person but bungled the interview so badly that he wound up kissing her at the end it. Finally, almost hysterical, he told Mary that he actually *hated* her and only hung around the Edwardses' to be near Matilda, whom he loved like he might die of it. All of this, it should be understood, was so grossly out of character for Lincoln that he himself began to fear for his sanity. Mary too recognized that her beau was non compos mentis, so she finally let him go, but she was not the type to hide that her pride, at least, had been wounded. In her mind, Abraham was honor-bound to marry her, and she told him so.

Matilda, meanwhile, blasted the hopes of both Lincoln *and* Speed with the revelation that she had been in love with someone else all

along. Apparently she had met a man on the train into town, and he had gotten the drop on all of Springfield. With that, the deliriously dysfunctional foursome blew apart. Matilda married her secret somebody. Joshua sold out his store and moved back to Kentucky. Lincoln became suicidal with self-reproach for conduct unbecoming himself. And Mary was left to sadly survey the wreckage and hope that, one day, "her Richard would be himself again." (Her reference was to Shakespeare's *Richard II*. In the play, the young king falls from the throne, paces a prison of his own making, and is driven almost insane by loneliness before he is finally murdered. The character is nothing like Lincoln, but Mary's implication is clear: if the king had only loved his people a little better, they would not have been so willing to see him destroyed.)

Lincoln's various 1840 heartbreaks — Matilda's overlooking him, Joshua's abandoning him, Mary's loving him — all corresponded with a low point professionally and financially, and collectively made him, as he said, "the most miserable man living." Unable to face society, he committed himself to the care of a physician and lolled in bed for long hours, unable even to rouse himself to appear before the legislature. His confinement, variously termed his "crazy spell," "Duck fit," or "hypo," marked his severest — and most productive — confrontation with the depressive demons that had dogged him since adulthood. Shuddering under the covers, Lincoln came to an understanding with himself: "To remain as I am is impossible," he realized. "I must die or be better." In truth, he did neither. He remained for the rest of his life suspended in the melancholic's limbo between "better" and "dead." But he did learn how to function there. Suicide, he decided, was unnecessary because he was in important ways already dead. The Fates were leading him along a path with turns that represented choices he had effectively already made and an endpoint that was in every sense fatal. The inevitability of it all comforted Lincoln, as it does most depressives, because it means that surrender to life is the only logical course. By February of 1841, Lincoln was well enough to write Speed, "It seems to me I should [be] entirely happy, but for the never-absent idea, that there is *one* still unhappy whom I have contributed to make so. That still kills my soul." His use of the word "kill" is telling. At approximately the same time, he confided in a female friend, "Mrs. Butler, it would just kill me to marry Mary Todd." Lincoln, it appears, would be killing himself either way. Certainly, this was a case for the Fates.

Two years after their frightful breakup, Lincoln accepted an invitation from a mutual friend to be Mary's escort on a scenic tour in nearby Jacksonville. He did it knowing full well what it might mean. But he had gotten all the chances out he deserved, and nothing had materialized. Mary hadn't forgotten him. He hadn't forgiven himself. Neither of them had married in the meantime. The Fates, it seemed, had spoken. On November 4, 1842, five weeks after their Jacksonville reconciliation and two hours after their decision to wed, Mary and Abraham stood in the Edwardses' parlor, among their hastily assembled friends, and took their vows. The groomsman, James Metheny, remembered that Lincoln, "look[ing] and act[ing] as if he was going to slaughter," had come to him that evening and said, "Jim, I shall have to marry that girl." Asked by the Butlers, with whom Lincoln boarded, where he was going, he said, "To Hell." Even his wedding ring was inscribed with a curse: "Love is Eternal."

So why did he do it? Certainly, Lincoln was uniquely unequipped to deal with a charge that he was "honor-bound" to do something. "I want in all cases to do right," he had written during a previous love scrape, "and most particularly so, in all cases with women." But in marrying without love Lincoln did not do right. A martyr to his honor, he was evidently blind to the fact that in sacrificing his own happiness, he would not necessarily secure Mary's. In a veiled reference to marriage, Lincoln told Speed that his father had always told him, "If you make a bad bargain, hug it the tighter." But Lincoln would not, perhaps could not, hug Mary tighter. Instead, for the whole of his marriage, he would absent himself in all kinds of ways. He would hide in the drugstore, with the men around the potbellied stove; he would hide in his law office among his books or his cronies; he would hide at the hustings, among the people. If his Shakespeare was handy, he could hide in full view of Mary. Staring into a fire or out a window, Lincoln could achieve a trancelike state of absentia that was actually alarming.

Gradually it would dawn on Mary that this man did not love her. He endured her, indeed pitied her, and for that if for nothing else, she felt inclined to punish him. His distractedness, after all, ruffled her feathers where they were thinnest: she could not stand to be slighted or ignored. Then again, you do not hit a man in the face with a block of wood, you do not force him out of the house without pants, you do not chase him around with a knife, without being vaguely conscious that you've crossed some kind of line. And indeed, over the course of their marriage, Mary *was* dimly aware that she drove her husband away and dragged him back in an endless recrudescence of their original courtship. As she herself admitted, "I doubtless trespassed, many times & oft, upon his great tenderness & amiability of character." Mary, it should be noted, was not given to such self-criticism, especially the kind that really hurts. Nor was she accustomed to seeing things from another's perspective. That she said this, knew this, and admitted this about her conduct toward her husband is singular. But in all decency, she *had* to say this if she loved Lincoln at all. And whatever her faults, Mary loved this man. She just sometimes had an appalling way of showing it.

One example will suffice for the rest. One day while Mary was chasing her husband around with a knife, it became suddenly clear to both of them that they were being observed by a stranger. Immediately, Lincoln whirled around and took control of his wife physically. That he always could have done so was one of the reasons she was chasing him in the first place. But what does it say that he *allowed* her to chase him around with a knife? Isn't that a kind of love? And, as it was the only kind Mary could expect, wasn't that another reason to chase him? Like most married couples, Abraham and Mary completed each other in all sorts of ways, good and bad. She stitched up his clothes and his manners. He endured her as few others would have. And behind it all, making it work, was the "engine that knew no rest," their mutual (if differently motivated) desire for advancement.

III.

A YEAR AFTER the Lincolns' marriage, Robert Todd came to Springfield to visit his four oldest daughters, all of whom had taken up residence in the city (Ann had by then replaced Mary in the Edwardses' marital halfway house). Three of his girls were now married, and they had collectively borne him six grandchildren. The youngest of these was the Lincolns' new addition, Robert, named in his grandfather's honor. Considering the number of children he had to support, Robert Todd was very generous with the Lincolns. Immediately upon his arrival, he pressed a twenty-five-dollar gold piece into Mary's hand and promised to help her in any way he could afford. In the next six years, he deeded eighty acres of Illinois land to the couple, gave them a total of $1,100, and allowed Lincoln to prosecute one of his debt cases and keep the proceeds.

In 1846, Lincoln was elected to Congress. On their way to Washington, he and his wife decided to stop in at Lexington. Mary hadn't been home in seven years. With the exception of his father-in-law, Lincoln hadn't met any of his new Kentucky relations. The journey was a fatiguing ten-day trip by stage, steamer, and train, and they made it with their two boys, Robert, now four, and Eddie, less than two, already tubercular and three years from an early grave.

As the Lincolns' carriage ambled down Lexington's Main Street, the three youngest of the Todd girls, Emilie, Elodie, and Kitty, bustled into crimson dresses, white boots, and ruffled aprons. At ten, Emilie had a dim recollection of her older sister, who had left when she was three. At seven and six, Elodie and Kitty were meeting a stranger. The girls had just taken their places in the parlor when their older cousin Joseph Humphreys burst into the house. "Aunt Betsey," he panted, "I was never so glad to get off a train in my life." Apparently he had traveled the Frankfort-to-Lexington leg near a couple of utter brats and a long-legged father who not only didn't spank them or shut them up but who actually "looked pleased as Punch and sided with and abetted the older one in mischief." The sound of carriage wheels interrupting his account, Joseph looked out the window and was shocked to see the very family he had described. "Good Lord, there they are now," he yelped before bounding out of the house.

Of all the girls, Emilie remembered the Lincolns' entrance best. "Mary came in first," she later wrote, and "to my mind she was lovely, [with] sparkling blue eyes [and] smooth white skin." Lincoln was another story. Clad in a long black cloak and mammoth fur cap, he looked to her like the giant of "Jack and the Beanstalk." Terrified, she stood behind her mother's skirt while the giant made his introductions to the rest of the room. Finally, he turned to her, lifted her into his arms, and said, "So this is Little Sister." It was the name he would call her for the rest of his life. "His voice and smile," Emilie remembered, "banished my fear of the giant."

The Lincolns stayed for three weeks. It was their first real vacation together, and it came at a pivotal moment for Abraham politically and personally. He was on his way to Congress, where he would practice politics on a new level. Heretofore, his attention had been directed toward Illinois issues. Now he would have to think nationally. Mary introduced him to Henry Clay, and Lincoln undoubtedly heard Clay's speech on November 3, 1847, in which he denounced the Mexican War: "This is no war of defense," Clay noted. "It is Mexico that is defending her firesides, her castles and her altars, not we. . . . [We must] disavow, in the most positive manner, any desire on our part to acquire any foreign territory whatever for the purpose of introducing slavery into it."

Such transition periods tended to make Lincoln wistful. He spent long hours in the Todd library, where he committed William Cullen Bryant's "Thanatopsis" to memory. Like the poet, Lincoln was a man "sick at heart" and plagued by "darker musings." As many of his contemporaries noted (and all of his biographers have said), Lincoln wallowed in the certainty of death and arose with "melancholy drip[ping] from him as he walked." But few have understood that for Lincoln the effect was as revivifying as a bath. Like most depressives, he fixated on the certainty of death because it is sometimes the only certainty in a mad, miserable world. This, of course, is the main message of the poem too: death's dark tide, sweeping all before it, looking almost like relief, is about upon us, so in the meantime, live.

The primary purpose of the trip, though, was for Lincoln to get to know his in-laws. Given their mutual affection for Whig politics and the law, he and Robert had plenty to talk about. Robert was too polished an aristocrat, however, to appreciate a "rough diamond" like Lincoln. And he would always regard Ninian as the finest of his sons-in-law. Lincoln fared a little better with Betsey. Despite his reputation for awkwardness around the opposite sex, Lincoln could be quite charming in the society of older women. His facility with language and deep knowledge of poetry made him a whiz with a bon mot or a honey-eyed compliment, and his chronic sincerity helped the latter to stick. Lincoln also established a mutual rapport with his wife's oldest half brother, Sam. According to friends, Sam was a "jovial" spirit, "all soul, all fun, and all fire." A seventeen-year-old student at Centre College in Danville, he came home to roughhouse with his new nephews, Bob and Eddie. Swelling with his avuncular role, he swaggered about the house, teased Mary for being so much shorter than he was, and taught Bob to call him "Uncle Sam," a gag he never tired of.

Of all the emotional connections made, however, the strongest bound the Lincolns to the youngest Todd girls: Emilie, Elodie, and Kitty. For Mary, the little girls provided a much-needed antidote to the overwhelming maleness of her own household. She loved the masculine world of politics, of course; she loved her husband, her two sons, and the two more yet to come. But she loved the feminine world of bonnets and bows too. She would never have a daughter to dress up and fuss over and gossip with and then cling to in old age. But she did cling to the idea that she could be for her younger sisters what Elizabeth had been for her — a guide into womanhood.

Lincoln too was charmed by these youngest Todds. All his life, he'd had a marked weakness for children generally and little girls specifically. Of the three, Emilie took the deepest root in his heart. By common consensus, she was the most attractive. (Indeed, according to one family story, she was so irresistible that as a toddler she had been kidnapped by a couple whose sole defense was that they couldn't help themselves. They "were considered good people," a witness said of the kidnappers, but Emilie's "uncommon beauty overcame [their] sense of right.") Emilie also made a deep impression on the Lincolns' son Bob. For three weeks, the two played noisily, romped about the house and yard, and laid the foundation for a friendship that would span more than seventy years.

There was one Todd whom the Lincolns conspicuously did *not* meet. Fourteen-year-old David had run off to fight in the Mexican War. Robert might have hoped that the boy would at least get some discipline in the service. Instead, David's experiences only made him wilder. Growing up in an army camp, he learned to curse, drink, gamble, and indulge. In Mexico he acquired a taste for travel and manly adventure that remained strong for the rest of his life.

IV.

THE MEXICAN WAR doubled the size of the United States — and multiplied a hundredfold the agitation over the slavery question. Kentucky, poised painfully between North and South, was particularly riven. In 1849, Robert faced reelection to the state senate — but this time he would really have to run. His opponent, a fellow Whig named Oliver Anderson, was a large slaveholder and an outspoken advocate of the institution. "I am," he announced, "what may be called a *thorough proslavery* man. So far from admitting the institution to be a necessary evil, I believe it tends to exalt the free population and would be unwilling to give it up, even if by a word I could remove the negro population to Africa." Robert, of course, belonged to the older Bluegrass school. He had servants — not slaves — and as they poured his wine, he talked in broad terms and with a full mouth about the distant day when they would be sent back to Africa. He had never personally freed a slave, of course, but neither had he purchased any. In the senate, he had consistently opposed the importation of slaves into the state, and he genuinely hoped that in the fullness of time the institution would die of its own unpleasantness.

In the polarized politics of 1849, all these quite moderate and once dominant attitudes made Robert Todd an immediate emancipationist. Suddenly he found himself pressured to say how much he liked the institution—a sentiment that was both untrue and, to his mind, uncouth. Indeed, the entire 1849 campaign was conducted in an ungentlemanly style Robert deplored. His name was libeled and his positions distorted; he was out in all weathers trying to defend himself to the plebs, chasing he-didn't-know-what anymore. After one particularly long speech, he collapsed with the chills and died nine days later at the age of fifty-eight.

A lawyer with years of experience wrangling over estates, Robert spent his closing hours drafting his own will. The bulk of his property he left to Betsey, including the house on Main Street, its contents, and its slaves. The remainder he divided equally among his fourteen children. The will was presented to the Fayette County Court the September after his death. If no one had challenged it, approval would have been the work of a moment. But into the legal breach stepped George Rogers Clark Todd, Robert's youngest son by his first wife. His father's will, George argued, bore only one witness's signature—not the two required by law. It was therefore invalid, and the entire estate, including Betsey's portion, would have to be liquidated—slaves, stocks, land, and furniture—and divided up between the heirs.

It was a devastating blow to his stepmother, who had raised George from infancy. And that's exactly why he did it. Highly intelligent, George was the most schooled of all the Todd males. He had graduated from Centre College in 1843 and the Transylvania medical school in 1848, where he had been an outspoken advocate of autopsies. An excellent anatomist and dissector, he ultimately became a skilled pathologist and surgeon. But George had a host of problems, most of which began at birth. He had been, however innocently, the cause of his mother's death, and it may have plagued him, probably encouraged his interest in medicine, and certainly stranded him awkwardly between the first and second iteration of Todds. By the time he came of age, his stepmother had had as much of the Parker-Todds as she could take. Yet George hung around longer than all of them, living at home through medical school. Battles were inevitable—and exacerbated by

George's drinking, which got steadily worse. Unlike most of his brothers, who drank heavily but convivially, George drank in anger. He had killed his mother coming out of the womb. He was short, myopic, and "inferior looking." He stuttered so badly that people routinely thought he was feeble. When in his cups, he forgot his problems, stuttered less, and could be, among his friends, charming and even fascinating. But alcohol also loosed his rages. He became the kind of man who wanted to sue life for damages. For the rank unfairness of his dead mother, bad eyes, and tangled tongue, the world owed him something, and when his father died, George meant to collect.

The legal wrangling would go on for years. Through it all, George's conduct would be shockingly vindictive. He didn't care that some of the household items had been Betsey's before marriage — he wanted them sold anyway. He didn't care that some of the slaves had emotional ties to the area — he wanted them sold anyway. He didn't care that his uncles would have to pay top dollar to buy back their sister's own bed and teacups — let them pay. He didn't care that he was effectively liquidating his father's memory. He was chasing something else — an equal portion of his father's love, equal to the penny.

The entire family was sucked into the quagmire, including Lincoln. By common consensus, he was elected to represent the older siblings' legal interest in the affair. In the end, George mostly had his way. Betsey's brothers saved her things, but they could not save her house. She and her children moved into Buena Vista, the summer home that had belonged to her family. Each sibling was then awarded an equal share in the resulting settlement, but each had to subtract from that amount any money that Robert had given them over the course of his lifetime. In the case of the Lincolns, the result was a negative sum, which made the entire proceeding a little more galling.

V.

ROBERT'S DEATH had more consequences than the legal ones. The father of all the children, he had been the symbolic linchpin holding them together. His removal triggered a sort of family diaspora, especially among the boys.

George was the first to go. He relocated only forty miles from home, but he moved the most completely away. No one wanted him around, and he knew it. To his self-pitying litany of afflictions he now added that he was the black sheep of his family. Setting up as a physician in Cynthiana, Kentucky, he boarded with a local lawyer, James Rolland Curry. Not long after, George married Curry's youngest daughter, Anne. With insufficient funds to set up housekeeping, the couple continued to live with Anne's father. They toured Niagara in 1851 and had a daughter, Mattie Dee, in 1853. By then, however, George had returned in earnest to the bottle. Despite living under his father-in-law's roof, he came home drunk and raged at his wife, who, though not the cause of them, had not been the solution to his problems. Curry's patience finally snapped when he caught his son-in-law forging documents. Curry not only threw George out of the house but threatened to prosecute him if he ever returned to Kentucky. George was hastily packed up and driven out of town in the dead of night by one of Curry's sons-in-law. Anne was granted a quick divorce on the grounds of cruelty. She never remarried and was remembered by a cousin as forever after "a broken-hearted woman."

"Uncle Sam," the oldest of the Humphreys-Todd boys, was also set adrift by his father's death. A recent college graduate, he didn't have enough money to buy a house of his own and couldn't move back in with his mother, who was, thanks to George, living in tight quarters. With few other options, Sam accepted an invitation to reside on a dead uncle's sugar plantation. In any age money has gravity, and the family members who have the most of it draw satellite relations into a low orbit about them.

That gravity had first begun to build around Betsey's uncle, James Brown, who had been Louisiana senator (1813–17; 1819–23) and U.S. minister to France (1823–29). (He is also famous for blabbing to Alexis de Tocqueville about New Orleans's quadroon concubine system.) While a senator, Brown had purchased Roseland plantation in St. Charles Parish. Not much was made of it until his nephew, Betsey's older brother, John Humphreys, took it over and converted it to sugar. Louisianans had been growing sugar since the 1750s, but it did not become a true cash crop until 1817 when ribbon cane was introduced. The ensuing sugar boom lasted until the Civil War and made Louisiana's cane fields twice as profitable as the most productive plantations of the Cotton Kingdom. In 1824, John Humphreys secured his investment by marrying into an even richer sugar family, the Kenners, who were to Louisiana sugar what Carnegie would later be to Pittsburgh steel. John's luck ran out in 1835 when he died at the age of forty-six, but by then his money had reached terminal gravity. His older brother,

David, had gotten rich selling flour to the sugar planters. His younger brother Alexander had moved to Roseland and married into the Delhommers, another wealthy sugar family. And a parade of nephews, Humphreys and Todd, were on their way south.

It is unlikely that Sam performed any actual work on the plantation. Probably, as with most of the local planters' sons, he spent much of his time in New Orleans. Unlike them, he had very little capital to fall back on. In 1856 he married twenty-year-old Clelie Cecile Royer, the daughter of a French-born gardener, Charles Royer. Five years and three babies later, Sam was still living with the Royers and working as a clerk. By then, however, his prodigal younger brother, David, had arrived in the city to spice things up.

David's career as the prodigal son had begun in 1846, when, at the age of fourteen, he had run off to fight the Mexicans. In many ways, the boy Betsey and Robert knew never came back. He never returned to school, never settled down. Instead, with nothing to anchor him, he drifted into a series of reckless ventures. After the Mexican War, he joined the California gold rush. He did not make his fortune (indeed, he's listed as a Yolo County farmhand in the 1850 census), but he made sure to send a few trinkets home, just for show. In large families, siblings are under enormous pressure not merely to distinguish themselves but to differentiate themselves. David appears to have seen himself as The Adventurer of the Todd family, and he sent his mother and sisters occasional bulletins to remind them (and himself) of just how colorful his life had become.

When gold lost its rush, David shipped out as a freebooter. The 1850s was a big decade for such things. Narciso Lopez kicked off the craze in his 1850 attempt to "liberate" Cuba from the Spanish. His campaign ended a year later with his public garroting in Havana. Despite this, the American mania for freebooting continued, and each year a fresh crew of scofflaws would set sail under the broad banner of Manifest Destiny to try their luck at toppling some part of Spain's dwindling American empire.

The exact extent of David's involvement in freebooting is unknown. In 1851, he was certainly in Chile, fighting in what historians now call the First Succession Revolution. Though his exact movements are undocumented, he bore the stamp of the experience forever—a Chilean national flag tattooed in full color on his left arm. This was not his only tattoo. Over the years, he accumulated an anchor on his right arm, crossed guns and a shot and game pouch on his right breast, and a heart pierced with an arrow on his left breast. By twenty-five, David was a highly decorated soldier in America's rogue army.

Like most rogues, David had to slow down eventually. Older, fatter, and no richer for his adventures, he finally settled in New Orleans. Sam was there, and the town suited him: bustling, sinning, easy to get to — or away from. From there, a good breeze might blow him anywhere in the world. Once he moved to the city, however, it is unclear where he actually worked. Certainly by 1857 (and until 1861) he was working for W. W. Crane & Co., a carriage repository on Carondolet. Carrying a "complete assortment of Carriages from the best manufactories," Crane advertised itself as a home of guaranteed low prices and encouraged purchasers with "cash and approved paper" to come on down and "examine [their] stock before making selections elsewhere." In other words, David Todd worked at the nineteenth-century equivalent of a car dealership.

With Sam and David established in New Orleans, there was apparently some pressure applied on their youngest brother, Aleck, to join them. Redheaded and fiercely affectionate, Aleck was too close to his mother and sisters to want to leave Kentucky, however. At twenty-one, he was still living at home and helping his mother around the farm. Finally he took his inheritance in the form of land and built a log cabin a day's ride west of Lexington. Though rough-hewn and in a sparsely settled region, his home was "furnished very fine," according to a witness, and "attended by negro servants."

This diaspora of Todd males left firstborn Levi the only son remaining in Lexington. Unfortunately, Levi lost his compass when his father died. He had always been his father's first lieutenant. Now that his general had lost the war, what were his orders? There were no books to keep, no errands to run. He had not the first idea how to dig down and build something on his own. Instead, he clung to his father's final vision — that litigiousness might somehow correct the injustice of poverty. Levi's filings were staggering in number and brazenness, but for as long as he waited at the docket, his suit never came in. Indeed, by the late 1850s, Levi found himself more and more on the other side of the aisle, repeatedly hauled into court for debts that supported neither business nor family but only his "unfortunate habits." By 1859 his wife, Louisa, had had enough and filed for divorce. In her petition, she claimed that Levi had a "confirmed habit of drunkenness" and a "cruel and inhuman manner." "Wholly unfit to have the charge of any of these children," she said, "he has no estate and for some time past has made little or no provision for the maintenance of his family." Knowing that he would react violently, she made sure that the divorce petition included an injunction to "enjoin & restrain the Def't Levi O. Todd from disturbing or in any wise interfering with the plaintiff or any of the children."

VI.

THE TODD SISTERS fared a bit better in the wake of their father's death. The four oldest had already relocated to Springfield and there established a bulwark against family disintegration. True to her promise to herself, Mary waited until her sister Emilie came of age and then invited her to spend the winter season in Springfield. Emilie arrived in December 1854 before the legislative session and the fetes that accompanied it. The way Mary figured it, if her attractive sister arrived early in the season, she could meet all the town's most promising men in one go and have her pick among them. And indeed, Emilie caused an immediate sensation. Pronounced "sprightly and pretty," she was drawn into an almost continuous party. "There seems no bounds to the spirit of gayety and dissipation just now," a Todd cousin said of the season. "There has been one party and sometimes two or more every evening for two weeks and a disposition still to keep it up."

Unfortunately, the winter of 1854–55 proved a very trying time for the Lincolns, politically and personally. In the fall, Lincoln's friends had nominated him for the state legislature, a move that infuriated Mary. As a legislator, Lincoln would not be eligible for the U.S. Senate, which she rightly saw as within his grasp. Determined to make him senator, she marched to the newspaper office while he was out of town and had his name stricken from the list of nominees. Lincoln returned to find himself caught awkwardly between his friends and his wife. "When L. came home," remembered William Jayne, a Lincoln partisan, "I went to see him in order to get him to consent to run. This was at *his* house: he was then the saddest man I Ever Saw — the gloomiest: he walked up and down the floor — almost crying and to all my persuasions to let his name stand in the papers — he said 'No — I can't — you don't Know all — I say you don't begin to Know one half and that's all.'" Not understanding that Lincoln meant that his wife wouldn't stand for it, Jayne went to the paper and had Lincoln's name reinstated. Lincoln was then roundly elected, but in what the newspapers described as a "family decision" he immediately resigned, a move that alienated voters. "The People of Sangamon County," remembered Jayne, "[were] down on Lincoln — hated him." As a rebuke, they elected a Douglas Democrat to replace him.

All of this was merely a prelude to that winter's greater political humiliation, to which Emilie literally had a front-row seat. Having resigned from the legislature, Lincoln was now cleared to make a run at the Senate. He and Mary kept a minute account book of all the legislators (who then voted for senator) with their affiliations and allegiances. By their calculation, Lincoln had a good chance. Admittedly, his Whig Party was then in disarray, but a majority of the legislators stood against the Douglas Democrats, and Lincoln was seen as the leading opposition voice in the state. Even Douglas granted that Lincoln had a greater understanding of the "territorial question" (how to handle slavery in the Mexican cession) than most of his opponents in Congress. Confident, Mary and Elizabeth planned a grand party in what they presumed would be the Lincolns' honor, and all three sisters — Mary, Elizabeth, and Emilie — filed in to the statehouse gallery to witness Abraham's triumph.

On the first ballot, Lincoln led the field with forty-five of the needed fifty-one votes. It was hoped that five anti-Nebraska Democrats who had voted for Lyman Trumbull would now swing for Lincoln and the thing would be practically cinched. On the second ballot, however, the rogue Democrats refused to budge. If the Douglasites were to be defeated, it would have to be Lincoln's people who swung for Trumbull. "Disappointed and mortified," Lincoln had trouble choking down the fact that he and his forty-five votes would have to yield to Trumbull and his five. "[I] could bear defeat inflicted by [my] enemies with a pretty good grace," he told an acquaintance afterward, "but it was hard to be wounded in the house of [my] friends." Nevertheless, Lincoln instructed his people to throw their weight behind Trumbull, and Trumbull was elected senator.

The balloting over, everyone retired to the Edwardses' party, which was awkwardly reconfigured as a tribute to Lyman Trumbull. Lincoln bucked up with his customary magnanimity. Asked by Elizabeth if he was disappointed, Lincoln extended his hand to the victor and replied, "Not *too* disappointed to congratulate my friend Trumbull." Mary was less graceful in defeat. She suspected, and not without reason, that Trumbull's people were guilty of some double dealing, and she was livid that her husband should have been the one to concede. It only made it worse that Trumbull's wife, Julia Jayne, had been Mary's bridesmaid and one of her closest confidantes. The whole thing was just too rich: here she stood, in her sister's parlor, amid the preparations she had mentally made for herself and her husband, toasting the ascension of Mr. Five Votes and his backstabbing wife. From that day forward, Julia would be dead to her. Mary was probably glad to have Emilie along for moral support, but she must have been mortified that her younger sister had borne witness to such a public humiliation. Emilie did not actually vacate Springfield until June (and both sisters would remember the trip fondly), but there was no denying that the defeat had put a severe damper on Emilie's stay.

The larger purpose of the trip, however — finding Emilie a husband — was quickly met on her return home. Barely unpacked from her Springfield sojourn, she met a first-term member of the General Assembly, Benjamin Hardin Helm. At twenty-five, Hardin was exactly the sort of man Emilie's father would have liked — affable and ambitious, pedigreed and promising. Hardin's father, John Larue Helm, was a former Kentucky governor and the acting president of the Louisville and Nashville Railroad. His mother, Lucinda Barbour Hardin, was the daughter of Ben Hardin, former United States senator. Hardin was their firstborn and, like that rare child of privilege, seemed genuinely happy to carry the burden of the family's expectations. Completing his general education at fifteen, he enrolled at the Kentucky Military Institute for three months to get a jump on his military education. On his sixteenth birthday, he had matriculated at West Point and after the normal course graduated ninth in the forty-two-member class of 1851. In that day, the academy's highest graduates were assigned to the army's corps of engineers. Helm, however, preferred the dash of the cavalry. He had attended the Cavalry School for Practice in Carlisle, Pennsylvania, before being posted to Fort Lincoln on the Texas frontier.

The 1850s was a bad time to be in the army. The Mexican War over, Congress had become stingy with promotions. They believed such official discouragement would naturally winnow the bloated force down to a peacetime level. Heroes of the Mexican War (Robert E. Lee included) suddenly faced stalled careers. Those who hadn't participated in the Mexican War (Helm included) faced far worse. Most were garrisoned along lonely frontiers; many gave themselves over to boredom and alcohol; and some very promising soldiers quit the service altogether.

Helm's post was about a two-day ride west of San Antonio. It had been constructed in 1849 as one of eight new frontier garrisons strung between the Red River and the Rio Grande. Named after an officer who'd died at the battle of Buena Vista, Fort Lincoln wasn't much to look at. Constructed of log and limestone, it included barracks for two companies, a commissary, two storehouses, a hospital — and then nothing else for miles. The installation was situated on the west bank of Seco Creek, which during dry spells became a series of milky limestone pools. But it was in its own way beautiful. Built on high ground in open country, Fort Lincoln offered a commanding (and spectacular) view. The hundred soldiers who manned it were charged with protecting settlers, safeguarding military and commercial traffic along Woll Road, and hunting down Indian raiders, real or imagined.

Helm had been in Texas for only six months when he began to experience health problems. The doctor diagnosed him with inflammatory rheumatism — a painful swelling of the major joints, especially those of the lower extremity. The news was depressing. From boyhood, Helm had dreamed that a life in the saddle would bear him to distinction; now it offered a grimly painful prospect. That Fort Lincoln was to be abandoned compounded the difficulty. The frontier was moving west, and Helm's dragoons would move with it. Given his condition, the idea of rougher accommodations and a rougher detail carving out the next fort might not have appealed to Helm. Instead he obtained a leave of absence and returned to his father's home in Elizabethtown, Kentucky, to wrestle with his options. On the one hand, he saw himself, and was seen by others, as a military man with a bright future. On the other hand, now back in Kentucky amid the comforts of family and family connections, he found that the rough and rawboned existence of a frontier fort-sitter had lost its luster. While he had been off nursing saddle sores in the middle of nowhere, his father had become governor of a state. The way Hardin began to figure it, in a nation at peace, a life in politics opened an avenue to distinction broader and less bumpy than a life in the army. Resigning his commission on October 9, 1852, he decided to remake himself as a lawyer-politician like his father. With his customary zeal, Helm returned to the classroom, where he had always excelled. He graduated from the University of Louisville's law school in 1853, and topped that off with a six-month advanced course at Harvard. Once back in Kentucky, he organized a law partnership with his first cousin, Martin Hardin Cofer, and was quickly elected to the General Assembly.

Thus, by the time he met Emilie, Hardin's reputation was again on the rise. He had segued deftly from one career to another, and although he moved in his father's wake, no one doubted he was his own man. Privilege, talent, and likeability occasionally create a compelling compound, and apparently they did so in Helm. Like Ninian Edwards, he was a governor's son and perhaps too mesmerized by his own ascending star. But Hardin was less elitist than Ninian, more willing to work, and more romantic. Almost as soon as he met Emilie, he fell utterly in love with her.

To be fair, Emilie Todd was the period's ideal of adorable. She was petite, modest, doe-eyed, and raven-haired. She had some of the mischief but none of the cruelty of a belle. Indeed, she acted like a girl who would mate for life. Hardin was similarly disposed. Not exactly handsome, his face and eyes were soft and innocent. His receding hair tended to make him look younger rather than older, like an open-faced baby. He did have one drawback — a prim sense of right that occasionally made him preachy. "Study hard and make yourself a smart woman," he advised his sister, Lucinda. "Make Ma & Papa proud of you [and] always try to be amiable in your disposition. You have been sick a great deal and it has made you peevish." "Ours is a profession that requires time & patience," he instructed his brother George, who was also studying law. "Though it may become somewhat irksome it becomes you to bear it like a man." Once they were courting, Emilie came in for her share of minute advice as well: "Tell your mother not to let you eat green apples," he instructed her precisely.

The couple married in Frankfort on March 26, 1856. Almost immediately, Hardin returned to the legal circuit. In addition to serving three counties as district attorney, he was also stumping for Millard Fillmore. (Fillmore had already been president; he had ascended to the office from the vice presidency when Zachary Taylor died of acute indigestion in 1850. In 1852, however, the antislavery wing of the Whig Party had passed Fillmore over and secured the nomination of the war hero Winfield Scott. So thoroughly was Scott trounced that one Whig representative rightly exclaimed, "We are slayed. The party is dead — dead — dead!" Thus, in 1856, Fillmore was running as a Know Nothing, a new party pledged to do something about the rising tide of immigration.) New to politics, Hardin was rather elated to have joined the fray. "[I] have just finished another *whaling* Fillmore speech & I think with some credit to myself," he wrote home. "None of the Sag-*Nitch* orators have as yet attempted to reply to me nor have I any opposition . . . though I may stir it up before I finish." Occasionally, Hardin did stumble into a town less sympathetic to boilerplate nativism. In Curdsville, for instance, he found himself in danger of being run out of town. "[What] a terrible Catholic *hole!*" he interjected. "I was interrupted a great deal & I presume I would have got a dreadful beating if the *rascals* had had the courage to try their hands." Even these moments were energizing, however. "The excitement of speaking & the active exercise," he exclaimed, "is doing me much good both *physically & mentally.*" The only drawback was that he missed his wife in ways Lincoln had never missed Mary. "I *can't* keep your image out of my mind," he wrote home. "Your presence is essentially necessary to my happiness. While I write I have your daguerreotype open before me but it only increases my [long]ing to see you. Dear Emma, I am almost foolish about you."

The Helms and Lincolns remained close throughout the 1850s. They did so despite the widening gulf between their respective sections, and they did so deliberately. The few letters that survive give every indication that dozens were written. And each one seems consciously constructed as a bridge, emphasizing shared memories, shared views, and shared affection. "Altho' Mr L- is, or was, a *Fremont* man," Mary explained to her sister, "you must not include him with so many of those, who belong to *that party,* an *Abolitionist.* In principle he is far from it — All he desires is that slavery shall not be extended, let it remain where it is." Having thus excused her husband's political position, she then admitted that hers was much closer to Emilie's. "My weak woman's heart was too Southern in feeling to sympathise with any but Fillmore," she wrote of the 1856 election. "[He] feels the *necessity* of keeping foreigners within bounds. If some of you Kentuckians had to deal with the 'wild Irish,' as we housekeepers are sometimes called upon to do, the south would certainly elect Mr. Fillmore next time."

Admittedly, the Helms and the Lincolns did not see each other often. Emilie was too "delicate" to travel in these years. But Hardin spent a week with the Lincolns in 1857, and he and Abraham developed a genuine rapport. Despite the age difference (twenty-two years), the two had a lot in common. Both were political. Both liked to tell anecdotes of long hours spent circuit riding and speechifying among the yokels. Most important, both had grown up in the same region around Knob Creek, Kentucky. Over the course of the week, Helm caught Lincoln up on the almost forgotten names of his childhood. Helm's law partner and cousin, Martin Cofer, for instance, had married the niece of Sarah Bush Johnston, Lincoln's stepmother. The two shared a mutual fondness for many such people and places. And though they did not see quite eye to eye on the subject of slavery, at base they were both Kentucky moderates. Hardin's parents owned sixty slaves, but he didn't own any, and he firmly believed that Kentuckians would go for compensated emancipation. For his part, Lincoln had no problem with such a program. What he most wanted was for the institution to be put firmly back on the road to ultimate extinction, where the Founding Fathers had quietly left it for dead. Given their affability and adaptiveness, Lincoln and Helm spent long nights arguing over means rather than ends, just as Kentuckians before them had done for generations. In each other's company, they could indulge the hope that the nation too might find such happy common ground.

Mary had been charmed by Hardin also. Indeed, her experience of becoming more deeply acquainted with Emilie and her husband had been so pleasant that she began to indulge the idea of inviting her youngest sisters out to Springfield too. "I have often wished that *Dedee* was here," she wrote in 1857, referring to her second youngest sister, Elodie. "I hope another winter, both Kitty & herself will come out & we will endeavour to make it as pleasant as possible for them." It would be a couple years before the invitation could be accepted, however. And by then, Lincoln had been elected president of the United States.

3

1861: Divided We Fall

I.

TO LINCOLN, the winter of 1860–61 seemed to be dragging on interminably. "I would willingly," he told a friend, "take out of my life a period in years equal to the months which intervene between now and my inauguration." He was not in a hurry to be president, per se. Rather, he found the limbo of president-elect excruciating. Inundated by correspondence, besieged by office-seekers, journalists, and advisors, he was under enormous pressure to say something about the "distracted" state of the country. His election had divided the nation, and the nation wanted to know what he was going to do about it.

To all such inquiries, Lincoln said as little as possible. He met all comers with a glad hand, plied them with funny stories, and sent them on their way before they could complain. This was all very deliberate. The South's secession, Lincoln believed, was an emotional, not a logical, response to his election. The incendiary language of a few Southern demagogues could not forever shout down the good sense of the Southern people as a whole. All they needed was time. If Lincoln said nothing that could be mangled in translation, Southerners' anger would ebb; their fears would subside; they would come to a place where they could be reasoned with. In their hearts, they knew that slavery needed to be abandoned. In their bones they knew that the Union vouchsafed a democracy unique in all the world. Lincoln genuinely believed that if he kept quiet and then reasoned with them directly, "the people . . . [would] set all right."

He was wrong, of course. In the end, Southerners walked out with a zeal he never foresaw. His blind spot was partly political, mostly personal. Lincoln was a sentimental, but not an emotional, man. He was given to depression but not anxiety. He was incredibly ambitious but not very passionate. Thus he could not be easily insulted, angered, panicked, or persuaded. His countrymen were different. His own wife was afraid of thunderstorms and occasionally hit him with chunks of wood. His own friends sometimes drank too much and said things they didn't mean. But always in the morning they were their sober selves again. Lincoln had learned from experience that when people he cared about went on an emotional bender, his best bet was to put his nearest son on his shoulders and heave the boy leeward to wait out the storm. Eventually, all regretted their acts of temper and again listened to reason.

To Lincoln, then, his inaugural address was critical. On March 4, he would speak publicly and substantively for the first time on the great issue of secession. Newspapers would have to carry his speech verbatim. His words could be misinterpreted but not misreported. He would have one chance to reason directly with the American people. Like most Americans of his age, Lincoln believed that words could change the world. The country's great speeches were sacred texts — and, like all politicians, Lincoln dreamed of making just such a speech himself. As William Seward later noted, Lincoln truly believed it would be possible to turn back the tide of secession with one address.

Unfortunately, he had no place to write the speech. His home and office were overrun with callers, and he had scarcely a moment to himself. Finally, his brother-in-law Clark Smith, who had married fifth-born Ann Todd, offered a solution. On the third floor of Smith's store, at the back of a storeroom, there was a door to his private office, and through that, there was a small room with an old slant-topped merchant's desk. It wasn't very glamorous, but it was definitely private, and it was Lincoln's to use if he wanted it. Lincoln accepted. In mid-January, he began working in earnest on his address. The texts he referred to most while preparing it were the other great speeches that had stared secession down: Daniel Webster's 1830 dismantling of the doctrine of nullification in his second reply to Hayne and Henry Clay's speech in support of the Compromise of 1850. Lincoln's first draft was a coldly firm and eminently reasonable document. The lawyer in him laid an airtight case before the jury of the American people. He had aimed the speech at the nation's head. Only later would he learn to aim for its heart.

While Lincoln worked on his inaugural, Mary left for a fortnight in New York. Her husband's new salary would be more money than they had ever known, and she had a decade of pent-up shopping to do. Clark Smith went as her escort and guide. His shop advertised the "Best Ladies Goods in Illinois," so he knew a thing or two about fashion. Mary's primary concern was for her clothes. Any hint of "western rusticity," anything outré, she knew, would give a determined enemy a point of entry for stabbing at places more vital. Like her father before her, she was determined to show that a Lexington-born blue blood had all the class of any eastern counterpart.

For Mary, shopping also satisfied deeper psychological needs. She derived a strange comfort from material possessions. Pretty things were permanent. They couldn't leave her, couldn't hurt her, couldn't die. The right button or bonnet string brought her an odd mental composure and compensated (in small ways) for even the worst catastrophe. Her preoccupation with them would eventually border on the pathological; for now it just gave her an unfair reputation for vanity.

Once home, Mary began planning the occasion at which she would debut her new clothes. The Lincolns' farewell reception was scheduled for February 6. Four of Mary's sisters helped her prepare: Frances and Ann, who lived in Springfield; Margaret, who came in from Cincinnati; and youngest-born Kitty, who was visiting from Lexington. At nineteen, Kitty had just come out. Like so many of the Todd girls, she had traveled to Springfield to sample a wider society away from the watchful eye of her mother. As host to the president-elect, Springfield was in a celebratory mood, and Kitty basked in the glow. Though surrounded by eligible men, she fell hardest for a young friend of the Lincolns', Ephraim Elmer Ellsworth.

Of course, the entire country was then in love with Ellsworth. At twenty-three, he was the most talked-about young man in America. His military company, the Zouaves, had recently concluded a national tour, performing their synchronized drills in their trademark baggy trousers, high gaiters, brocaded blue jackets, and red fezzes. As the esprit of his corps, Ellsworth became the country's model man, the beau ideal. This was, in fact, his life's ambition. Born of modest means, he had dedicated himself to becoming a paragon of masculinity — respectful, abstemious, modest, and commanding. Lincoln, noting the disparity in their heights, pronounced him "the greatest little man [he] ever met." Ellsworth had all the qualities Lincoln admired and didn't possess: physical grace, rigid bearing, personal attractiveness, and a sunny disposition. He was particularly good at roughhousing with the little Lincolns, Willie and Tad. In the fall of 1860, Ellsworth had relocated to Springfield at Lincoln's urging. He had studied a little law and traveled with Lincoln to make speeches in support of his candidacy. With Robert away at college, Ellsworth became a sort of surrogate son to the Lincolns. His pairing with Kitty Todd seemed very natural. Though Ellsworth had a fiancée to whom he was quite dedicated, he was a gracious flirt, and he and Kitty got on famously. By the end of her stay, Kitty was smitten.

Shortly after their farewell reception, the Lincolns moved into a hotel and readied their house for new renters. The details of the inaugural trip were set. As Lincoln shifted his focus from where he was going to where he was leaving, he became nostalgic. As long as the winter had been, he did not now want to leave. Springfield was the only home he had really known. By train, stage, and foot, he made the trip to Coles County to visit his stepmother. It was an emotional reunion — and an emotional re-parting. When he returned, he told his law partner, William Herndon, not to take his name off their sign. He would be back, he said, and they would go on as if "nothing had ever happened."

Lincoln left for the train station at seven-thirty on the morning of February 11. Arriving early, he stood in the waiting room near the platform and allowed his friends and neighbors to pass by and shake his hand for a last time. The mood was wistful. Lincoln's "face was pale," noted a witness, "and [he] quivered with [an] emotion so deep as to render him almost unable to utter a single word." After he boarded the train, a crowd of almost a thousand bunched around the back and demanded a proper goodbye. Looking out from the rear platform on a sea of faces, "almost all of whom [he] could recognize," Lincoln found it difficult to maintain his composure. "No one," he told his friends, "can appreciate my feeling of sadness at this parting. To this place, and the kindness of these people, I owe everything. Here I have lived a quarter of a century, and have passed from a young to an old man. Here my children have been born, and one is buried. I now leave, not knowing when, or whether ever, I may return."

Lincoln felt markedly better after the train departed. He was off on a new adventure, focused again on the road ahead. Making the trip with him were his immediate family, William Wallace, Elmer Ellsworth, his private secretaries, John Nicolay and John Hay, and a host of reporters in an adjoining car. The meandering trip to Washington would take twelve days and cover almost two thousand miles. The touchstones of his speeches along the way were humility, homeliness, and hope. As always, he got the greatest mileage out of his own ugliness. In seeing the American people and allowing them to see him, he was, he said, getting by far the better of the bargain. "I hold myself without mock modesty, the humblest of all individuals that have ever been elevated to the Presidency," he told a crowd. "I am [a man] without a name, perhaps without a reason why I should have a name." Regarding himself "but an accidental instrument" of a strange election, Lincoln joked that he was too ineffectual to do any real damage in four years. "No great harm can be done by [me] in that time," he said, "[but] if anything goes wrong . . . and you find you have made a mistake, elect a better man next time. There are plenty of them." By refusing to take himself too seriously, Lincoln encouraged his countrymen to do the same. In their hands, not his, lay the future of the country. "You need only to maintain your composure," he told a crowd. "If you, the PEOPLE, are but true to yourselves," he noted, "then why shall we not, as heretofore, be recognized and acknowledged as brethren again, living in peace and harmony one with another?"

II.

LINCOLN'S INAUGURAL EXPRESS had made it as far as New York before the Southern people inaugurated their own president. The "man and the hour" were officially met at one P.M. on February 18, 1861, when Jefferson Davis mounted the steps of the Alabama state capitol in Montgomery and looked out on a sea of fluttering white handkerchiefs. Southerners, he told the crowd, were at last one people "united in heart." Reunion with the North was "neither practicable nor desirable." "We have entered upon the career of independence," Davis declared. "[If] reason [does not] guide the action of the government from which we have separated . . . the suffering of millions will bear testimony to the folly and wickedness of our aggressors." It was neither a moving nor a particularly eloquent address, but it had one unequivocal virtue — its meaning was lost on no one. "A Government is formed for the South," noted one observer, "and no idea of reconstruction is entertained."

The inaugural exercises complete, men and women returned to their homes and hotels to prepare themselves for the Confederacy's first social event, a levee to be held in Davis's honor at Estelle Hall. Tiffany & Company of New York had shipped $30,000 worth of jewelry to Montgomery in the days preceding the gala. Confederate belles would celebrate their independence in federal chokers and chains. By dusk, "every house, little and big, was illuminated from the Capitol to the Exchange," and rockets and Bengal lights were being thrown steadily across the width of the street. The receiving line formed at about eight o'clock and quickly bunched up behind the voluminous skirts of the carefully coifed ladies. With the press of bodies, the temperature in the hall rose steadily toward the unbearable, and by ten o'clock the crowds began to disperse, the weary for their beds, the stalwart for a dance being organized at nearby Concert Hall.

Two of the more conspicuous females at the reception were Elodie Todd and Martha Todd White. Martha was the tenth-born of the fourteen Todds. She had met and married an Alabamian, Clement White, as a teenager and now lived with him in Selma, fifty miles west of Montgomery. Thirteenth-born Elodie was twenty, unmarried, and still living with her mother in Kentucky. She had come to Alabama to visit her sister in the past, but never before had she gotten the kind of reception she got in 1861. Her and Martha's status as Mary Lincoln's sisters made them celebrities at the Davises' ball. "Of course they attract considerable attention, and are the toast of Southerners," reported the press.

As the single sister, Elodie was in particular demand. She was not, in her own estimate, a beauty. "I am just as they say in K[entucky]," she quipped, "the ugliest of my Mother's handsome daughters and simply plain Dee Todd. I am used to being called so and I do not feel it at all." Elodie was being coy, however. With a fine figure, sweet face, and courant black curls, she had men spinning in and out of her circle all night seeking introductions. Many men may have fallen in love with Elodie that night. History records only one: Nathaniel Henry Rhodes Dawson. Nathaniel was an acquaintance of Martha's and a Selma neighbor. Though only thirty-two, he looked and felt older. His hair was gone. His parents were dead. He had lost two wives already, each of whom had left him with a baby daughter and a desponding heart. But gazing at Elodie, standing in the center of the whirl of Confederate becoming, he felt suddenly sure of life's enormous possibilities. "I made up my mind [right then]," he later recalled, "to make the star mine in whose beams I had wandered."

III.

ABRAHAM LINCOLN was inaugurated two weeks later. He spent the day before the ceremony retouching his address. Most of his advisors had approved the original text, but Secretary of State Seward had found it too provocative, with too few touches of affection. Lincoln agreed and made the changes. In the evening, he went to hear John J. Crittenden's farewell speech to the Senate. Crittenden, who had taken over fellow Kentuckian Henry Clay's role as a sectional go-between, hadn't gotten enough votes in support of compromise, and packed galleries listened as he poured shame upon the assembly. "What man is there here that is not of a blood, flowing . . . through every State in the Union? And we talk about not compromising a family quarrel. . . . In the name of God, who is it that will adopt that policy? We are one people in blood; in language one; in thoughts one; we read the same books; we feed on the same meats; we go to the same schools; we belong to the same communion. . . . It is our infirmity to have . . . difficulties. Let it be our magnanimity and our wisdom to compromise and settle them."

They were difficult words for Lincoln to hear. Crittenden, like so many others, had chosen the metaphor of "family quarrel" because it resonated with literal truth. Many American families would quarrel in the months ahead — none more than the president's. And yet the president was, as much as anyone, to blame. People had approached him with Crittenden's compromise — extending the 36° 30' line to the Pacific — and he had rejected it. For him, slavery was an evil; it was protected where it existed, but it should not be allowed to spread. Having always held this opinion and having just been elected for it, Lincoln thought it ridiculous that he should compromise it away now. "The tug has to come," he said. On the question of slavery in the territories, he and his party would "hold firm, as with a chain of steel."

Lincoln was inaugurated the next day, the fourth of March, a little after noon. With him on the platform were his wife and sons, Mary's sisters Elizabeth and Margaret, and their cousin Elizabeth Todd Grimsley. Watching her cousin, Lizzie thought that he delivered his address "with all the dignity, calmness and composure of one accustomed to delivering presidential inaugurals." Of the speech itself, she noted, "Who shall say that [it] will not go down the ages as a model of clear diction, dispassionate dealing . . . and tender poetic appeal?"

The speech is best known for its peroration, and rightly so, for surely it is one of the prettier things Lincoln ever said: "I am loath to close. We are not enemies, but friends. We must not be enemies. Though passion may have strained, it must not break our bonds of affection. The mystic chords of memory, stretching from every battle-field, and patriot grave, to every living heart and hearth-stone, all over this broad land, will yet swell the chorus of the Union, when again touched, as surely they will be, by the better angels of our nature." The entire effect is musical. Hearing it once and not reading it closely, the audience would have had a vague sense that they were eavesdropping on heaven, a place where chords swell with the angels' touch, where Americans all, past and present, are bound together, a congregation singing from their souls. For the duration of this passage and for a few seconds afterward, the idea of war must have seemed far away.

For all its beauty, however, the passage does not stand up to scrutiny. In fairness to Lincoln, this was not his best stuff, and indeed, he hadn't written it — he had rewritten it. The original idea was Seward's, though his version was far clumsier: "I close. We are not, we must not be, aliens or enemies, but fellow-countrymen and brethren. Although passion has strained our bonds of affection too hardly, they must not, I am sure they will not, be broken. The mystic chords, which proceeding from so many battle-fields and so many patriot graves, pass through all the hearts and all the hearths in this broad continent of ours, will yet harmonize in their ancient music when breathed upon by the guard-ian angels of the nation." Much has been said of Lincoln's stylistic im-provements, and his version *is* more lyrical, but they are substantially the same text and suffer from the same flaws. In both cases, one has to ask, where exactly is this music coming from? Whether the chords are proceeding through (Seward), or stretched between (Lincoln), the idea that they connect every heart, hearth, field, and grave in the coun-try surely conjures an image of a complex network, not an orderly in-strument. If the instruments in both speeches are identically clumsy, however, the musicians playing them are substantially different. In Seward's, the angels who set the music in motion are our guardians, the heavenly minions who've always looked after God's people. In Lin-coln's, *we* are the angels; *we* make the music. It is *our* better nature that can remind us that we are threaded through the heart to all our fellows; it is when *we* sing that we send a sympathetic vibration down the line, setting the rest of us to singing too.

Even if Lincoln had worked out all the kinks of style and sense, however, the famous passage has a larger problem: it seems, as it was, tacked on. The overwhelming message of the speech is not that the two sides *shouldn't* separate but that they *couldn't*. First, and most obviously, separation was illegal. But as important, it was impractical, impossible. The two sections were physically bound to each other. Whatever problems they had would only be aggravated by trying to pretend otherwise. The North would be *less* likely to surrender fugitive slaves. The South would be *more* likely to import new slaves. Disunion couldn't solve the divisive slave question; it could only further irritate it.

Seward, like Crittenden, had tried to save the national family by saying that its members ought to love one another. In his first inaugural, Lincoln reminded the national family that whatever they *ought* to do, there were certain things they could not help but do. They were a family, whether they liked it or not, whether they liked one another or not. In this way, he put the American family, and through it the Todds, on a more reliable foundation. Their love might rise or fall, but their relation was permanent. "Suppose you go to war," Lincoln reminded them all; "you cannot fight always; and when after much loss on both sides, and no gain on either, you cease fighting, the identical old questions . . . are again upon you."

It would be four years before Lincoln's words were fully understood. The speech he had hoped would save the Union fell on deaf ears. Southern papers hated it, of course. But a large number of Northern papers savaged it too. "Wretchedly botched and unstatesmanlike," reported the *Hartford Times*. "One of the most awkwardly constructed official documents we have ever inspected," seconded the *Philadelphia Evening Journal*. "A loose, disjointed, rambling affair," echoed the *Chicago Times*. The *Baltimore Republican* called it simply "the death-knell of peace."

Waiting on Lincoln's desk the next morning was an urgent request to reinforce Fort Sumter. He had made a promise to hold federal installations, and he intended to keep it. At four-thirty A.M. on April 12, rather than see Sumter resupplied, Confederate forces opened fire on the lurking shadow in Charleston Harbor. Perhaps the two sides couldn't go on fighting always, but a fight was exactly what they wanted now.

IV.

AFTER SUMTER, three of the Todd brothers could not get into the Confederate army quick enough. George, Sam, and David all turned their backs on the Union wing of their family with scarcely a pang. In a way, burning their bridges actually helped to make their emotional experience of disunion more complete. More than most Southerners, the Todd boys had truly seceded from something — and Southerners were willing, for now, to congratulate them for it.

With a medical degree and dissecting experience, George easily found a commission as a surgeon. He was ordered to report to Richmond, where he could be assigned to a needy regiment. With fewer skills, Sam had to sign on as a private in a New Orleans company of Chasseurs à Pied, a militia group famous for its Frenchified drill and fancy dress. (Once in camp, however, he began to have health problems and had to return home.) David's exact movements are cloudier, obscured by his own braggadocio. His version, which he loved to tell (and which grew taller with each telling), went like this: Before joining the Confederacy, he traveled to Washington to visit the Lincolns. He went not as a brother, however, but *as a spy*. Cloaking his Confederate sympathies, he pressed Lincoln for details about the government's war footing, and, chump that he was, Lincoln not only failed to see through the designs but offered to make David minister to Brazil. David was playing a risky game, however. Federal detectives had been watching him closely and persuaded the president to have him arrested. They were apparently not much brighter than Lincoln, however, because David "promptly and completely befuddled and outwitted his stupid captors" by claiming that, in all decency, he should be allowed to attend a wedding in Georgetown before he was taken to jail. Availing himself of a "favorable opportunity," he "slipped out, jumped into a hack, and, compelling the hackman to drive him to the Potomac River, succeeded in crossing it, and escaped to Richmond, where he joined the Confederate Army!"

What of this actually happened and what is part of David's rich fantasy life is impossible to determine. Like most tall-tale tellers, David wrapped kernels of truth in loving layers of bunkum. But which is the kernel? Did he try to see the Lincolns? Did he even go to Washington? Did he, perhaps, attend a wedding in Georgetown, drink too much, and regale attendees with a story that, with a few tweaks, would eventually become this one? No one will ever know. No family member, newspaper, or third party confirms any aspect of David's tale. The story is important, then, not because it is true but because it is what David wished were true. First and last, he would view the war through the prism of manly adventure.

What can be verified is this: Possibly with Sam, David traveled from

But while Nathaniel was lost in romantic reverie, Elodie found herself entwined in family dramas. As expected, news of her engagement had not gone over well. For each excited letter she wrote she received an admonition in return. One of the sternest came from Mary Lincoln, who was rather appalled at the idea of one of her favorite younger sisters marrying a Confederate captain. "Sister Mary . . . receives the news seriously," Elodie told Nathaniel, "and writes me a long letter on the subject of matrimony and adjoins me that I am a great deal better off as I am. She ought to know as she committed the fatal step years ago, and I believe another such letter would almost make me abandon the idea." She received a similar sermon from her mother, who traveled to Selma to deliver it personally. "Your captain," Betsey told her, "has filled your head with ideas that I have been all my life trying to keep you from possessing." Given such reactions, Elodie decided to delay informing her youngest brother, Aleck, who could be possessive. "I intend writing to him that he must make up his mind to give me up to you without a word," Elodie told Nathaniel, "but I believe he will take the idea of my marrying very much to heart and grieve that I would prefer any one to him."

Even as she was defending her decision to her family, she was doubting it herself. Nathaniel had told her, "Circumstances have made me love you more than I dreamed that I was capable of"—but he had never examined the circumstances. Hundreds of miles from a home that seemed in his dimming recollection "perfectly fabulous," Nathaniel could easily see Elodie as a symbol of all he would return to, a glorified abstraction. But he seemed easily to forget that she was a person with problems and peccadilloes of her own. In her letters, Elodie corrected the rosy excesses of his domestic reveries. When Nathaniel called her beautiful, she called him a flatterer and insincere. When he called her gentle, she advised him that she had a temper of her own and not the amiability he, *"lover-like,"* attributed to her. A woman of irreverent wit, she could not resist poking occasional fun at Nathaniel's chronic ardor. A few days into his army service, he had managed to drop a trunk on his head—the gash required stitches and left a permanent scar. "I am sorry to hear that you are *battling* already," Elodie wrote sympathetically. "[I] would prefer your escaping as many scars as possible but do not think of returning home *without some* as you will never be accounted *brave and bold.* Kitty says she fears you will come home limping or without arms, Matt [Martha] says without a head, so you can see what a subject of concern you are in the family."

New Orleans to Montgomery after Sumter. He may have had some remaining contacts in the army from either his tour in the Mexican War or his days as a freebooter. Even without these, he had legitimate military experience and a garrulous, bellicose temper. If he fell in with the right tough-talking crowd over drinks, he had an ability to make important friends quickly. Regardless, something turned the trick. On May 1, he traveled to Selma with good news. He had secured a first lieutenancy, with a promise of a captaincy in three months.

Elodie was dismayed by the news. She was proud of her brother and sympathetic to the Southern cause. But if the times were stirring, they were also starting to get a little scary. Unlike her brothers, she thought the gathering storm looked more ominous than glorious. Her mother had written her that it was time for her to return to Kentucky, and she was inclined to agree. Home was the place to be in a crisis. About then, there was a knock at the door. It was Nathaniel Dawson.

Nathaniel had been quietly courting Elodie for two months. Under the pretense of lending books or sending food or flowers, he had attached short bits of poetry or his own romantic sentiments. Elodie had been flattered by the gestures, but not much more. In fairness, Nathaniel hadn't put his whole heart into it. His second wife had been dead only a year, and he wasn't sure he was ready to risk his heart a third time. He had poured more of his energy into his militia group, which had been drilling for about a month. When Jefferson Davis called for three thousand volunteers from the state of Alabama, Nathaniel asked his men if they wished to offer their services. The vote was taken "without a dissenting voice," and the Magnolia Cadets hastily prepared their kits. "Tho' the step is one that will call for some sacrifices," Nathaniel wrote a friend, "I hope it will give me that entire, constant employment that seems so much to relieve the troubles of this life." For him, the army offered an escape. "My own home is so dark & desolate," he noted, "that I will hardly miss its absence and I can expect no trials that can equal those of the past year. I would fly from them if I could." But as he was preparing his kit to leave, it struck him that his home wouldn't look any brighter when he returned. He could fly from it, but if he lived, he would have to fly right back again. So he marched over to Martha Todd White's and asked Elodie for her hand.

Elodie was taken aback. Nathaniel's notes hadn't hinted at anything quite *this* bold. Indeed, her whole problem with the man had been his reserve. He had always seemed just a little "cold, not unfeeling [but] undemonstrative, [as if he] did not care for friendship or love either."

And yet here he was, all impulsiveness, asking her to be his wife. She was impressed. There was another problem, however. Her mother would be shocked. "Ever since I can remember," she noted, "I have been looked upon and called the 'old maid' of the family and Mother seemed to think I was to be depended on to take care of her when all the rest of her *handsomer daughters* had left her." But then she thought about it. Her brothers were making commitments and damning the consequences; couldn't she do the same? So she said yes. "[They may] think I am committing a sin to give a thought to any other than the arrangements they have made for me," she said of her family, "but as this is the age when Secession, Freedom, and rights are asserted, I am claiming mine."

Elodie and Nathaniel had only a few days together before he had to leave. The Magnolia Cadets had been ordered to Dalton, Georgia, where they would be mustered in as Company C of the Fourth Alabama Infantry Regiment. From there they would head to Lynchburg and then to an encampment across the Potomac from Washington, D.C. Elodie helped Nathaniel pack. She and Martha sewed the Cadets a company flag, which was presented on April 24 in a ceremony at Watts' Hall. Two days later, the couple walked to the dock on the Alabama River south of town, where Nathaniel got on a paddleboat. He watched the shore until he could not see Elodie anymore, and then he sat down and wrote her a letter. "We are speeding on our way over the water," he noted, "and at each revolution of the wheels, the distance between us is lengthened, but the ties which bind us are only increased." It was the theme that would become the foundation of their courtship. Though "almost strangers" when Nathaniel left, they would fall in love by mail. "You say we hardly know each other," Nathaniel wrote Elodie after a few months in camp, "[but] I think differently. I know you from your letters intimately." "Had I not been a volunteer," he continued, "I never would have known how rich were the imaginings of your mind and how pure and beautiful were the flowers that grow in the garden of your heart." With each letter, they revealed a little more of themselves in the safer spaces provided by paper and pen. "[By the time] we are joined in the holy bonds of marriage," Nathaniel claimed, "we will have discovered in each other many latent qualities of head and heart that, otherwise, would have been known only after long years of association." Certainly the distance was a hardship; certainly nothing could compare to spending time together. But while most couples had a merely perfunctory and artificial courtship, Elodie and Nathan-

iel were enduring a trial by fire. "Do you not think," Nathaniel ask[ed] "that the circumstances which will prevent our marriage at any cert[ain] time will have a tendency to strengthen and increase our love for e[ach] other? When tried and made to pass thro' an ordeal we generally co[me] out stronger and better." In Dawson's mind, then, distance did not much compromise their love as help to constitute it. As the chasm t[hat] opened between them grew deeper, their longing grew deeper to fil[l] the forced space tested and redoubled their devotion.

And Nathaniel was nothing if not devoted. He worshiped Elo[die] he claimed, with a kind of "Eastern idolatry," and he regularly tur[ned] toward Selma and kissed the miniature attached to his watch fob. [He] liked it when love took material form, and he often sent personal [ob]jects folded into the pages of his letters — pressed flowers, leaves, p[eb]bles, scraps of material, a lock of his hair, a bit of gold lace from [his] sword belt. When Elodie requested that her letters be burned afte[r he] read them, Nathaniel refused, telling her they were "sacred writi[ng]" and had to be preserved. He took considerable trouble to make s[ure] the letters were returned to her for safekeeping, but he kept tw[o of] them on his person at all times — and reread them constantly. W[hen] he had no new letters to fire his imagination, he took long walks ac[ross] the flattened grasses of camp to some secluded spot to be inspire[d by] his own sentimentality. "I am disposed to be romantic," he explaine[d to] Elodie: "Scenery and circumstances by which I am surrounded alw[ays] affect my disposition." At Quantico Creek he sat on a hillock pic[king] violets, staring bemusedly at a Union gunboat on the river. "I can [see] the men aboard plainly," he noted, "and sometimes fear the sorry [little] wretches will throw a shell at me." At Harpers Ferry he chose a [van]tage overlooking the confluence of the Shenandoah and the Poto[mac.] "You have [from here] a lovely view of the surrounding country, fi[elds] and farms," he noted, "while, just at your feet, the waters of the [two] noble streams . . . mingle together in friendly sympathy. . . . In the [dis]tant fields one sees flocks of sheep and herds of cattle, browsing [upon] the rich clover and luxuriant blue grass [under] a blue and broade[ning] horizon." From such a scenic lookout, the idea of war and the mo[not]ony of camp life seemed far away — the distance between him and [Elo]die began to close. "I see your image in the beautiful morning," he [told] her, "and in the beautiful country around me. You *color* everyth[ing."] Commemorating the moment, Nathaniel carved Elodie's initials i[n a] rock. "If fortune favors our love," he told her, "and we live, I will b[ring] you here that you may see for yourself."

Elodie was being playful, of course. In other letters, she expressed greater concern for Nathaniel's well-being. And in fairness, she was an often distracted lover. Already, in choosing Nathaniel, she had cut herself off in important ways from Mary, the closest of her Northern siblings. If Kentucky failed to secede, she would be cut off from her mother, her sisters, her home. Betsey and Kitty had come to Selma immediately after Elodie had announced her engagement. But a few weeks later, her mother began to talk of returning. "I will miss her so much," Elodie noted, "and feel as tho I am *deserted,* but the truth is I am a *deserter* myself, and you are much to blame for my becoming such." It was unusual for Elodie to blame Nathaniel in this way. She had made her own choice, and she did not regret it. But if Kentucky didn't secede, she might. "What is to be the fate of home?" she asked. "I cannot divine and will not think [about] Kentucky."

V.

THOROUGHLY SOUTHERN in its social customs, increasingly Northern in its economic interests, the Bluegrass State was a unique hybrid of the two regions. Kentucky had more slaveholders than most of the states that had already seceded, but they tended to own fewer slaves. Put another way, Kentucky had a relatively large number of people with a relatively small stake in the institution. At 20 percent, the state's proportion of blacks was significantly less than that of South Carolina, Georgia, or even Virginia. This relatively low ratio of blacks made white Kentuckians less prone to the Deep South's night-sweat visions of "the dusky sons of Ham leading our fair daughters to the altar." But they agreed with their Southern brothers and sisters that the national government had no right to interfere in a state's domestic affairs. In 1861, Kentuckians clung to the commitments that Henry Clay had made for them: to the South, to slavery, and to Unionism. Unsure how to translate those commitments into policy while the rest of the South seceded, Kentucky's legislature declared the state neutral — which most understood was the equivalent to its putting its head in the sand. Still, it was one of the few things they could agree upon, so in it went.

Boiling beneath the surface of neutrality was what one witness called "domestic pandemonium." Despite the neutrality proclamation, citizens could not help but notice the massive divide opening beneath their feet. Some families shouted across it. Others pleaded across it.

But it was difficult to ignore. "Kentucky has not seceded & I believe never will," Crittenden wrote his son George. "She loves the Union & will cling to it as long as possible. And so, I hope, will you." George did not. With his father preaching compromise in the legislature, George joined the Confederacy without a note of explanation. He rose to the level of major general, as did his brother Thomas — in the Union army.

The Breckinridges were tied in a similar knot. John C. Breckinridge, ex-vice president and ex-presidential candidate, remained in the U.S. Senate, but only to heap abuse upon the incoming administration. He then resigned to become one of the Confederacy's more accomplished generals. His uncle, Robert J. Breckinridge, by contrast, was referred to by Republicans as "the strongest and sturdiest champion of the Union cause South of the Ohio." He made speech after speech trying to keep the national family together. "If we desire to perish," he noted, "all we have to do is leap into this vortex of disunion." Then he got a letter from his son Robert Jr., saying he was joining the Confederate army. "Be, if you please sir," the young man wrote, "as lenient as possible in your thoughts of me." Breckinridge was both heartbroken and appalled. While he had been busy making Union speeches, his own son had been carried off by the hotheads. "[Your brother] has hopelessly ruined himself," he wrote bitterly to his other son, Willie. Willie too joined the Confederacy. "Whatever may be in store for me," he wrote his father, "I shall never forget your kindness to me."

Even the Clays were not immune to the secession fever. Four of the Great Compromiser's grandsons fought for the Confederacy, three for the Union. Indeed, by 1861, the Kentucky state motto, adopted in 1792 — "United We Stand, Divided We Fall" — was beginning to look less like a pledge of unity than a predictor of disaster. "[Secession] has divided States [and] Counties," one Kentuckian noted, "[and] produced discord among neighbors, old friends, and even families. . . . A gloom is over this once happy land, the future all dark . . . and the whole fabrick of our government tottering to the fall."

It remains one of the war's enduring ironies that the two men battling for Kentucky were Kentuckians themselves. Abraham Lincoln and Jefferson Davis were born a hundred miles apart, Lincoln at Hodgenville and Davis at Fairview. Given his Kentucky birth and the precarious position of his wife's family, it was only natural for Lincoln to see the Bluegrass State as both the literal and the symbolic battleground for Union. "I hope to have God on my side," he is supposed to have said, "but I must have Kentucky."

And in the end he did. By publicly respecting Kentucky's neutrality but quietly undermining it in favor of the Union, Lincoln played a masterful game of chess in the state. But to make it work he had to allow Confederate sentiment (and manpower, and material) to be leeched off to Tennessee. "Fifteen hundred Kentuckians, armed only with hatchets, passed here en route for Richmond a day or two since," one witness noted. "These are the men for any emergency." Kentucky, more than any other state, would live the "Brother's War." Two-fifths of Kentucky's white soldiers would fight for the Confederacy, three-fifths for the Union — a ratio closer to half than any other state's.

As Kentuckians themselves, the Lincolns were preoccupied by such divisions. Both followed developments in the state closely and read all the Bluegrass papers they could lay their hands upon. Kentucky's personal significance to Lincoln is most evident in his tendency to exaggerate its political significance. "I think to lose Kentucky is nearly the same as to lose the whole game," he said tellingly. "Ky gone, we cannot hold Missouri, nor, as I think, Maryland. These all against us, and the job on our hands is too large for us. We would as well consent to separation at once, including the surrender of the capital." For Lincoln, if he could save Kentucky he could save the Union.

He seems to have felt the same way about his brother-in-law Hardin Helm. The younger Todd boys, he knew, were beyond his reach. But if he could save Little Sister's husband, he would have done all he could to save the Todds. Shortly after Sumter, Lincoln summoned Hardin to the White House. He had given the matter careful thought. He knew that Hardin had grown tired of shagging about the circuit as a country lawyer. He knew that he had a growing family and was short of money. He knew that he loved the army and that his health forbade a field command. He knew that he was good with details and figures. And he knew that he would never raise his hand against fellow Southerners. Knowing all these things, Lincoln crafted the perfect solution and sealed it in an envelope. He would appoint Hardin a major in the army's paymaster corps, give him an annual salary of three thousand dollars, and, if he wished, post him to the West, where he could remain a neutral amid the coming unpleasantness. This was the highest appointment Lincoln could make without congressional approval, and in making it he expected to pay a political price. Already newspapers were complaining about the "100 Todds" hovering about the hog trough, "all wanting offices." Two weeks earlier, while considering Cousin Lizzie for postmistress, Lincoln allowed that they had a right to complain. "Will it do for me to go on and justify the declaration that Trumbull and I have divided out all the offices among our relatives?" he asked. In appointing Hardin, he expected to pay a price with the army too. Many of the captains in the service wanted the envelope he was about to give to Helm, and some of them deserved it.

Lincoln was offering Hardin more than a position, however; he was offering him an alternate vision of his life. As paymaster, Hardin would never have to ride a horse or shoot a gun. He would be one of the youngest majors in the regular army. He could buy a nice house, raise a nice family, and occasionally visit the Lincolns, where "Little Sister" Emilie would prove an ornament in Mary's court. The magnanimity of the president's gesture was not lost on his brother-in-law. "The position you offer me," Hardin said, "is beyond what I had expected in my most hopeful dreams. . . . It is the place above all others which suits me." Lincoln urged him to consider it carefully, free of outside influences, and to do what was right for his family. "You have been kind and generous to me beyond anything I have known," Hardin said at the conclusion of their interview. "I wish I could see my way."

Disregarding the president's advice, Hardin sought out his contacts in Washington. Among others, he bumped into Robert E. Lee. Lee foresaw dark times ahead and said so. He regarded Virginia's decision to secede as "the beginning of sorrows" and admitted to a clerk, "I am one of those dull creatures that cannot see the good of secession." Nevertheless, he followed his state out of the Union and resigned from the army he had served most of his life. "With all my devotion to the Union," he wrote his sister, "I have not been able to make up my mind to raise my hand against my relatives, my children, my home." Undoubtedly, this was the advice he gave Hardin: Don't be on the side opposite your people. But Hardin was in a different position from Lee. Kentucky hadn't left the Union — and wouldn't. And either way, Hardin would be raising his hand against his relatives. His own father, while critical of the Lincoln administration, was deeply committed to neutrality and the Union. His sister had recently written him a mournful letter after seeing "five hundred [Kentucky] troops go off . . . for the South." "Oh it made me feel really sick," she admitted. "I could scarcely keep from crying. The tears would come to my eyes in spite of myself. . . . I felt all the time just as I would at seeing two brothers preparing to fight. Oh it is awful."

Hardin, in short, was no George Crittenden; he was not intemperate, hotheaded, or rebellious. The "good son" was his own self-appointed role. Could he really turn down his brother-in-law, disappoint his father, and take up arms against his own? "I had a bitter struggle with myself," Hardin admitted to a friend. "The most painful moment of my life was when I declined the generous offer of my brother-in-law."

VI.

ON MAY 19, Hardin arrived in Montgomery to see what the *other* president was prepared to offer. The meeting proved a disappointment. If he really wanted to serve the Confederacy, Jefferson Davis told him, he should return home and work tirelessly for Kentucky secession. On his way back to Louisville, Hardin undoubtedly stopped over at Selma. By then there was quite a congregation of Todds in the city. Martha lived there; Elodie's visit was now effectively permanent; Sam and David had just come through; and on May 9 Kitty and Betsey had arrived to talk Elodie out of her engagement or, failing that, to celebrate it. Selma would become for the Southern wing of the family what Washington was for the Northern wing — a center of gravity, an emotional base.

Betsey Todd did not stay long, however. As Kentucky drifted more firmly into the Union column, she had a difficult choice to make. If she didn't get back, she would be a sixty-year-old widow cut off from home and all its securities. If she did make it back, she would be cut off from her Confederate sons and daughters. This topped her list of worries, but there were others. Elodie, whom she had always counted on as a companion in her old age, seemed firm in her decision to marry a man she didn't know. Mary, with whom she had finally gotten on good terms, had invited her to the White House, and there was no good way to say no, though she would obviously have to say no, because most of her sons were in the Confederate army. Even though she hoped Kentucky would secede, she found herself attending Union prayer meetings, because they were one of the few places where people were still praying for peace. The emotional complexity of it all was just too much for an old woman. At home, she figured, she could at least pretend that things were normal.

Kitty decided to stay. Elodie needed her, and she wasn't ready to admit that her coming out had been cut short by war. The truth, though, was that almost immediately after her arrival, Selma became a ghost town. The young men disappeared with their regiments. The women nested in their homes, sewing socks and writing letters. Selma suddenly seemed to Kitty like an abandoned rail station at the end of the world. Elodie could empathize. "The gaiety of Springfield and the extreme dullness of this place must indeed be striking," she admitted. "I think [Kitty] is perfectly willing to leave now for some other place more congenial to her tastes." Of course, part of what Kitty missed about Springfield was flirting with Ellsworth. Though now in the Confederacy, she persisted in jokingly describing the Union colonel as her love interest. "Kitty says if you take her beau Col. Ellsworth prisoner just send him to her and she will see that he does not escape," Elodie told Nathaniel. But he did not find it funny. Her countrymen were choosing sides, and Kitty would have to do the same. "Tell Miss Kitty you will claim her and that she must live in Ala[bama]," Nathaniel wrote. "I will not . . . let her throw herself away on Col. Ellsworth as she must have a Confederate Col. for her beau." A few days later, on May 24, he made the case more crassly: "Tell [Miss Kate] that I have a special desire to kill Col. Ellsworth . . . as I do not think he is good enough for any sister of yours."

Ellsworth died the same day. The morning after Virginia seceded, 13,000 Union forces moved quickly to secure the capital by establishing a foothold south of the Potomac. By the light of an unusually bright moon, troops and horses poured across the city's three bridges and advanced on Arlington Heights and Alexandria. Ellsworth's regiment had been chosen to approach Alexandria from the east by steamer. Their orders were to secure the waterfront, sever the rail lines, and occupy the telegraph office that connected the town to Richmond. They did not expect resistance. A message had been sent from the *Pawnee*, already docked at Alexandria, informing any Confederate forces that they had one hour to vacate the town.

Ellsworth's troops landed just as dawn broke. The town was quiet. A few Confederate sentinels fired indifferently at the boats as they approached, but they quickly ran off to rejoin their regiments. Ellsworth sent one company to deal with the rail lines, left the bulk of his men at the docks, and picked seven men to accompany him to the telegraph office. One of them was Edward House, a correspondent for the *New York Tribune*. "We passed quickly through the streets, meeting a few bewildered travelers," House remembered, "[until] all caught sight of the Secession flag, which has so long swung insolently in full view of the President's House." The flag flew over the Marshall House, a second-class inn; to Ellsworth it seemed ostentatiously large and impudently high, and it hung in his face like a red cape in front of a bull. "Boys," he said, "we must have that down before we return." House expected that he meant that they would come back to it after they had cut the telegraph line, which Ellsworth had before "appeared to regard as very seriously important." But Ellsworth seemed suddenly mesmerized by the flag. He was, after all, not regular army but a young magnificent drillmaster for whom insignia, uniforms, sashes, and symbols were extremely important. Then too, he was Lincoln's friend, and the flag, in view of the White House, had too long flown impudently in the president's face.

The detachment made for the Marshall House. Bursting in, they startled a man who was not yet fully dressed. "What sort of flag [hangs] above the roof," Ellsworth demanded. The stranger "declared he knew nothing of it, and that he was only a boarder there." Ellsworth then bounded up the stairs to the "topmost story, whence, by means of a ladder, he clambered to the roof, cut down the flag . . . and brought it from its staff." The party then began to descend the stairs, Corporal Brownell "leading the way, and Colonel Ellsworth immediately following with the flag." They had not yet reached the first landing when the stranger they had first met stepped from the shadows and leveled a double-barreled shotgun at Ellsworth's chest. Ellsworth didn't see him; he would go out of the world obliviously folding up the Confederate standard. "Brownell made a quick pass to turn the [stranger's] weapon aside," House reported, "but the fellow's hand was firm, and he discharged one barrel straight to its aim. . . . I think my arm was resting on poor Ellsworth's shoulder at the moment; at any rate, he seemed to fall almost from my grasp. He was on the second or third step from the landing, and he dropped forward with that heavy, horrible, headlong weight which always comes of sudden death." The assassin then turned the second barrel on Brownell but somehow missed. Brownell responded by discharging his rifle in the man's face. "The wound," House admitted, "was the most frightful I ever witnessed." Just to be sure, Brownell ran the man through with his bayonet. As the echoes died away, a moment's stunned silence was followed by pandemonium. Unsure whether they were under general attack, the men instinctively pulled together while Brownell reloaded. The doors of several rooms opened hesitantly, but no one approached. The area secure, they turned Ellsworth over. He had a two-inch-diameter hole in his chest, directly in front of the heart. In stunned silence, they carried his body back up the stairs, laid it out on a bed, composed its limbs and features, and covered it with the Confederate flag.

News of Ellsworth's death shocked the nation. He was the first notable casualty of the war, and the effect of a little spilled blood was electrifying. This is how war works, of course. One death justifies the next; each feeds a cycle of revenge that must run its course. The North mourned Ellsworth, to be sure. Flags flew at half-mast, church bells tolled, and thousands came out to view the body, first in the East Room of the White House and then in New York City Hall. But beneath the mourning, observers noted a trace of something else: an undercurrent of swelling anger, indignation, and even rage. "Perhaps in a manner we cannot understand," noted one Northerner, "God will accomplish more by [Ellsworth's] death than He would by his life. . . . His death will consolidate the North as one man." A preacher, sermonizing on Ellsworth, agreed. "We needed just such a sacrifice as this. . . . [People will now say] 'Let the war go on!'" A correspondent for the *New York Times* wondered that the loss of one young a man should have such a galvanizing effect on the national psyche. But somewhere deep in its consciousness, the country knew there was about to be a lot of this. Ellsworth was a harbinger of all those promising boys who would be absurdly cut down. "Shot by an innkeeper," doesn't look great on a headstone. Neither does "died of dysentery." And yet this is exactly where the country was headed, and the faint whiff of betrayed expectations amplified the sense of rage.

It was different for the Lincolns, of course. For them Ellsworth was more of a son than a symbol. Particularly because he had spent so much time playing with Willie and Tad, he had seemed like a grown-up version of their boys, or a version they hoped their boys would grow into. Lincoln was in the White House library when an officer gave him the news. For some minutes he stared blankly out the window across the Potomac. Two visitors came in on urgent business and tried politely to rouse him, but he didn't seem to notice. "He did not move," said one, "until we approached very closely, when he turned round abruptly, and advanced toward us, extending his hand. . . . 'Excuse me,' he said, 'but I cannot talk.'" The men assumed he meant that he had laryngitis. "To our surprise the President [then] burst into tears, and concealed his face in his handkerchief." "We stepped aside in silence," remembered the visitors, "not a little moved at such an unusual spectacle, in such a man in such a place." "It was his first personal realization of what the war meant," remembered a friend. "He did not foresee the hundreds of thousands who were to fall before the great strife would be ended. He afterward learned to bear the loss of thousands in battle more bravely than he bore the loss of this one in the beginning of the contest."

Mary Lincoln was deeply affected too. She twice visited Ellsworth's body at the Navy Yard and sobbed through the funeral the next day. Ironically, she was presented with the bloody Confederate flag that had enshrouded Ellsworth's corpse. (Embarrassed, she stuck it in a White House drawer and forgot about it until, with that capacity unique to children, Tad fished it out and waved it grandly in front of his father's guests, much to the chagrin of everyone involved.) Of the funeral, Elizabeth Grimsley correctly noted: "This is only the beginning of terrible scenes I fear through which we will have to pass."

Kitty's reaction to her crush's death is unknown. She wrote immediately to Mary but the letter has not survived. Undoubtedly it was a letter of condolence, if not commiseration, for a man who had been an important part of their recent bond. Worried about her sister, Elodie reassured herself that Kitty and Ellsworth had been only "excellent friends, *nothing more*." Even so, Nathaniel was in an awkward position. He had admitted (however jokingly) that he wanted to kill Ellsworth, and on the very day that the man had died. Worse, he didn't particularly want to take it back. As far as he was concerned, Ellsworth had gotten what he deserved for invading the South. "Providence seems to have cut him off as soon as he touched our soil," he wrote Elodie. "There is a great bitterness felt on our side, and we will kill all we can lay our hands on." He was dimly aware, though, that the hardening of such sentiments was precisely what threatened to tear Elodie's family apart. "I am anxious for your sake and your family that you should have peace," he wrote her, "for it must be unpleasant to have them divided." Unpleasant didn't begin to cover it. Two of her sisters on opposite sides were grieving the same man, her mother was declining White House invitations and yet attending Union prayer meetings, her brothers were in the Confederate army, her brother-in-law was commander in chief of the army arrayed against them, and she was left hoping it wouldn't come to war while her fiancé wrote about killing "all he laid [his] hands upon." The situation was more than unpleasant, and Ellsworth's death had brought it all into sharp relief. In this sense, his death was a harbinger for the Todds too. For them, the conflict would always be far messier than it was for anybody else. Neither love nor hate would be allowed to flow as they do best, in smooth and uncrooked channels.

VII.

FOR TWO MONTHS after Ellsworth's death, the war settled into a languid positioning game around Washington, D.C. The irony of Nathaniel's being encamped in arms across the Potomac from his would-be brother-in-law was not lost on him. "How singular that I should be engaged to the sister of Mrs. Lincoln," he marveled jokingly to Elodie. "I wish you would write her to that effect so that in case of being taken prisoner I will not be too severely dealt with. Do you not think it was a very politic step in me to engage such an advocate at the headquarters of the enemy?" Elodie found the whole thing a little less amusing. "Pray do you think to inform Bro. Abe would do any good? He would make you suffer for yourself and my being such a secessionist too, and you must be too cute to get into their hands."

In any war, the momentum to action reaches a point at which it cannot be stayed. With the three-month enlistment periods of his volunteers running out, Lincoln was under considerable pressure to mount an offensive on Richmond. The general in charge of the operation, Irvin McDowell, pleaded with the president for more time to mobilize and train his troops, despite the lateness of the hour. Here Lincoln gave a famous response: "You are green, it is true; but they are green also. You are all green alike." Coincidentally, the two armies were alike in another way: they had the same battle plan. McDowell's plan was to feint against the Confederate right, then attack the left en masse. P.G.T. Beauregard, commanding Confederate forces on the field, had the exact same plan: feint right, drive left. If everyone had executed properly, the result of the Civil War's first major engagement would have been an almost comical whiffing, followed by pell-mell advances on the enemy capitals. Of course, as it happened, everyone did not execute properly. McDowell came the closest — and he lost.

Federal forces began stirring at two in the morning on Sunday, July 21, but they almost immediately fell behind schedule. Groping around in the dark, they bottlenecked in the roads behind slower-moving units and artillery pieces. As a result, McDowell's diversion went off before his main attack force was fully in place. The curtain went up before all the actors were on the stage.

At about six A.M., the Confederate colonel Nathan "Shanks" Evans, positioned at the extreme Confederate left, began taking fire near a modest stone bridge spanning Bull Run. His orders were to defend his position until Beauregard could launch his main attack away at the right. But Evans quickly suspected a ruse; the federals weren't pressing hard enough. They were massing for something, and whatever it was, he didn't want to face it alone.

Nathaniel's Fourth Alabama, with the rest of Barnard Bee's brigade, were among those ordered to the stone bridge. The news was a great irritation to Bee, who assumed, with the rest of the Confederate high command, that all the action was going to be on the right. Nevertheless, at seven A.M. the Fourth Alabama began a double-quick four-mile march toward Evans's last known position. They were almost upon it when Bee realized that Evans had shifted a mile to the left and appeared to be taking heavy fire. Riding ahead, Bee reconnoitered Evans's position and was elated. He had figured out what Evans knew only too well, that the federals had feinted right and were massing left. "Here is the battlefield, and we are in for it!" Bee exclaimed. Already exhausted and desperately thirsty, Bee's men formed their lines a few hundred yards behind Evans and were immediately ordered to advance and take up a position on the right. Shortly thereafter, other reinforcements, Georgians under Francis Bartow, arrived and took up a position on Bee's right. Together the three brigades, Evans's, Bee's, and Bartow's, comprised 4,500 men. They were arrayed against the Union's main attack force, more than twice their numbers and swelling. Nevertheless, they were ordered to advance. "Up, Alabamians," Bee yelled. "Go!" And then off Bee buzzed to some other part of the field, leaving the Fourth's assault to its colonel, Egbert Jones.

Egbert J. Jones had much to prove — to himself and his men. A forty-year-old Huntsville lawyer, he had been a soldier in the Mexican War but never saw any fighting. His election to colonel had been contentious. Most of the south Alabama companies, including Nathaniel's, preferred ex-governor John Winston. His political connections, they figured, would ensure them a prominent place on the battlefield. They had acquiesced in Jones's election through the spring, but when he began a new regimen of daily drills and fatigue details, they bucked. Jones, they decided, didn't have the mettle to lead the Fourth. "Seven of the ten captains, including myself, have told his friend that in our opinion he should resign," Nathaniel informed Elodie. "I fear that the Reg. will never be worth much as the Col. is utterly incompetent, and we have no respect or confidence in him. I feel demoralized to be under the command of such a man." Jones was mortified by such sentiments. Unsure how to respond, he sought out General Joseph Johnston, who said that the rogue captains had two options: they could formally charge Jones with something or they could button their lips. The captains backed down, but the incident further stoked their contempt for Jones. Instead of buttoning their lips, they flapped their gums, circulating reports of their colonel's utter worthlessness. Their gripes became the common gossip in Selma. "Having heard some gentlemen conversing on the never-ending subject of war," Elodie wrote Nathaniel, "I was surprised that they spoke so freely of Col. Jones as being totally unfitted for the position he occupies and what a terrible thing it would be if [we] should have a fight . . . for no other fate but being cut to pieces awaited the 4th Regiment if he commanded or else they would disgrace themselves by running." In the face of his unpopularity, Jones struck a deal: if the men would follow him through the first battle, he would show them what he was made of.

Thus, at the call of "Up Alabamians!" Jones went roaring forward, the Fourth Alabama with him. They made it farther than any regiment participating in the charge before withering federal fire dropped them to their bellies. They were now strewn about a low cornfield that sloped up a hill a hundred yards to the Yankee line. It was a frustrating position, and they would be there for an hour, in some of the toughest fighting at Manassas. The two-foot corn provided very little cover; shot and shell rained down on them from above; the sound was deafening; and only adrenaline kept them from collapsing of heat prostration and thirst-induced exhaustion. To move, it seemed, was to die; to stay was to die — or be driven insane. "My first thought was, 'This is unfair,'" one soldier remembered. "'I didn't come out to fight this way; I wish the earth would crack open and let me drop in.'"

Of course, the earth does not crack open, and no one drops in. Each man has a reality to face: What do I do now that there's nowhere to go? Some men fold, some go berserk, some just drift back into their heads, leaving their body to do its duty while they watch from another world. And this is just what happened in Nathaniel's company. Some few feverishly jumped up, aimed, fired, and dropped to their backs to reload. A private next to Nathaniel attempted the maneuver. "[I] watched him as he fired and saw his hand fly up as if the gun had rebounded. [He] said to me, 'My arm is shattered.'" Another hot-blood had better luck, actually picking off the Union color bearer. "I waited until I saw him good," the soldier remembered, "that is, till I saw his body down to his hips. I drew as fine a bede on him as any one can with a rifle, and pulled the trigger, and down went the stars and stripes." For the most part, though, the captains were successful in getting their men to hold their fire until the Yankees tried to advance, then to rise and fire in unison. It worked. Four times the Yankees tried to sweep the Alabamians from the field; four times they were repulsed. And through it all, Colonel Jones sat "conspicuously on his horse, as calm as a statue."

But while the Alabamians had been holding their ground, the rest of the Confederate force was in a steady retreat. Evans's, Bartow's, and Bee's men had shown a lot of grit in slowing the federal advance, but they could not stop it. As they withdrew, the Fourth Alabama was left abandoned in its cornfield, outflanked and nearly engulfed. Even then it was not Jones but General Bee who ordered them to fall back. Under the circumstance, a retreat was a trickier maneuver than the advance had been. Upright and with their backs to the advancing federals, they made easy targets. "[We] retreated under a shower of bullets poured upon [us] from the front, right and left, followed by the Yankees themselves," remembered one soldier. "It was a matter of perfect astonishment, to all, that a single man of [us] escaped alive."

Nathaniel almost didn't escape. While he was negotiating a fence, a shell took out one of the timbers and sent him flying ten feet to the ground. He arose disoriented and hobbled by a bad sprain. As he staggered forward another man was shot right next to him. The next hit was Jones. Of course, he had probably made up his mind to die before the battle had even started. He may even have been a little relieved when the shell tore through both thighs and knocked him from his horse. His men might respect him now; they might wish they hadn't been so small; his honor might be redeemed. All this might have been accomplished with a wound that wasn't as mortal, but Jones would have to take the rough with the smooth. "Don't run boys," he told his retreating regiment, and off they ran.

Though they had lost their colonel, the Fourth did not panic. They fetched up south of Mathew's Hill and decided to make another ill-advised stand. To their right, they had been heartened to see a well-formed column, some clad in gray, exactly where they expected Bartow to be. Unfortunately, it was the Sixty-ninth New York, which "opened a murderous fire" on their ranks. Their lieutenant colonel and major both fell. The Fourth now had no field officers left, and they were practically surrounded. This time, the retreat was less orderly. "Everything was in great confusion," Nathaniel remembered. "The Yankees were following us and . . . flanking us on both wings. . . . The disorder was indescribable. Col. Law was now wounded, Col. Jones reported dead, and either with or without an order, for I heard none, the regiment . . . retired in confusion, and brave men had to run for their lives."

By the time they reached safety, the Fourth was demoralized. They had shown their backs, turned tail; they were disgraced. It would be days before they realized all they had accomplished. They thought they had been fighting in the cornfield against another regiment like themselves, one that finally overran their position and sent them flying. But when reports on both sides became public, they realized that they had faced four *different* regiments; they had sustained the heaviest casualty rate in the battle of Manassas; they had been among the last Confederates to flee the field; and they had helped to stall McDowell's main attack force long enough for reinforcements to arrive, roll back the Union gains, and ultimately win the battle for the Confederacy.

For now, though, they were reeling. Their hasty retreat had scattered them to the rear, and the effect of battle was catching up with their bodies. About 150 members of the Fourth Alabama were eventually rallied and taken in again. The majority, including Nathaniel, had had enough. Forty percent of their regiment lay on the field killed or wounded or had gone missing. They had all been malnourished for weeks, sleep deprived for days, weakened by camp diseases, dressed in wool on an oppressively hot day and marched six miles at the double-quick right into combat, where they had witnessed terrible things happening to people they cared about. They were, in short, done — Nathaniel as much as any of them. Dazed, he hobbled about the rear, helping the wounded until he became "so fatigued and lame" that he "got into the shade and remained there until the firing ceased and the prisoners were coming in and the battle over." Occasionally, he saw a familiar face and asked about his company. All assured him that it had been "cut to pieces."

The next day Nathaniel wrote home from the battlefield. He crowed a little about the extent of the Confederate victory, but for the most part his mood was contemplative. "The scene presented was horrible," he admitted. "Dead line the road all the way. . . . I counted in one small spot . . . one hundred dead Yankees. . . . [They] presented an awful appearance, and I thought perchance that the fortunes of man might place me in a similar position." True to himself, Dawson gathered some bullets and picked a flower from where General Bee had been killed. He sent them to Elodie with his letter: "During the fight when the bullets fell like hail, I thought of you as far away, at church, on your knees, praying for my safety, and I was nerved and strengthened to do my duty. . . . You are the idol of my heart, and I am so grateful for your love."

Elodie too was sobered by the bloodshed. "As much as I thought I loved you," she wrote Nathaniel, "it was not until yesterday and today which has caused me to realize the devotedness and depth of the love that is in my heart for you and how crushed and torn it would have been had you been snatched from me by death's relentless hand. . . . It is with a thankful heart that I write and hear of your safety while so many others, more deserving of mercy than I, are sorrowing over their loved dead."

The casualties at Manassas sobered the nation as well. As news of the rout poured into Washington, Lincoln and his cabinet members huddled around Winfield Scott's desk in the War Department, reading grimmer and grimmer dispatches. A thousand men had died; in one eight-hour battle the nation had lost more than half as many as they had in the entire Mexican War. Striding back to the White House in the evening, Lincoln was accosted by Robert Wilson, an old acquaintance from his New Salem days. When Wilson asked him for the latest news, Lincoln tried to brush him off, saying that "it was contrary to Army Regulations to give military information to parties not in the military service." "I don't ask for the news," Wilson replied, "but you tell me the quality of the news — is it good, or is it bad." Leaning down to Wilson's ear, Lincoln "said in a sharp, shrill voice, '*damned bad.*'" It was the first time Wilson had ever heard Lincoln curse, but when he "became fully acquainted with the details of the fight . . . [he] became satisfied that . . . no other word would have conveyed the true meaning of the word bad." As Lincoln predicted, the recriminations proved loud and long. The battle had seemed to confirm the South's martial superiority, and the federal army would spend the rest of the year retooling.

While it did so, Elodie clung to the idea that the North would now let the South go: "Would that . . . this glorious victory . . . would satisfy our enemies and woo gentle peace to diffuse her gentle smiles again over our beloved country." But she knew better. "I look straight forward as far as I can and all around and above and yet all looks gloomy

and dark. I have never for a moment doubted that anything but success would attend us, but I have thought of the many who would and
must die to purchase it. . . . I do not now think of peace for a moment;
fighting alone can accomplish our end and that hard and bloody."

Nathaniel too was depressed in victory. He spent a few days after the
battle "engaged in writing to the friends of [the] killed and wounded
and found it a sad task." "The absence of over twenty from our ranks,"
he said, "has made quite a gap in the company and cast a deep gloom
over us all." Like Elodie, Nathaniel now wanted it to be over, almost
as soon as it had begun. He wanted to go home, get married, move
on. "I long to be yours, entirely yours," he wrote Elodie pathetically, "I
will feel as if my labors were ended and that I had a right to enjoy the
comforts of home under the soothing care and affection of my noble
ladylove, one whom I adore and worship more than my country. . . . I
frequently lie on my blanket at night, looking up to the blue canopy of
heaven studded with stars, and dream of those days [of our courtship]
as among the halcyon hours of my life."

Almost immediately after the battle, however, Nathaniel was beset
by more embarrassing problems. Though the Fourth Alabama's overall
conduct was unimpeachable (38 killed and 208 wounded out of 750
engaged), rumors that Captain Dawson had shamefully fled the field
circulated in camp and around Selma. For a man of Nathaniel's quiet
dignity, the imputation of cowardice was almost too much to bear. He
made minute accounts of his conduct to anyone who would listen,
including the newspapers, and confessed to one of his friends that it
might be better if he never returned from the war. He fantasized about
throwing himself into the path of enemy gunfire and promised to meet
with pistols any man willing to repeat the charges to his face. (Ultimately, the allegations proved as baseless as those that had been leveled against the departed Egbert Jones. A man who wanted Elodie for
himself had circulated the rumor to embarrass Nathaniel and, once
exposed, had apparently disappeared.)

Though it did not stick, the cowardice charge soured Nathaniel on
the military and convinced him that petty politicking would ruin the
Confederacy. By his reckoning, there was something wrong with an
army in which a man would "stoop to such baseness" as to falsely ac-
cuse another of cowardice. Then too he began to chafe under the con-
straints of army life. For company-grade officers especially, army discipline marked the first time they were expected to do as they were told,
not as their class prerogatives allowed. The most galling of these con-

straints from Nathaniel's perspective was the army's refusal to grant leaves of absence and its threat to force all volunteers to remain in service for the duration of the war. More than a breach of trust, these moves made it possible that Nathaniel would not be able to marry Elodie for a period of some years, a prospect he found both offensive and alarming, given the rumors floating around about rivals. "I am willing to lay down my life for you," he told Elodie, "but the idea that I am to do so without having been married to you is a harrowing one." Without the sanction of law and God, Nathaniel's relationship with Elodie, and through her his reason for fighting, were faced with illegitimacy. "I have never felt so anxious," he wrote, "upon any subject, as to close the term of my service in order that I might be with my loved Elodie. . . . I know that unless we are married this spring, I will become useless to the country." At the outset of the war, Nathaniel had determined to see the conflict as a defense of female integrity, as a vindication of Elodie's rights and liberties. Now the simple synonymity he had always assumed between his fiancée and his country was breaking down; the Confederacy was forcing him to choose between them, and he made the choice easily. "You tell me that you have made up your mind to be *secondary* to your country," Nathaniel wrote his beloved, "[but] *you are my country*, and can be *secondary* to nothing." His own life could be sacrificed, he agreed, and all that he had — except her. "I am not a Roman to give my wife for my country," he summed it up, "[because] without [you] I would have no country to live for and to die for."

VIII.

JUST AS THE NATION was psychologically unprepared for the number of Manassas dead, it was physically unprepared for the number of prisoners and wounded. Richmonders opened their homes to injured Confederates, but they were overwhelmed by the tidal wave of enemy soldiers who inundated their rickety prison system. In charge of that system was David Todd. Over the next two months, he would become the deserving scapegoat for all its shortcomings.

How he came to the post is a bit of a mystery. After securing his lieutenancy in Montgomery, he traveled to Richmond, where he was appointed as an aide to General Theophilus H. Holmes. By late June, he was preparing to ship out to Staunton to join the forces massing for battle. But on July 1, he and a fellow Kentuckian, the poet Theodore

O'Hara, were redirected to the office of General John H. Winder, provost marshal of Richmond. Winder was in charge of the city's security generally, and he made David the commandant of the prisons, a series of converted tobacco warehouses along the James.

George too was in the city in his capacity as a surgeon, ministering to the many wounded. He tried to see David but was spurned. His resulting mood may have had something to do with his conduct in the lobby of the St. Charles Hotel, where he swore so heavily and slandered the Confederate government so violently that he was arrested by local citizens. According to the *Richmond Dispatch,* George "revil[ed] prominent leaders of Confederate State forces as 'd —— d traitors' and indulg[ed] in other opprobrious epithets towards the South and its defenders." Between his "incendiary language" and speech impediment, George was deemed a "suspicious character" and "conveyed . . . to the cage." A search of his person revealed a letter from Abraham Lincoln, heightening his captors' suspicions, but George assured them that it was all a mistake and that he "regarded Lincoln as one of the greatest scoundrels unhung." The incident was mildly embarrassing to the Todds because it made the papers, but it was nothing compared to what they would soon face. Of the altercation between her brothers, Elodie said, "[I] hope they will yet make friends. [David] should remember [that George] is our father's son and for his sake endeavor to forget and forgive the past. Unforgiving as I am, I would do so." Forgiveness was not David's long suit, however, and his lack of tact would prove a grave liability in the months ahead.

The 1,421 prisoners taken at Manassas were a subject of intense interest among Richmonders. Guests raced to the windows of their hotels to "get a peep" at them as they were force-marched through the street. Gauntlets thronged their path to the jail, cursing, ridiculing, and spitting on them. The jails themselves became "the picture-gallery of the town" as "crowd[s] of idlers," churchgoers, and society women drawn in slow-moving carriages all strained to catch a glimpse of this newly foreign thing: a Yankee. "The square was for weeks packed with Rebels," recalled an inmate. "Whenever they caught [sight] of a Federal officer, [they] hooted at and insulted him . . . men, women, and even little children scarcely old enough to walk." The frenzy was fully supported by the local papers. Yankees were compared to zoo animals, lunatics, or worse. "Behold how they multiply," noted the *Richmond Whig* of the Yankee. "They multiply . . . [like] the Chinese . . . the aphidae, and all the other pests of the animal kingdom. Pull the bark from a decayed log, and you will see a mass of maggots, full of vitality, in constant motion and eternal gyration, crawling over one another, creeping under one another, all precisely alike, all intently engaged in preying upon one another; and you have an apt illustration of Yankee numbers, Yankee equality, and Yankee prowess." Another reporter pointed out the obvious absurdity: "One would think live Yankees must have undergone some wonderful transformation of late. Do the ladies and children, who are so eager to get a peep . . . expect to see them [sporting] horns and hoofs? Yankees have been common enough among us, heaven knows, [before now]." But a "wonderful transformation" had occurred. Brothers were now enemies. Northerners were now "infidels," "invaders," and "pests." Men who spoke the same language, shared the same history, and worshiped the same God were suddenly not always recognizable to each other as human. Struggling to outdo one another in their zealotry, "the newspapers proposed the most inhuman treatment," remembered one inmate, "coolly urging [our] hanging and close confinement, while from outward manifestation, one would have supposed we were confined in Hades, with howling devils yelling for our blood at the gates."

The commandant within the gates, David Todd, was a curious choice for such a delicate detail. According to one account, he consistently "pretend[ed] that the duty [was] irksome & that his martial spirit wearie[d] for the tented field and blood 'galore.'" His second in command was Sergeant Henry Wirz, later commandant of Andersonville and executed for war crimes. Together the two made a terrifying pair. According to prisoners, Todd took "personal delight in human blood and suffering," and Wirz was his ever-willing "pupil." "I think Wirz thought that cruelty pleased Todd," remembered one inmate, "so he tried to imitate him." "There was something in Todd's voice and manner," recalled another, "that always indicated a desire to commit some cruel wrong." According to witnesses, David's orders were borne along in a sea of insults. He heaped "foul and scurrilous abuse" upon the inmates "at every visit." The symbol of his authority was the sword. He "invariably" came in with it drawn, and he occasionally left with it bloody. Once "he struck an invalid soldier in the face" with the flat of the blade because the man hadn't fallen in quickly enough. On another occasion, he stabbed a Union sergeant named Whitcomb through the thigh for standing near a lamp that hadn't been extinguished precisely at lights out. Significantly, prisoners remembered that David did not seem in control of such violence; he seemed possessed by it. Recalling the stabbing of Whitcomb, one prisoner described David's sword thrust as a "paroxysm"; another said it seemed as if he had just stabbed the first man he saw; a third said he had lunged into the crowd without seeming to aim at all. Given such descriptions, it seems likely that David had been drinking. According to one witness, he was "drunk during nearly the entire period of his authority at the prison." This squares with the fact that the morning after the stabbing, he sent someone in to appeal to Whitcomb as a fellow mason to keep the matter quiet. Whether or not he sincerely regretted its results, certainly by morning David had slept off his "paroxysm."

The bottle does not explain everything, though. David Todd, a prisoner noted, seemed to take pains to ensure that the life of a federal officer was "one of daily indignity and hardship." He required, for instance, that prisoners be escorted in twos to the latrine and that no one be allowed to use the privies after lights out. The order seemed reasonable. Unescorted prisoners, particularly at night, were more likely to escape. But given the high number of prisoners and low number of guards, the order effectively meant that only one-third of the inmates made it to the latrine in a given day. The rest were left to befoul the floors or, in the case of the sick, who were rarely evacuated, themselves. Within a week, the prisoners were living amid pools of their own accumulating filth. "The floor of the rooms in which we were at first confined unfortunately was not level," remembered one, "so that a foul stream . . . from the sink settled on one side of the room to the depth of one or two inches." On one occasion, a prisoner "became insane and, tearing his clothing to shreds, spent his time splashing" about the cesspools. Poisoned by their environment, many of the inmates developed diarrhea. Their intestines in knots, seventy to eighty of them awaited the "privilege" of being taken to the latrine in lines "from twelve to twenty-five feet long" for most of the day. At least one prisoner remembered this as the worst, and least talked about, aspect of captivity. If anything, David profited from the situation he had created. Some of the Union troops had just been paid before Manassas and so had between five hundred and one-thousand dollars in gold among them. They used the money to buy privileges, such as a trip to the privy or better food. When they ran out of gold, they "sold one article after another to the guards." How much of this money ended up in David's pocket is impossible to say.

Another of David's orders was deadlier. Most of the prison buildings were hastily converted tobacco warehouses. Bars were added to the windows along the ground floor, but to save time and money the upper-story windows had been left unbarred. Each prison was surrounded by guards, so there seemed little chance that an inmate could jump from a window to make his escape. Nevertheless, David ordered that any man who stuck his arm or head out a window would be liable to have it shot off. He was seeking to control not escapees but spectacle. During the day, inmates and the crowds engaged in shouting matches across the prison yard, and David despised the feeling that he was running the town zoo. Again, though, the order had a pernicious side effect, which may have been what David liked best about it. His guards were bored country boys. Inebriated and squinting down their rifle barrels, they wiled away the hours trying to get a bead on Yankees who drifted too close to the windows. Occasionally, they fired.

How many prisoners were injured and how many were killed as a result of David's order is difficult to determine. The *New York Times* estimated the number of wounded at six to eight, the number killed at three, before Todd's order was finally rescinded. Confederate papers were less likely to comment. Describing one of the potshots, the *Richmond Whig* noted that a guard had fired only after he had repeatedly warned the prisoner to step back and had received only a "volley of abuse, mingled with oaths" in return. "The sentinel instantly raised his musket and fired at the scamp, but the ball missed," the paper reported almost disappointedly. "Some of the prisoners are very saucy and need taking down a peg or two." But when one of the prisoners *was* taken down, the paper reported it only obliquely. "A Yankee prisoner named Gleason ... died very suddenly yesterday at the Confederate States Prison No. 1," the article noted: "cause, concussion of the brain." The paper did not mention that the concussion was caused by a bullet. Though no witness puts David Todd at the scene of any of the shootings, the prisoners knew he condoned them. His order had "furnished a convenient excuse for repeated malicious firings into the building by drunken or evil-minded guards," none of whom were punished during his tenure as commandant.

But the charge that made David infamous was the claim that he desecrated corpses. Between the overcrowding, the unsanitary conditions, and the substandard fare, it was only a matter of time before disease became rampant in the jails. Winder and others had been repeatedly warned that they would face an epidemic if conditions did not improve, but there was little they could do or knew to do. They tried to keep pace with overcrowding by acquiring and converting other warehouses along the James, and they encouraged the prisoners to clean out their sinks. Past that, they had neither the resources nor the impulse to do any better. Inevitably, then, prisoners began dying of neglect and disease. This was not a scandal in itself. "The mortality among the Abolition prisoners now in Richmond is considerable," the *Richmond Dispatch* noted breezily on August 9. "We regret this . . . [only] because the parties have not had time to repent of their folly and wickedness in combining with others to cut [our] throats." Within the prisons, however, it was difficult to be as blasé about the mounting number of corpses. Among other things, they stank, and David was particularly offended by the aroma of dead Yankee wafting through his jails. What he did about the problem is a point of controversy. According to David, he repeatedly petitioned for the bodies to be removed and, when they weren't, he and his men removed them themselves. The *Charleston Mercury*, which took up David's side, claimed that "the bodies [had begun] to putrefy and to endanger the health of the prisoners," forcing David to act on his own initiative. But the *Mercury* is alone in this construction of events. According to other witnesses, it was routine practice for the Yankee dead to be roughly handled and roughly buried, often in "Negro graveyards" among their "friends." Moreover, after David had succeeded in cleansing his jails of bodies, yet another prisoner died, and, unsure what to do with the corpse, the guards took it to headquarters. Unable to both carry the body and ring the bell, they dropped it on the porch and rang for Todd. Finding a dead Yankee on his doorstep, David became "so exasperated" that he "kicked the body out into the street, where it laid overnight."

Even the staunchly rebel public was dimly aware that David had gone too far. Prisoners, they felt, should be gawked at, spat upon, and maybe even hanged — but it crossed the line of Christian decency to beat a man after he'd quit the mortal coil. That David had kicked the corpse in a public street and left it there didn't help. As night fell and day rose on a single dead Yankee — cold and getting colder alone in the road — there was something almost pitiable about the scene, and pity was the last thing the rebel public was in the mood to feel. This time Winder had to act. David had been occasionally volatile, insubordinate, and embarrassing, but now he had proven himself a public liability. It would not be enough to replace him. He would need to be dressed down. On the evening of August 9, Winder had David Todd arrested "for having acted contrary to the orders . . . of the military department of Richmond." David demanded a trial so that he could vindicate his course, but by August 18, he had been relieved of duty. His tenure as commandant had lasted less than two months. He would be dogged as a "desecrator" for the rest of the war.

In all fairness, there are factors that mitigate David's conduct. In virtually all wars, the issue of how to treat captured enemy combatants becomes an early problem. In the run-up to the conflict, ideologues vilify the enemy, justify the violence, and create a heady atmosphere for hating that makes any abuse of prisoners seem almost laudable. In this sense, David's harsh treatment was in keeping with newly minted attitudes toward the pestilential Yankee. His task, moreover, was certainly unenviable and probably unmanageable. The crowds at the gates demanded blood, the rebel public demanded tighter security; the Union public demanded leniency; and the prisoners demanded the impossible — to be treated as gentlemen. David could never have satisfied them all. With no protocols in place and more prisoners arriving all the time, the Richmond jail system was a disaster — and David Todd made the perfect lightning rod for the resulting storm of controversy because everybody knew his name.

Given the delicacy of his situation, what David most needed to display was tact — a trait not among his virtues. Instead of establishing order, system, or discipline at the jails, he sought only to compel obedience to his personal authority. Like many slave owners, he may have thought the two were the same thing. Regardless, his unsystematic use of violence gave him the reputation of not a strict disciplinarian but an indulgent sadist, which he perhaps deserved. Moreover, if everybody knew his name it was because he constantly told them. David rarely missed a chance to mention his White House connections. He reveled in his celebrity, even his notoriety. He relished the opportunity fate had given him to spit on Lincoln from the close range of a relative. "A favorite expression of his," remembered one prisoner, "[was] 'I would like to cut "Old Abe's" heart out.'" Such sentiments only cemented the sense that David Todd was on some sort of vindictive crusade. Acquaintances were left with troubling questions: What kind of man turns so violently against his family? What kind of man would cut out his brother-in-law's heart? In trying to underline the strength of his patriotism, David had only cast suspicion on the weakness of his character. He relished the most disturbing aspects of being a jailer in a brothers' war, and Winder had been right to relieve him, right to reprove him.

Once reproved, David went on a bender. He got a room at the Powhatan, one of the city's best hotels, and spent his time indulgently drinking, feeling sorry for himself, and fornicating. The lifestyle took its toll. One night after taps, two prisoners, surgeons Gray and Le Boutillier, were roused by a sentry and hastened to David's hotel room. The scene that greeted them was frightful. David was thrashing about and "spouting blood [from the mouth] like a harpooned whale." "Walls, chairs, floor [and] bedding were stained with it," Gray remembered, "and [there was] more coming." David's dramatic blood-geyser elicited no sympathy from the doctors. Like the rest of the prisoners, they thought Todd was an insufferable ass who had done more than any one man to make them miserable. Why, Gray wondered, had he awakened enemy surgeons to tend to him instead of his own doctors? The severity of the case, however, intrigued Gray. He admitted later that he had never seen "such a pulmonary hemorrhage, except following a penetrating wound of the chest." Remembering a Latin phrase he had learned in medical school — *Fiat experimentum in corpore vili* (Let the experiment be made on a body of no value) — he set about to stop David's bleeding, thinking that "here surely was a '*corpore vili*.'" Finally, the patient (as well as the hemorrhage) was brought under control. Gray and Le Boutillier were sent back to the prison hoping the world, or at least they, had seen the last of David Todd.

Strangely, though, the incident convinced David that the Union doctors were now his friends. A week after his hemorrhage, he galloped ceremoniously up to the prison and formally invited the men to dine with him that evening. They were hardly in a position to say no. When the doctors arrived at David's room at the Powhatan, they were surprised by the spread. Their host had gone all out, and Gray had to admit that it was an excellent dinner, considering what a "humbug Todd was." Of course, David himself dominated the conversation — as both subject and speaker. "He . . . claims to be & probably is, a brother of Mrs. Lincoln," Gray noted, "& [he] says Mr. Lincoln offered to send him as minister to Brazil, but that he rejected with scorn an office from an abolition President. He lies no doubt. He is a fearful braggart & a coward too withal." Perhaps David was lying. But it would be an oddly specific lie. Unknown to Gray, he *did* have some experience in South America, and Lincoln *had* worked assiduously to keep his wife's family members on his side of the divide. Gray's skepticism is understandable, though. David probably was lying, and throughout the dinner, he told story after improbable story "of which he was ever the hero."

"I suppose he would have talked himself into another hemorrhage," Gray decided, "if we had not [finally] broken up." Taking his leave, Gray noticed an abundance of female undergarments strewn about the room. "[You] had better forego [your] pleasant vices for a time," he told David, or "[you will be] drowned in another bleeding." "[I] was not born to die in [my] bed," David responded airily. "I am sure he may die in such fashion as pleases him as far as I am concerned," Gray wrote acidly in his diary.

Gray had every reason to be bitter. Why was David Todd, widely regarded as the most draconian jailer in Richmond, formally entertaining Union prisoners? Granted, he may have felt that he owed the doctors something for their assistance, but surely he could have paid them money rather than served them supper. The truth is probably simpler: having alienated everyone else, David had no one left to eat with. In his own raging and bibulous way, David Todd was at war with everybody. Whether kicking corpses, barking orders, or embarrassing his superiors, he had a tendency to lash out indiscriminately, just as he had that night with his saber. And just as on that night, his wild thrusts usually resulted in self-inflicted wounds. He invoked his connections to the White House so that he could rhetorically sever them. But in repeatedly raising them, he ensured that they would never be completely cut. His vilest denunciations of the Lincolns did not prove his patriotism, but only his vileness. And so when it came time to call a doctor to attend to his health, he called *Union* surgeons from the jail. And when he wanted to entertain, he invited *Union* prisoners, whom he otherwise tortured, and dined them lavishly at his own expense, if only because he wanted a (literally) captive audience for tales of his valorous youth. David, in short, had no friends on either side; he had burned through them all so spitefully that he was left alone in his own self-gored hotel room, the site of all the indulgent sinning, which, he must have known, was slowly killing him. Predictably, he turned to one of the few people who still cared about him. "We received a letter from my brother David this evening," Elodie wrote her fiancé in early September. "[He] says those terrible bleedings of his lungs were produced by the excitement of his arrest. I feel so sorry for him. He is so mortified and hurt at the manner in which he has been treated [and] declares he will play janitor no longer. . . . It makes me angry to have anyone offend my brothers or sisters. I would prefer their harming me."

She might have been more careful what she wished for.

IX.

IT WOULD BE a few months before David Todd's conduct at the Richmond prisons erupted into a national scandal. The corpse-kicking charge was made in the *New York Times* in October, but it was quickly denounced by the *New York Herald*. "This news concerning Todd involves alleged atrocities on his part which are too revolting to be true," the *Herald* noted. "We cannot believe them. They are malicious inventions." Why then had the *Times* printed them? According to the *Herald*, "little villains" at the rival paper had printed the story as a "back-handed blow" at the administration. Lincoln himself attempted to make a grim joke of the rumors when he scolded Lizzie for traveling without military escort to Mount Vernon. "Cousin Lizzie, have you taken leave of your senses?" he asked. "Can you compute the amount of trouble you would involve General Scott and myself in, if a member of my family should be captured? And the enemy would be only too glad to get you in their clutches, particularly your cousin David Todd, now in charge of the rebel prison in Richmond." Reporters, though, were beginning to nose around the story. Already, the first lady was not liked. Her clothes, her shopping, her involvement in politics and patronage, all cut against the grain of the times. With the war under way, the public expected its women to be silent, self-sacrificing supporters of their men. Mary was none of these things: she spent too much, ate too much, said too much. But here in her brother David was a more serious charge. In the spring, when peace was still a possibility, the newspapers had seen her Southern connections as a bridge to reconciliation. After Manassas, they came increasingly to see them as a bridge to treason. David's conduct would give Mary's enemies an excuse to think the worst, and an opportunity to hit her where she was truly vulnerable. To avert suspicion (and cover her flank), Mary insisted that all her incoming correspondence would pass through her husband's secretaries first. And to make sure people knew where she stood, she told a reporter that "by no word or act of hers should [David] escape punishment for his treason against her husband's government."

This comment, carried widely in the press, eventually made its way south to Selma, where Elodie was flabbergasted. "I do not believe she ever said it," she noted, "and if she did and meant it, she is no longer a sister of mine nor deserves to be called a woman of nobleness and truth." To Elodie, Mary's remark had broken the unwritten rules governing the Todds' peculiar situation. Obviously, the family was divided *politically*. But *personally*, they needed to love each other as always. How else could they respect themselves? How else could they endure? Family members did not love one another by choice, Elodie believed, but by definition, even if they had to do it in spite of themselves. Thus, she and her sisters loved Mary as a person, but even if they hadn't they would "love & respect her as the daughter of a Father much loved & whose memory [was] fondly cherished." Like breathing, then, familial affection was involuntary, and from it Elodie drew her simple rules of conduct. The Todds could disagree with Lincoln but not disrespect him. They could insult his politics but not his person. As she explained it to Nathaniel, "There is not one of us that cherish an unkind thought or feeling toward him and for this reason we feel as acutely every remark derogatory to him, except as a President."

Elodie's neighbors did not make such fine distinctions. The execrableness of Abe Linkhorn's character was one of the few things everybody agreed on; cursing him became a national pastime. "I never go in Public that my feelings are not pounded," Elodie noted, "nor are we exempt in Matt's own home for people constantly wish he may be hung & all such evils may attend his footsteps." She tried not to take it personally, but who would she be if she didn't? "We would be devoid of all feeling or sympathy did we not feel for [the Lincolns]," she told Nathaniel. "I wish I were not so sensitive, but it is a *decided weakness* of the entire family and to struggle against it seems for naught."

Elodie's touchiness on the Lincoln issue did not play well in the Selma ladies' circle and infused a local society already divided and volatile. By the summer of 1861, the town had uneasily grouped itself into two camps, one associated with the men of the Selma Blues regiment, the other associated with the men of the Magnolia Cadets. The Cadets had left Selma in such a rush that the women of the town had not had time to organize a proper sendoff. The Blues, by contrast, had hung around for weeks after they were organized to parade in their uniforms and indulge in local hospitalities. The disparity was too much for Cadet partisans. They chided the Blues for being too dainty to eat army rations and too comfortable to ever leave Selma. The Blues did depart eventually, but the divisions remained an essential part of the town's social calculus. "It seems strange to me that so few are together and all helping for the one and the same cause," Elodie noted, "that they *cannot work together* cheerfully and happily in place of actually working against each other and throwing as many obstacles in their way as possible." "I do not know of anything that has been tried," she claimed, "that has not been opposed by another party."

These divisions played themselves out most viciously at the tableaux, the fundraising soirees organized by the Selma ladies' circle. Every month or so, the women of the town put together a program of charades, skits, dancing, and musical entertainments designed to solicit donations from remaining local gentlemen. These donations, of course, had to be distributed between the Blues and the Cadets, a process that became so bitter, Nathaniel threatened to return the money sent to his men. The social politicking became even more rancorous when it was decided to hold separate tableaux for the two regiments, and it was Elodie's touchiness on the Lincoln issue that cemented the antagonisms for the remainder of the war. Fond of singing, Elodie had participated in several of the earlier soirees and had been present when an organizing committee suggested a skit that ridiculed Abraham Lincoln. She was incensed. "That is a privilege I allow myself exclusively," she explained, "to abuse my relations as much as I desire — but *no one* can do the same before me." The committee relented, and the Lincoln scene did not appear at the tableaux. A few months later, however, she received the program for the first soiree organized for the exclusive benefit of the Blues: the skit was on the evening's agenda. Elodie was irate. "I must confess that I have never been more hurt or indignant in my life," she wrote Nathaniel. "What have we ever done to deserve this attempt to personally insult and wound our feelings in so public a manner? We have suffered what they never have and perhaps never will in severing ties of blood." It was bad enough that her callers regularly told her that Lincoln should be "caught and hung." To savage him at a public function was too much. "You do not know all we have taken from some of the people of this place, no not one half," Elodie wrote her fiancé. "*Pride* has kept us from showing how we felt. I am afraid I shall never love Selma, and I feel thankful that I am not dependent on its inhabitants for my happiness."

With this incident, the loose division in the Selma social circle became a deep rift. "Society [here] has undergone a change," Elodie explained, "and is now divided into two distinct classes." The first class, calling itself the Anti-Whites, was composed of Blues partisans. The second class, calling itself the Whites, after Elodie's sister, Martha White, comprised Cadet-backers and anyone who thought the Lincoln skit had crossed a social line. With everyone clear on the sides, women who had insulted each other only obliquely heretofore came straight to the point. "There has been a *war here in words*," Elodie reported, "and the *Victory* is not yet awarded."

X.

AT THE WAR'S beginning, the Todds' division had made them minor celebrities. Those who had publicly turned their backs on each other had underlined their ardent patriotism. Those who had clung to each other had underlined their enduring affection. For all, secession had created an almost pleasant drama, a moment when one could rise and be counted. That moment was fleeting, as was the celebrity. By year's close, the country was not interested in the Todds' sad drama anymore. The emotional tenor of the country had grown harder, more bitter. A family had to be on one side or the other, not both.

Of necessity, the Todds' public stance toward one another hardened too. Their very existence implicated one another, and so they attempted to deny that existence, or at least its emotional import. Mary no longer read her mail. With the postal system divided, the Southern wing of her family couldn't have easily written her if they'd wanted to, and they didn't want to. By the end of the year, the Todds had turned away from their divide. They did not reach across it, or even yell across it; they existed to each other now as a memory, or as a concept. As Elodie noted, "If my family did not get their names published occasionally, I would not know they were alive."

But privately, with the exception of George and David, affection remained like flowers beneath the snow. "You see I am sad today," Elodie confessed to Nathaniel, "and you may be right in thinking I take the cares and troubles [of my family] to heart too much, but I have tried in every way to drive them from me and I cannot. Tho' I employ every moment & take no time for thought, yet they find their way to me." "Would to heaven we had never had occasion for this Unnatural War," Elodie admitted. "Surely there is no other family in the land placed in the exact situation of ours, and I hope there will never be [another] so unfortunate as to be so surrounded by trials so numerous."

As awkward as it had been, it was not as awful as it would get. The war was widening, swallowing more. By the end of the year, Hardin Helm had organized his own regiment. "This separation I sincerely hope will not continue long," he wrote his wife, Emilie, upon leaving, "but Dear Em I have gone in for the war and if God spares my life I expect to battle to the end of it." Aleck too had made his decision. He gave his sweetheart a picture of Kitty and an oversize ring of gold that David had sent him during his prospecting days. He hoped the gifts would secure her promise to wait for him until he returned.

"You do not know how strangely and badly I feel," Elodie told her fiancé at year's end. "[Once] we were altogether a happy household. Those were happy times, but now I forbear to draw the contrast, the dark view of the picture. It is more than enough to feel the difference, which I do most keenly, and am hoping each hour, each day may produce a change that will enable us once more to be a reunited family. But I fear there will be some missing from the family circle." And in this she was unfortunately right.

Robert Smith Todd, the patriarch of the Todd family, had six children by his first wife and eight by his second. While widely respected, he was never particularly successful. He died a disappointed man in 1849.

The eldest of the Todds, Elizabeth Todd Edwards was a mother not only to her children but to her younger sisters, including Mary Lincoln.

Ninian Edwards and Abraham Lincoln came up in the Whig Party together. Although Ninian found him "mighty rough" and occasionally resented his success, he also saw Lincoln's brilliance.

Frances Todd went out with Lincoln a couple of times but decided that he was the "plainest man in Springfield." She later married William Smith Wallace, the doctor who owned the drugstore beneath Lincoln's law office.

William Smith Wallace, the namesake of the Lincolns' third son, Willie, traveled with Lincoln to Washington and was appointed a paymaster in the Union army.

Abraham and Mary Todd Lincoln in 1846, four years after their marriage.

Ann Todd Smith, fourth-born of the Todd girls, did not always get along with her sister Mary.

George Rogers Clark Todd was a brilliant surgeon, but, enraged by a stutter, myopia, and alcoholism, he became the self-described black sheep of the Todd family.

Clark Moulton Smith, a Springfield merchant, provided Lincoln with the sanctuary in which he wrote his first inaugural address.

Charles Henry Kellogg, after attending Lincoln's inauguration and pestering the president for a federal job, traveled in the bosom of the Confederate army, effectively committing treason.

Margaret Todd Kellogg also attended Lincoln's inauguration. Nevertheless she was compelled to leave her home in Cincinnati because she was seen, not without reason, as pro-Confederate.

Samuel Todd, after an extremely brief Confederate career, was killed on the second day at Shiloh.

David Todd's short tenure as commandant of the Richmond prisons ended in scandal and allegations of murder. His meritorious service during the siege of Vicksburg could not redeem his reputation.

Martha Todd White was the (partly) innocent cause of the greatest, but not the only, Todd scandal to plague the Lincoln administration.

Emilie Todd was the Lincolns' "Little Sister."
Though she married a man who became a
brigadier general in the Confederate army, she
remained close to the Lincolns and even stayed
in the White House during the war.

Emilie and her husband, Benjamin Hardin
Helm, at the time of their marriage.

Benjamin Hardin Helm rose to command the Confederate "Orphan Brigade," so called because it was shot
through with Kentuckians who couldn't
return home to their unseceded state.

Alexander Todd, the Todd sisters'
collective favorite, was killed near
Baton Rouge in 1862.

Elodie Todd attended Jefferson Davis's
inaugural and there met her future husband,
Nathaniel Henry Rhodes Dawson.

Kitty Todd traveled to Springfield to celebrate Lincoln's ascension to the presidency. As the war dragged on, however, her allegiance to the South deepened.

Mary Todd Lincoln as she looked during the Civil War.

Abraham Lincoln as he appeared during his presidency.

4

1862: "Blood Galore"

I.

THE DAVID TODD prison scandal broke in January 1862 with a long exposé in the *New York Herald,* the very paper that had come to his aid the preceding October. Based on the revelations of an exchanged prisoner named James Gillette, the article confirmed rumors already afloat about the Richmond jails. "The treatment of our brave boys was cruel in the extreme," the *Herald* noted. Their quarters had been filthy, their meals rancid and infrequent, their medical care nonexistent, and it was all the fault of one man — David Todd. "A more tyrannical man than Lieutenant Todd it would be difficult to find after a search of years," the paper claimed. He had a "heart [in which] not one drop of pity seem[ed] to linger." Most gravely, the *Herald* charged that Todd had directed the execution of three soldiers for the minor offense of peeping out a window. The article was specific: the executed soldiers were M. C. Beck and C. W. Tibbetts of the Seventy-Ninth New York Militia and R. Gleeson of the New York Fire Zouaves. Here, published *in New York,* were the names of three New Yorkers murdered by Mrs. Lincoln's brother. David Todd, the *Herald* concluded, was nothing short of "a monster."

Other Northern papers quickly followed suit. There was little else to cover in the way of war news. Armies were in winter quarters. The major battles that had been fought were all Union defeats, and rehashing those would only sap morale. What Northerners needed was a sign that they remained a superior people, and the abuses at the Richmond prisons answered that need nicely. In news accounts, Todd was an "extravagant" reprobate who conformed in every particular to the image of the Southerner in the Northern mind. Tyrannical, intemperate, and vile, he was the very monster Northerners had expected, and the more they read about what he had done to their "brave boys," they more he rekindled their wrath. "From all sides come stories of the acts of this sneaking, savage, cowardly scoundrel," reported the *New York Times* in February. "[Todd] seems fitted by nature for the position of a plantation overseer. . . . [He] wants no better amusement than to come into the prison on a forenoon and to kick the helpless, crippled and wounded." "The notorious Lieut. Todd was singularly vicious and brutal," echoed a pamphlet published in the same month. "[He] seldom entered the room without grossly insulting some of the inmates. . . . It is not to be wondered . . . that this ferocious and vindictive monster should be regarded with feelings of the deepest horror and detestation."

Such charges fell lightly on David. To his mind, he had given the Yankees only what they deserved. After his embarrassing dismissal, he "recuperated" for a month at the Powhatan before traveling to northern Virginia to join Colonel Tom Taylor's First Kentucky Regiment as an assistant quartermaster. Taylor was a Frankfort, Kentucky, native. He probably knew David personally and was happy to extend him the opportunity. Thus, despite the ignominy of his being arrested and relieved of command, David's career in the Confederate army had not suffered much. His new position, he told his sister, suited "his taste better than any other."

But if David Todd did not suffer for his conduct, there remained the question of whether his sister Mary would.

II.

NEITHER MARY LINCOLN nor her husband had been particularly well received in Washington. Both were seen as provincials — rough-hewn prairie people elevated beyond their talents or deserts. To the abolitionist Lydia Child, Mrs. Lincoln "look[ed] more like a dowdy washerwoman" than a first lady. Her opinion of Mr. Lincoln was even harsher: "I never see old Abe's *pictur* without thinking that his lanky neck looks as if he was made to be hanged." (This from a noted humanitarian.)

But Lincoln had a tendency to grow on people. The first time the cabinet met, each member thought himself a better man than Lincoln.

A few months later, Secretary of State William Seward wrote his wife with the flatness of fact: "The President is the best of us." Even Lydia Child warmed to Lincoln eventually. "With all his deficiencies, it must be admitted that he has grown continually," she wrote a friend. "I think we have reason to thank God for Abraham Lincoln." Of course, Lincoln could not, and did not, win everyone over. Many would never deviate from the belief that he had only an affable mediocrity. But no one who met him questioned his decency or his dedication to his country. He worked sixteen-hour days for the entirety of his presidency. He seemed to meet everyone with "a cool head, a firm hand and an honest heart."

Mary Lincoln was another story. She did not grow on people. Rather the opposite: popular opinion moved steadily against her. It is vaguely possible that the Northern public would have ignored the David Todd revelations if Mary had established herself as a beloved and self-sacrificing patriot of the Union cause. Instead, by the time story broke, they were prepared to believe the worst. Indeed, the idea that Mary Lincoln was a blood relation of a deranged rebel commandant seemed quite in keeping with two other scandals, entirely of her own making, which broke at the same time.

To understand these scandals requires a short tour of Mary's unusual psyche. Much of her adult life Mary Lincoln was dogged by charges that she was "half-crazy," "part-insane," "demented," or "deranged." Today, psychologists prefer more precise diagnoses — narcissistic personality disorder being the lead contender. Like most disorders, this one is rooted in childhood and is complicated, but it can be boiled down: All children crave love, attention, and recognition of their unique qualities. Some children, not getting (and never reconciling themselves to not getting) these things, erect on the ruin of their childhood expectations an ersatz self that can demand and take them, heedless of the consequences to others. This was Mary Lincoln in a nutshell. Lost in a large household, not getting her due strokes from her dead mother, absent father, and preoccupied stepmother, she invented a new reality to live in, one in which she was uniquely insightful and deserving. Her own feelings and opinions became magnified in importance and expression. The feelings and opinions of others grew distant and disposable. Thus, her reaction to another's advancement was invariably, "Why should *she* benefit?" And her reaction to another's misfortune was always, "Why *shouldn't* he suffer?" Lincoln was not entirely exempt from this trend in her thinking. Certainly, as the hot coffee dripped down her husband's scalded face, Mary felt no immediate pang of conscience for throwing it there. But when he accepted such treatment with a sad understanding, she was inclined, occasionally, to allow him to comfort the wounded child in her who was, at base, the malevolent architect of such things.

In ascending to the White House, Mary had launched herself into a manic period of self-display. She spent lavishly on dresses and jewelry, often looking ridiculous for the effort. One witness at a state dinner said it appeared that she had a flowerpot balanced on her head, and he lamented that a woman who had once milked her own cows now insisted on displaying "her own milking apparatus" to every man present. She shocked official Washington by wearing a lilac dress to the state funeral of Edward Baker, a sitting senator killed in action and one of her husband's closest friends, the man for whom her dead son Eddie was named. When gently informed that black might have been more appropriate attire, she coolly responded, "I wonder if the women of Washington expect me to muffle myself up in mourning for every soldier killed in this great war?" War or no, Mary meant to take her turn on the stage. The problem was one of audience. The reality she had fashioned for herself was like a one-way mirror; she could admire her reflection in it, but the rest of the world saw right through it. What she needed were others who would stand on her side of the mirror and admire her in it too.

Unfortunately, the people willing to play this game tended to be unsavory. Meeting for long hours in the White House Blue Room, her salon of intimates included Oliver "Pet" Halsted, a shady arms contracts promoter described by insiders as "brilliant" and "dashing" but also "dangerous." "He plays many hands at the same time," a friend admitted, "at a full consideration of his own best chances." Another Blue Room regular was "Cap" Dan Sickles, "one of the bigger bubbles in the scum of the [legal] profession," according to one witness, "swollen and windy, and puffed out with fetid gas." Sickles was infamous for gunning down his wife's lover in broad daylight, in front of witnesses, in the middle of a Washington thoroughfare. The paramour, Philip Barton Key, was the nephew of the chief justice of the United States and the son of Francis Scott Key, author of "The Star-Spangled Banner." Sickles was nonetheless acquitted of murder, in the first-ever use of the temporary insanity defense.

Even with a homicide to his credit, Sickles was not the most infamous rogue to penetrate Mary's inner circle. That distinction belongs to the Chevalier Henry Wikoff, whom Mary established as her "major-domo in general and in special, as guide in matters of social etiquette, domestic arrangements, and personal requirements, including her toilette." Born in America, Wikoff had spent most of his time in European capitals. "He has seen more of the world than most men," admitted one journalist, "has mingled with society of every shade and grade . . . can talk of love, law, literature, and war; can describe the rulers and thinkers of his time, can gossip of courts and cabinets, of the boudoir and the salon." Coupled with the Chevalier's Old World sophistication, however, was more than a dash of Old World decadence. He had been imprisoned in 1851 for abducting a tobacco heiress in Italy. *Scribner's* called his account of the scrape, *My Courtship and Its Consequences*, "one of the least creditable volumes ever put forth by a native American." No less a man than P. T. Barnum credited Wikoff with teaching him one of his first lessons in the art of hokum. Wikoff was, noted Washington officials variously, a "terrible libertine," a "world renowned whore-monger and swindler," an "unclean bird," a "vile creature," a "social Pariah," and a man with "a singular facility [for] thrusting his diplomatic fingers into other people's pies." "[It is] a disgrace to American society," wrote Lincoln's secretary, "that it suffers such a thing to be at large." Mary claimed that she kept men like Halsted, Sickles, and Wikoff around because they were powerful and could help her husband. The journalist Henry Villard suspected another reason: that Mary had an appetite for flummery so voracious that only the "most bare-faced flattery" could sate it — and these men were the country's flum-masters.

Scoundrels held another attraction for Mary. They could help her bend the rules and line her pocket while they lined their own. The stories are too numerous and well-documented to admit of doubt: men bribed the first lady to lobby her husband for jobs. Twenty thousand dollars bought a port collectorship. Diamonds bought a naval agency. To be fair, Mary's conduct was no more crooked than that of many politicians in that freewheeling day. It was, however, considerably more crooked than that of her husband, whom Mary considered a monomaniac on the subject of honesty. To her way of thinking, Lincoln could afford to take the high road only because she was willing to take the low, which was, after all, where a lot of politics was conducted.

Sometimes she sank too low, however, as in her dealings with William S. Wood. In early 1861, Wood had been responsible for the Lincolns' travel arrangements from Springfield to Washington. Somewhere along the way, he and Mary had developed a mutual regard.

Wood made Mary a gift of some very fine horses. Mary then, according to witnesses, locked herself in her room and refused to come out until Lincoln agreed to appoint Wood interim commissioner of public buildings. Wood got $2,000 per annum out of the deal; Mary got lax oversight of the $20,000 appropriation each administration received for making refurbishments to the White House. Together, Wood and Mary blew through the money in little more than a month. They traveled to New York and Philadelphia, bustled into and out of the finest stores, and took whatever would fit in the carriage back with them to the hotel. It was an orgy of purchasing and maybe more. In June, Lincoln received an anonymous letter warning him of the brewing "scandal of [his] wife and Wood." "If he continues as commissioner," the letter warned, "he will stab you in your most vital part." Lincoln heeded the warning, and Wood was fired.

Once sacked, Wood turned on Mary, threatening to throw a spotlight on her dirty dealings with the White House gardener. According to him, Mary and the executive groundskeeper, John Watt, had colluded to defraud the government of thousands of dollars in a vast web of phony billing. Mary hotly denied the charges. "[Wood] is not a good man," she wrote the interior secretary investigating the Watt allegations. "He is bitterly disappointed [at being] displaced — and is *capable* of saying any thing against those who tried to befriend him. . . . [In making such charges] he is either deranged or drinking." In truth, Wood didn't know the half of Mary's improprieties. With Watt to tutor her in the delicate art of book cooking, Mary had overcharged the Interior Department for state dinners, sold off White House furniture, taken kickbacks from merchants, drew money on flowers not delivered and labor not performed, and had Mrs. Watt appointed to a sinecure while Mary collected the salary herself. By the end of 1861, Washington was beginning to whisper. "Hell is to pay about Watt's affairs," Lincoln's secretary noted in his diary. "I think the Tycoon [Lincoln] begins to suspect him. I wish he could be struck with lighting. He has got William and Carroll turned off [removed], and has his eye peeled for a pop at me, because I won't let Madame have our stationery fund."

In February 1862 the whisper became a roar. The scandal was touched off not by Watt but Wikoff, who, among his other intrigues, was a spy for the *New York Herald*. In December, Wikoff had talked La Reine (as the Blue Roomers called Mary) into showing him an advance copy of her husband's annual message to Congress. Portions of the speech then made it into the paper, and an incensed Congress opened an investigation. Subpoenaed and deposed, Wikoff admitted that the information had passed *through* him, but he refused to name the original source. The head of the investigating committee gave him a couple days to change his mind, and then threw him in the capital prison. The Blue Roomers now had to scramble to save their queen. Sickles, a lawyer, appointed himself Wikoff's counsel and shuttled between the White House, the prison, and Watt's house, concocting a wildly improbable story. According to Watt's testimony, he had been idly perambulating about the executive mansion when he happened to catch sight of a parchment on the president's desk. A man of literary taste, he had been drawn to peruse the document and, given his remarkably retentive memory, had managed to remember much of it word for word. He then, again idly, rattled off the whole of the text to Wikoff in the course of a next morning's casual conversation. Watt's whole testimony was laughable in every particular, but by the time he gave it all Washington was abuzz with the report that Mary Lincoln was herself the source of the leak. To save his administration further embarrassment, Lincoln appealed to the Republican members of the committee, and the matter was dropped.

Lincoln was inclined to believe that his wife and her cronies had done something foolish but not worse. The public was less forgiving. Disturbing reports began to surface that Watt was a rebel sympathizer and that Wikoff was a foreign intriguer, possibly in league with the Confederacy. If Mary Lincoln was giving state documents to such men as these, wasn't it possible that she was a rebel too? The charge was ridiculous, of course. But there *were* spies in Washington. Mary *had* behaved imprudently, at least. And she *did have* a brother who liked to kick dead Yankees. The public may have misconnected the dots, but they didn't invent them. "Not a few bitter tongues," remembered a witness, began to "roundly [assert] that Mrs. Lincoln herself was in constant correspondence, as a spy, with the chiefs of the Rebellion. Through her they obtained the secrets of the Cabinet and plans of generals in the field."

Ultimately, though, it was not the Wikoff or Watt affairs that brought Mary's orgy of self-love to an end; it was the death of her son Willie. Four boys had been born to the Lincolns: Robert, Eddie, Willie, and Tad. Robert was cool and distant. Eddie had died in 1850. Tad was perhaps adorable but certainly ungovernable; he had a slight speech impediment and didn't really learn to read or dress himself until after he left the White House at the age of twelve. Willie was another story. Nathaniel Parker Willis, an author and an acquaintance of the Lincolns, thought Willie an old soul — self-possessed and substantive, though still full of mirth. He was like "a wild flower transplanted from the prairie," Willis noted, "unalterably pure and simple," "willing that everything should be as different as it pleased, but resting unmoved in his own . . . single-heartedness." Willis watched one day as Willie played on the White House lawn. Secretary of State Seward pulled up in a carriage with Prince Napoleon and his entourage. Playfully, Seward doffed his hat to Willie by way of salute; Prince Napoleon, perhaps thinking this was the protocol, did the same. Though only ten, Willie very gracefully "drew himself up to his full height, took off his [cap] and bowed down formally to the ground, like a little ambassador." As soon as Seward and the prince had passed, Willie fell back to playing as if nothing unusual had happened. "Genial . . . ingenuous and fearless for a certain tincture of fun," Willis noted; "it was in [the] mingling of [these] qualities that [the boy] so faithfully resembled his father."

In early February, Willie had fallen ill with what was probably typhoid fever, contracted from fecally contaminated drinking water. (In those days, water from the Potomac River — the city's septic tank and the army's latrine — was piped directly into the White House.) Whatever the source, the bacteria multiplied in Willie's bowel, causing his intestines to cramp, ulcerate, and then hemorrhage. After a few weeks of feeling like he was dying of a gut shot, Willie slipped mercifully into a coma and died. Mary was inconsolable, convulsive, hysterical. From the manic high of her reign as the Blue Room's "queen," she plummeted into a despair so black that Lincoln worried for her sanity.

Robert Lincoln worried for her too. Though less forbearing than his father, he had the older man's intuitive grasp of Mary's nature. She would need help getting ahold of herself. When once she lost her tether, it wasn't the work of a moment to find it again. With his father's permission, he invited his aunt Elizabeth to make a visit from Springfield. He was close to the Todds, and he recognized that they had a unique way of bringing his mother back to herself.

Elizabeth was shocked by her sister's condition on her arrival. Mary had confined herself to her bed, refused to dress, and left to others the care and comfort of Tad, himself brokenhearted and sick with the same disease that had killed Willie. Keeping her temper, Elizabeth gently coaxed Mary into her mourning clothes, but her letters home betray her disapproval. "[Today] I persuaded [your aunt] to put on

[her] *black dress*," she wrote her daughter, "[but it] painfully reminded her of the loss that will long shadow her *pleasures*. Such is her nature that I cannot realize that she will forego them all or even long under existing circumstances." Elizabeth admitted that "such language sounds harsh but the *excessive indulgence* that has been revealed to me fully justifies it." She was referring of course to the Watt and Wikoff affairs, rumors of which were still reverberating throughout Washington. Willie's death, Elizabeth told her daughter coldly, would be "a serious crush to [Mary's] *unexampled frivolity*."

Elizabeth took a softer line with Lincoln himself. She had always thought her brother-in-law an odd duck. It bothered her, for instance, that he would sit down to dinner and then forget to eat. It bothered her that he didn't seem to appreciate how much she and Ninian had done to further his career. But she had for Lincoln something she didn't have for her sister: respect. And she respected the fact that Lincoln's heart was unstrung. Willie had been considered — and had considered himself — "Mama's boy." Tad was Lincoln's charge — they could make mischief together, and Lincoln had a weakness for things with weaknesses. But of all the boys, Willie had the most promising mind and the most promising heart — and his father knew it. In Willie, Lincoln found a kindred spirit, and he had no hope to find another. Though he had hundreds of friends and a wife and children whom he loved, he was, in some new way, alone on the earth.

Recognizing a little of this, Elizabeth decided to try to cheer Lincoln up. She took him first to the White House conservatory, which she thought the most magical place in Washington. "[Here] the world is represented by flowers," she said, "[flowers] that Speak." Lincoln didn't really hear them, though. "I never was in here before," he told Elizabeth. "How Spring like it looks." A few days later, Elizabeth tried again, taking him on a stroll through Lafayette Park in spring. Lincoln was just beginning to open up about Willie when Tad, who had come along, locked the garden gate and hid the key. After a fruitless search, Lincoln, as usual, favored the boy by finding the trick clever.

Of course, Elizabeth had tried to cheer Lincoln up with the things that *she* found cheerful. But she had done it out of love. "Beneath what the world saw lurked a nature as tender and poetic as any I ever knew," she said of him. "I respect[ed] & love[d] Mr Lincoln ... He was a great man — a good man & an honest one." Lincoln returned the good opinion. "Do stay with me," he told Elizabeth one day. "You have such a power & control, such an influence over Mary — Come do stay." Elizabeth was ready to go, however. Though only forty-nine, she considered herself an old lady. She had long before lost the taste for fashionable places and found the "exertion of dressing and talking to strangers . . . irksome." She missed her garden and her baby's babies. A couple months after her arrival, she took the train back to Springfield.

Sometime after her departure a letter arrived for her at the White House. Curious, Mary opened it. Elizabeth had told her daughter to "be careful to refrain from alluding in an unkind way to her [aunt]," but Julia hadn't gotten the message. The contents, whatever they were, enraged Mary, and she did not speak to Elizabeth again for more than a decade. Any progress Elizabeth had made in reconciling her sister to her grief was undone overnight. Mary became obsessed with mourning attire, black stationery, and silence. She sent everything that reminded her of Willie away, including his friends (who were also Tad's friends). For his part, Lincoln returned to brooding and — with the spring campaign finally under way — to prosecuting a war.

III.

BY INCLINATION and insight, Lincoln foresaw that the Civil War would be won or lost in the West. He was a westerner himself, after all, and as a former land surveyor, he knew how to read a map. Thus, while the majority of his generals and an unforgiving public focused myopically on Virginia, Lincoln followed the advice of Winfield Scott and worried less about capturing Richmond than cutting the Confederacy in two along the Mississippi River. "The Mississippi is the backbone of the Rebellion," he concluded. "It is the key to the whole situation."

To break that backbone, Lincoln directed a massive military buildup of army and freshwater naval forces at Cairo, Illinois. Located at the confluence of the Mississippi and the Ohio, Cairo was the southernmost city in the Free States. And in February 1862, the federal force massed there began to roll down the river like a juggernaut. The Confederate commander in the theater, Albert Sidney Johnston, was immediately rocked back on his heels. He had stretched his defensive line from Columbus, Kentucky, just fifteen miles below Cairo, to Bowling Green, Kentucky, two hundred miles to the east. Between these two fortified points were two weaker installations, Forts Henry and Donelson, on the Tennessee and Cumberland rivers, respectively. In short order, a Union detachment under Ulysses S. Grant captured Henry and

Donelson and opened the way to Nashville, which fell on February 23. With the center of his line destroyed, Johnston was forced to abandon his entire defensive strategy and regroup farther south, at Corinth, Mississippi. In two short months, he had lost Nashville, a quarter of his army, and most of Tennessee and Kentucky. The Confederacy, which had been crowing about Bull Run all winter, was stunned into silence. "Richmond is very quiet," Nathaniel lamented to Elodie. "It seems to be conceded that a great battle is to be fought, and must be won, near Corinth."

The city of Corinth was what one observer called a "wretched place — the capital of a swamp." With 50,000 soldiers befouling it daily, it certainly became one — but it had claims to such opprobrium even before. Corinth had no businesses, manufactories, or supply warehouses of any military significance. The surrounding countryside was a forbidding tangle of oak, underbrush, and bog. The town seemed to have been willfully situated in the exact middle of nowhere. Considering this, however, it was an oddly accessible middle of nowhere. Two rail lines crossed in town — one conveniently oriented north-south, the other east-west. To accommodate water-borne traffic, a dirt road stretched northeast from town twenty miles to Pittsburg Landing on the Tennessee River. Corinth, in short, was humble but handy, and it became what one observer called "the 'Grand Point' at which troops [were] collected from all parts of the Confederacy for some great move."

Collected there too were three Todd brothers and two Todd brothers-in-law. Hardin Helm, now a colonel and commander of the First Kentucky Cavalry, had covered the Confederate retreat from Bowling Green. He and his men were then stationed at Burnsville, Mississippi, to scout the enemy advance and guard the eastern approach to Corinth. Encamped with him was Charles Kellogg, husband of Margaret Todd and an attendee of Lincoln's inauguration. A Northerner moving with, but not a member of, the Confederate army, Charles never appreciated the delicacy of his position until it was too late.

Also traveling with them was Aleck Todd, whom Hardin had appointed his assistant quartermaster. Emilie was undoubtedly behind the move, though Hardin didn't seem to mind. He was a protective older brother himself, and he had known for years that the Todd sisters coddled Aleck. He was their youngest brother, and since his abuse at the hands of his nurse they had united to shield him from further harm. Besides — easy to like, fiercely affectionate, and with an open, boyish face framed by thick red hair — Aleck was everybody's natural favorite. Temperamentally, he had all the feistiness of his brother David without any of the boozy malice. When the war started, he inscribed his diary, "Death to Yankees!" but directly beneath that he wrote: "Should this be found by the Union soldiers they will confer a favor by sending it by mail or otherwise to Alex Todd."

David was also at Corinth. His regiment, pulled west to boost Johnston's numbers, was somewhat desperate to distinguish itself. Their only winter action had been a farcical skirmish at Dranesville, Virginia, where they had fired on their fellow Confederates before being shot up by the Yankees. Among the slain was their colonel, Tom Taylor, who had been blown off his horse while his men "hastily abandoned" the field. In the wake of this "unfortunate affair" (as Nathaniel called it), David took a leave to attend to business and acquire better weapons for the regiment. In his travels, he stopped by Selma and regaled his sisters with colorful stories of camp life. Elodie was glad to see him in good spirits but thought him little recuperated from the pulmonary troubles of the preceding year. "He looks badly," she admitted to Nathaniel, "being just recovered from Typhoid Fever and Pneumonia, and certainly requires rest." David could not be prevailed upon, however, and by late March he had rejoined his regiment outside Corinth.

By then, Sam Todd had arrived too. In February, Louisiana's governor had called for the enlistment of a large group of ninety-day men to help boost Confederate numbers. Recovered from whatever camp illness had sidelined him the year before, Sam seized the chance. He enrolled as a private in Company H of the Crescent Regiment — derided as the "kid glove" regiment because so many of its members were New Orleans blue bloods. Sam was no dainty, however. Thankful for a second chance to rise and be counted, he was perfectly happy to roll up his sleeves. At thirty-two, he was one of the older privates, but, a blithe spirit, he threw himself into even the menial aspects of soldiering and drew compliments from his commanders for his enthusiastic sink digging and tent pitching.

Once the Confederate force, Todd boys included, was massed, the plan was to turn the tables on Ulysses S. Grant. His army had marched to within twenty miles of Corinth, crossed over the Tennessee River, and occupied the broad tableland beyond. Even with his back to a river, Grant gave no thought to his defensive position. Having pushed the Confederates all the way through Tennessee, he assumed they'd sit at Corinth and wait for him to push them some more. He would await the reinforcements of General Don Carlos Buell and then obliterate the city.

Johnston and his second in command, P.G.T. Beauregard, had other ideas. On the first or second of April, Hardin had telegraphed them that, based on his observations, Buell would not be able to rendezvous with Grant until April 6. This gave the Confederate force a window of opportunity. If it could march quietly to within striking distance of Grant on April 3, it could surprise him on the fourth before he was reinforced.

The plan was sound; the logistics a nightmare. Rightly, Beauregard thought an army could cover twenty miles in a day. He didn't have an army, however; he had a collection of raw volunteers. Ordered to roll out of Corinth at six A.M. on April 3, entire divisions were still lounging about the city well into the afternoon. By dusk it was clear that not enough of the army was going to be in position for an attack the following morning. Meeting with Johnston, Beauregard agreed that the offensive would have to be postponed until eight A.M. on April 5. As the meeting was breaking up, he did receive some good news. A Union cavalry commander, LeRoy Crockett, had been captured on patrol and was brought into the main camp. Among other things, he specifically complimented Sam Todd's regiment. "A fine set of soldiers you have," he told the Crescents' colonel. "If they were in blue I would have taken them for my own boys." More important, however, he admitted that his generals had no idea that the South was on the march. "They don't expect anything of this kind back yonder." The Confederates were a day behind schedule, but they still had the advantage of surprise.

On the morning of the attack, April 5, soldiers fell in at three A.M. to move from their camps to their assigned positions. Unfortunately, darkness and a torrential downpour again made coordination difficult. Roads backed up behind wagons. Some commanders went around; others waited around. By four P.M., the line had not formed and it was clear the Confederate attack would have to be postponed again. Beauregard was flabbergasted, apoplectic. His army was now two days behind schedule. Worse, they had not moved stealthily. In taking their positions, the men had talked loudly, laughed loudly, lustily cheered their commanders, and taken potshots at the local fauna. When the rain had stopped, hundreds of them had fired their guns to make sure they still worked. For kicks, an entire regiment squeezed off a volley in unison. If Grant had any sense, Beauregard figured, he would be reinforced and waiting for him the next morning. The attack, he decided, would have to be called off altogether. Johnston, however, had a reputation to redeem and overruled him. "Gentlemen, we shall attack at daylight tomorrow."

The resulting battle of Shiloh was an amazing mess. Despite the Confederates' many blunders, they achieved total surprise. Entire Union regiments were caught in their camps, jaws slackened against half-masticated breakfasts, arms up to their elbows in their washing pails. Hundreds of them, and by the end of the day thousands of them, simply panicked and sprinted for the river, where, according to one witness, they cowered behind a low bluff "deaf to duty and dead to shame." Reinforcements arriving at the landing insulted, struck, and threatened to shoot the yellow-bellies to no avail. The few who were inclined to budge only tried to pounce on the departing steamboats. These were bayoneted or pushed into the water and "suffered to drown each other in their own way." When Grant arrived from his headquarters upriver, his boat had to churn against a tide of soldiers trying to float to freedom on logs.

Unfortunately for the Confederates, their offensive wasn't much better organized. In the snarled oak and underbrush, whole regiments crisscrossed each other's paths, then circled around to startle each other in an open glade and blaze away at close range. Whether by zeal or ineptitude, reserve units almost immediately overran the lines they were supposed to reinforce. At the rear, the man in charge, Albert Sidney Johnston, might have been able to coordinate things better, except that he wasn't at the rear. He was leading the offensive, which has to be regarded as a tactical mistake, because it got him killed.

Of the Todd boys', only Sam's regiment was sucked into the maelstrom. At eight A.M., before the attack began in earnest, the Crescents were detailed to guard a tiny bridge over Owl Creek at the extreme left of the Confederate line. There they could presumably send up an alarm if the federals made any attempt to turn the rebel left flank. Marching up Purdy Road, they encountered no resistance. A random shell took off their drummer's head above the wispy beginnings of his beard. Undoubtedly, it was the first time Sam had seen anything like it. But for the most part, the federals were in retreat. Sometime before noon the Crescents happened upon the abandoned camp of the Sixth Iowa. The Iowans were gone except for their dead and dying. Despite this, the kid-glove regiment put their stomachs before their scruples and set to plundering the Yankee tents. (In their defense, they had barely eaten in three days. The order to cook five days' rations had come on April 3. "Not having any rations to cook," one of them had noted, "it did not take us long to obey." Instead they had left Corinth with five crackers apiece and sufficient humor to nickname their new bivouac Camp Starvation.) After a half-hour of ravenous pillage, the men began to remember themselves. One of the tents contained a Yankee corpse, his head upon his hand, his torso blown open. Riffling lost some of its appeal after that. Stuffing the last edible bits into their sacks and mouths, they wandered to their post at the abandoned bridge. And there they sat, practically forgotten, for hours.

By two in the afternoon, it was clear to every man present that the flank they were guarding was long gone and the enemy they were guarding against had probably gone with it. Now orphaned, and with no way of knowing where their own corps was, the Crescents wandered back down the road toward Shiloh Church, where Beauregard had set up headquarters. The general was nearly hoarse from shouting, but he was heady with victory. He felt sure he was driving all the federals into the river. "Go on, my brave boys," he told the Crescents. "Charge them and the victory is ours. . . . shoot low, shoot low."

The advice was good, though Sam's colonel wasn't sure what it meant in practical terms. Where were they supposed to charge? Whom were they were supposed to shoot low? Still a bit lost, the Crescents marched up the road a little farther, and, drawn by the din of battle, they stumbled through some thick underbrush and emerged in front of the Union position that what would come to be called the Hornets' Nest. Here, after a morning of freewheeling reverses, the federal resistance had stiffened along a three-quarter-mile wagon path (later known as the Sunken Road). Seven poorly coordinated Confederate charges had already been made against the position before the Crescents arrived. All were repulsed with heavy losses. The Crescents would be part of the eighth and final charge.

Facing the Crescents were the Seventh and Fifty-eighth Illinois, about a thousand men strong. Ill-advisedly, they had drifted forward from the Sunken Road into an open farmyard called Duncan Field. From the Duncan cabins and cotton bales, they had begun sniping at the Crescents the moment they spotted them across the field. Falling back into the edge of the thicket, the Crescents went down on their bellies. Yankee artillery had about gotten their range. "Balls and bomb shells," admitted one Crescent, "whizzed over our heads and burst in the air or carried away tops of trees." As they pondered their course, the Twentieth Louisiana came up on their right. After a conference with the brigade commander, Patton Anderson, it was decided that the two groups would make a general charge, the Crescents taking the Illinoisans on the left and Anderson's men taking the Union battery on the right.

Given the fire they were already taking, the order to charge came swiftly. At about three-thirty, Sam and the others sped across the open field toward the Hornets' Nest. The ensuing skirmish lasted only fifteen minutes and was unusual for Shiloh in that it occurred out in the open, where everyone could see each other perfectly. Their flank in the air, the Illinoisans knew they would have to return to the relative safety of the Sunken Road line, but they gave their ground grudgingly. A soldier making the charge with Sam remembered later, "The field was literally strewn with dead and dying [but still] we charged on." The onslaught dissipated like a wave dashed against a wharf, however, as the Illinoisans regained the road and the Twentieth Louisiana, on the Crescents' right, was cut to pieces by federal canister. There was no sense in pressing further, and Sam and the others fell quickly back across the field. Clearly, the Hornets' Nest was not to be taken from the front. Ten thousand Confederates had participated in the eight charges. Twenty-four percent of them had been cut down.

After their charge, Leonidas Polk, a general known as the "Fighting Bishop," pulled up beside the Crescents on the left and offered them another option. Detailing them to his right, he suggested moving through the woods north of Duncan Field and emerging in the rear of the Illinoisans. Despite a reputation as a poor field commander, Polk seemed almost alone in understanding that the northern Nest would be better flanked than fought through. And his plan worked perfectly. A federal line that had held out for six hours began to weaken within minutes. The Seventh Illinois, recognizing disaster, escaped to the rear; the Fifty-eighth Illinois recognized disaster too late and was flanked and pinned down in a little vale that would come to be called Hell's Hollow. With more Confederates now seeping around the right of his line, the Union general William Wallace sent word to the four regiments of Iowans at his center that they needed to pull up stakes too. What might have been an orderly withdrawal, however, became mass chaos when a Confederate bombardment began at four-thirty P.M. Lacking Polk's finesse, several division commanders had brought all available cannon into Duncan Field and trained them on the Nest. Lasting only five minutes, it was nevertheless the most massive artillery barrage ever seen on the continent. Flanks turned and center crushed, the Sunken Road line now collapsed upon itself. Like the Fifty-eighth Illinois, many of the men were driven into Hell's Hollow, where the Crescent Regiment and others picked them off with ease. With no other choice, the remainder surrendered, 2,200 in all. The Confederate mood was exultant. Literally and figuratively, it seemed that the sun was setting on the federals. Their resistance had been smashed. Beauregard, confident of victory, telegraphed Richmond with the good news. All that remained was a little mop-up work, and that could wait until morning.

For Sam Todd, the day had been a mix of new experiences and emotions. He had seen a man's head (mostly) blown off. He had seen people he knew and liked shot down. He had also felt a rush like no other. He had cheated death. Lying in a captured tent, riffling idly among its contents, he perhaps wondered if its owner had been so lucky as to live through the first day of Shiloh too.

Outside the tent, the Confederate army was completely disorganized by victory. Regiments camped higgledy-piggledy, nowhere near their lines. Thousands of men left camp altogether. Under the cover of darkness, in the midst of a downpour, to the groans of their own uncollected wounded, they scavenged the battlefield by guttering lamplight. They picked over the remains of overrun Yankee encampments, drinking from Yankee bottles and insulting the daguerreotypes of Yankee sweethearts. As dawn broke, they staggered off to Corinth to stash their swag. Like the bulk of their generals, they figured the battle was basically over.

Grant took a different view. As Hardin had correctly predicted, Buell's men, 25,000 strong, began arriving on April 6 and continued to arrive most of the night. One of them was Ambrose Bierce. He and the rest of the Ninth Indiana had debarked at Pittsburg Landing after nightfall. In what Bierce called the "black-dark" they shuffled along, inch by inch, "treading on one another's heels by way of keeping together," until they were finally led to their position in Grant's emerging battle line. "Very often," Bierce remembered, "we struck our feet against the dead; more frequently against those who still had spirit enough to resent it with a moan." At dawn, they got their first look at the battlefield. Near them was a "federal sergeant, variously hurt, who had been a fine giant in his time. He lay face upward, taking in his breath in convulsive rattling snorts, and blowing it out in sputters of froth which crawled creamily down his cheeks, piling itself alongside his neck and ears. A bullet had clipped a groove in his skull, above the temple; from this the brain protruded in bosses, dropping off in flakes and strings." "I had not known," Bierce later recalled thinking, "[that] one could get on even in this unsatisfactory fashion with so little brain." One of Bierce's men suggested putting the man out of his misery with a bayonet. Bierce said he thought not. "It was unusual, and too many were looking."

Forming a skirmish line, Bierce and his men were ordered to advance steadily across a field and probe the thicket beyond. Hidden there was the entire right side of the Confederate line, including Sam Todd and the Crescents. They watched as the federals obliviously approached them, then fired. To Bierce it seemed that the rebels had waited until they could count his men's teeth. "I can't describe it," he said, "the forest seemed all at once to flame up and disappear with a crash like that of a great wave upon the beach — a crash that expired in hot hissings, and the sickening 'spat' of lead against flesh." As Bierce and his men staggered back across the field, a young officer who had witnessed their sacrifice gravely reported the obvious to his colonel: "The enemy is in force just beyond this field, sir." At nine A.M., that force attacked.

The resulting second day at Shiloh was a little like the first in reverse. Though the Confederate line did take the initial offensive, it met far stiffer resistance than it had the day before. "From the time the wood was entered," remembered the Union general Lewis Wallace, "'Forward' was the only order; and step by step, from tree to tree, position to position, the rebel lines went back." Rebel resistance did not cave immediately. In some sectors, the Confederates rallied, charged, fell back, and rallied again. But the Union forces were more numerous, and they were fresher. Bierce said it was as if there were something electric running down the federal line. Despite their sleepless night, despite the volley they had taken when they had crossed the field, his men were alert and vengeful. Heads thrust forward, eyes expanded, teeth clenched, they "breathed hard, as if throttled by tugging at the leash." "If you had laid your hand in the beard or hair of one of these men," he noted, "it would have crackled and shot sparks."

Sam and the Crescents were held in reserve during this first Confederate charge. Standing at the back of the field near one of the artillery units, they screamed encouragements as their fellow rebels surged forward. The charging men quickly crossed the field, then disappeared into the woods beyond and were lost from view. A short while later, they reemerged, running flat out in sloppy retreat, hotly pursued by an onrushing Yankee brigade. The artillerists near the Crescents became suddenly frantic. They poured sixty rounds into the federals, but on they came. The Crescents too were staggered, almost frozen. Finally, one of the artillerists rode up and shouted, "For God's sake, boys, hurry up or our battery is gone!" Already many of the horses had been cut down. Some of the pieces were being pulled away, but others could not be moved without fresh mounts. Jolted into action, the Crescents advanced, as Sam's captain noted, "under the most murderous fire you ever had any idea of." As they reached the abandoned battery, the fight to regain the guns was fierce, often hand to hand. Finally, the Yankees shoved mud down the cannon vents to disable them and began to withdraw. The Crescents pursued them across the wheat field and had about gained the woods when they were ambushed by federal reinforcements.

Now it was the Crescents turn to run pell-mell to the rear. Sam's Company H sped back across the field, across a road, and down a hill to reassemble in a low ravine beyond. In the confusion, no one noticed Sam's absence. A moment later he staggered into view at the top of the hill. He had been shot through the back; his intestines protruded from the exit wound above his groin. About halfway to the ravine, he collapsed. Grabbing a blanket off a nearby horse, Lieutenant Seth Field and three others ran out to meet him. They rolled him onto the blanket and carried him back to an ambulance, which was already full of groaning men. Needing to get back to his command, Field quickly told Sam that he hoped his wound wasn't mortal. Sam knew better: "Ah, Lieut., I believe they have got me this time." He wasn't being original; wounded soldiers often said this. It had a sort of *joie de guerre,* a manly insouciance that implied that even being shot through the bowels was a part of life's rich pageant.

As it had gone for the Crescents, so it went for many Confederate regiments that day. "The enemy seemed retiring everywhere," remembered one federal, and "cheer after cheer [rang] through the woods. Each man felt that the day was ours." And so it was.

It was not Sam's day. He died en route to the hospital. No one in the wagon knew him well. The doctor went through his pockets and collected his effects. He was buried by the side of the road. His service with the Crescents had lasted a month; his experience of warfare had lasted one and a half days.

News of his death traveled slowly. He had died among strangers and been hastily buried in the middle of nowhere. It was almost as if it had never happened. As they did with most of Shiloh's missing, people figured Sam might have been captured or taken to some makeshift hospital. Isolated in Selma, Elodie knew only that no one was writing her. "Really these battles and rumored battles keep me miserable all the time," she noted. "It [is] utterly impossible to keep posted as to the whereabouts of my Brothers. When I think of [those] I perhaps may never see again, and of myself a stranger in a strange land, *unloved*, I feel as tho' I could bear no more."

Finally David tracked down the doctor who had collected Sam's things and learned the truth. "It is my sad task to transmit the unwelcome news that our poor brother Sam is no more," he wrote his sisters. "The report has been here for several days but I could not believe it as no one had seen him either dead or even wounded. . . . I cannot describe the grief of his widow & with sorrow write these few lines."

Once confirmed, news of Sam's death rippled out in the Northern press. The first lady's brother had died in arms trying to overthrow her husband's government. It was the sort of story that highlighted for Americans the curious nature of their own conflict. First published in major papers like the *Philadelphia Inquirer,* the story radiated out in smaller ones like the *Davenport (Iowa) Daily Gazette,* the *Chambersburg (Pennsylvania) Semi-Weekly Dispatch,* and the *Amherst (New Hampshire) Farmer's Cabinet.*

In the South, Sam's death was seen not as a curiosity but an abomination — and Mary Lincoln was held symbolically responsible. How could she have allowed her husband to kill her brother? He hadn't even done it himself but had *hired* people to do it, which only amplified the sense of the deep unnaturalness of the war. As reported in the *Macon Daily Telegraph,* "[Sam] died in defense of his country against the hireling invaders whom the husband of his sister, Mrs. Abraham Lincoln, sent to desolate our country and dishonour our people." The *New Orleans Delta* sneered, "It must be a pleasant reflection to Mrs. Abraham Lincoln, amid her vulgar attempts to ape royal fashions with her balls and soirees at the Federal capital, [to know] that a gallant brother should have thus fallen by the hands of her husband's mercenaries." The Georgia *Chronicle & Sentinel* linked Willie's and Sam's deaths together to complete the portrait of an uncaring monster dancing on the graves of brothers and sons. "The 'Lady of the White House' . . . holds high revelry after the recent decease of her own son and while her own brothers are pouring out the blood they derived from a common parent in the defense of the soil of her and their ancestors."

It would be difficult to find a private, in either army, whose death was more widely recognized in the national press than Sam's. Unknown before the war, he had had a military career lasting only a few months before he had died no more (or less) tragically than 620,000 men would go on to do. But to the psyche of the nation, Sam was significant. Like the Todds generally, he had become a proxy in the debates over loyalty and family that were taking place in every living room. Privately, many Northerners felt vaguely sorry for families like the Todds. Though they did not always like to admit it, many of them had had ties of kinship or friendship severed by the war. Had the Todds maintained dignified relations despite their hardships, they might have invited sympathy or at least pity. Instead, given Mary's extravagances and David's cruelties, Sam's death became just the latest plot point in what was becoming a disturbing national melodrama. Those who watched it unfold, if they saw themselves in it at all, felt only heightened feelings of dysfunction, anger, and embarrassment.

IV.

CHARLES HENRY KELLOGG was by most accounts a good-looking man, about six feet tall, with an "unusually heavy beard, the lower part of which [was] quite gray." (Existing photographs confirm the latter detail — his beard was significantly bigger than his head.) He and Margaret Todd, the oldest of the Humphreys Todds, married in 1847 and moved to Cincinnati. They attended Lincoln's inaugural, staying in the White House, and Charles began jockeying for patronage jobs with the rest of the Todd relations. In his case, however, administration officials objected. Kellogg, they claimed, was a rebel sympathizer who had been overheard making pro-Southern statements during his Washington stay. "While he was an inmate of your house," they informed Lincoln, "[he] advocated the cause of the secessionists." Unsure what to do, Lincoln held up the appointment.

A few months later, Charles wrote to the secretary of the interior, Caleb Smith, to suss out the cause of the delay. The two were old friends. Charles felt comfortable addressing him as "Dear Caleb," and Smith felt comfortable telling Charles the truth. His allegiance to the Union had been questioned. Incensed, Charles fired back a spirited denial. Thanking Smith for his "prompt & frank statement" of his case, he explained that whatever favorable opinion he may have expressed

or sympathy entertained for the cause of the South was "entirely dissipated at the bombardment of Sumpter." He could not and did not support any "armed rebellion against the constituted authorities"; he had
never and would never entertain or utter "a disloyal sentiment to [the
U.S.] government." "I do not make [these] statement[s] with any hope
of advancing my [application]," Charles claimed, "but to put myself
right personally with you & Mr. Lincoln, for whom I entertain feelings
of unlimited respect. The few weeks spent in Washington will *ever remain* the happiest spot in my life. May I beg of you to make known to
Mr. Lincoln my emphatic denial of all disloyal sentiment?"

Charles was lying. In a letter to Elodie a month after Sumter, Margaret admitted that she and her husband had "been [temporarily] compelled to leave Cincinnati . . . for expressing sympathy for the South."
More damning, Charles was secretly scheming to sneak across Union
lines into the Confederacy. It took him five months to figure out a way
in, but when the Confederate army retired from Bowling Green, he saw
a chance to retire with it. By March 1862 he had made it all the way to
Stevenson, in northern Alabama. There, while waiting for the train on
to Huntsville, he chanced upon a war correspondent for the *Savannah
Republican*. The two struck up a conversation, the substance of which
made it into the papers. According to the reporter, Charles identified
himself as "a resident of Cincinnati and a brother-in-law of Mr. Lincoln." He said that he had "relatives in Selma, Ala., and other places in
the South, and that Capt. Podd [Todd], who has had charge of the Federal prisoners in Richmond, was his brother-in-law." He also admitted
that he had been trying to get into the South for some time and gave
"a long account of the difficulties he had encountered, and the by-ways
he had been compelled to take" just to get to Stevenson. The reporter
was agog that Charles would broadcast so much information, but he
seemed oblivious to his situation. "He expressed himself very warmly
— somewhat too warmly— in favor of the South," the reporter noted,
"[and] says he *knows* it was the intention of the Republican leaders,
from the beginning, to force the South to the wall." Charles also claimed
to know that George B. McClellan, commander of all Union armies in
the field, had "sent large reinforcements from Washington to the West,"
leaving the capital vulnerable to attack. All of this information made it
first into the *Savannah Republican* and then into the *Charleston Courier*, where it caught the eye of Nathaniel Dawson. "[The article] introduces Mr. Kellogg as a warm advocate of our cause," Nathaniel wrote

to Elodie. "Call his attention to it, as it may get him into some trouble with his Yankee cousins."

Charles, however, was just getting started. At Huntsville, he joined up with Hardin Helm and the First Kentucky Cavalry. For ten days, and until he took sick, he stayed in their camp, slept in Hardin's tent, and generally mingled with the troops. After recuperating in Memphis for a week, he again caught up with the Confederate army in late March at Corinth. There he sought out General Albert Sidney Johnston, commander of all Confederate forces in the western theater, and "produced evidence to him satisfactory" that he was "true to the interests of the Confederacy." In the ensuing battle of Shiloh, Charles remained "on the field during the whole time assisting [doctors] at the La. hospital." Afterward, he continued on for a few days to tend the wounded and search for Sam.

His position was precarious, however. Johnston had given him permission to stay with the army, but Johnston was now dead. His replacement, P.G.T. Beauregard, was a very different man in a very bad mood. Having prematurely telegraphed Richmond that the battle had been all but won on the first day, Beauregard now found himself superintending a retreat. When Charles requested the pass back north that Johnston had promised, Beauregard refused. If Charles wanted a pass, the general curtly informed him, he'd have to get it from Richmond, and, in the meantime, he needed to leave the army. Sent on with no papers vouching for his character or allegiance, Charles then reported to the Confederate commander in Mobile, where he was taken into custody and imprisoned aboard the *Southern Republic*. He did manage to get a note to Elodie in nearby Selma, but by the time she made it to Mobile, Mr. K., as she called him, had been transferred to Montgomery. "I am greatly distressed on my poor Sister's account," Elodie lamented. "I fear we can do but little for him." At last alive to his peril, Charles wrote a long letter to the Confederate secretary of state, Judah Benjamin. "There is evidently some great mistake in this matter," he noted. "I remain incarcerated with felons & murderers & on rations purchaseable at forty cents per day!" Seeking to establish his Southern bona fides, Charles listed all of his Confederate Todd relations and a host of other men who could "testify to the persecutions [he had] borne at the north for [his] sympathies with the South in her present struggle." He iced the case with a little flattery. "Your public career has been watched by me with a great deal of interest," he told the Confederate secretary, adding that Benjamin's "great speech on the right of secession" had particularly won his admiration.

Something in the letter did the trick, and Benjamin ordered that Kellogg be sent on to Richmond for examination. There, jailed in the prison system so recently run by his brother-in-law, he was cross-questioned by S. S. Baxter, the commissioner charged with investigating civilian crimes against the Confederacy. Charles protested that he had only come south to aid his family, especially his mother-in-law. He was no spy and had no "political object" in the South. Baxter believed him. Charles was released on his honor in Richmond, though police continued to watch him.

Eventually Charles secured a pass back north. The whole experience had proven that he could stand on neither side of the line comfortably. The federals wouldn't give him a job, the Confederates had had him arrested, and all for the same reason: they didn't trust him. The Kelloggs have always been classed with the loyal wing of the family. Certainly, Charles was, like most of the Todds, torn about the war. And perhaps he had come south in part to help his mother-in-law. But along the way he had traveled in the bosom of the Confederate army; provided aid and comfort to the enemy at Shiloh's hospitals; revealed the vulnerability of the federal capital to a rebel reporter, and blabbed to countless people, including high-ranking Confederate officials, of his enthusiastic support for the South "in her present struggle." For all that the Confederate Todds did and would like to have done to destroy the Union Lincoln loved, only Charles Kellogg committed treason.

V.

SHORTLY AFTER SHILOH, Hardin Helm was promoted to brigadier general and assigned to John C. Breckinridge's reserve corps. Hardin's new command was not the whole but a part of the "Orphan Brigade," so known because it was shot through with Kentuckians who couldn't return home to their Unionist state. Hardin's regiments, however, contained no Bluegrass boys, which disappointed him. "I want to identify my destiny with them for weal or woe," he grumbled to his wife. But if he was unable to throw his whole heart into the new assignment, others of his organs cried out for him to leave his cavalry days behind. On May 4, he wrote his new commander with a delicate request for a leave. He was experiencing, he vaguely explained, a temporary "inability to perform the duties of a soldier." The supporting statement from the doctor provided only a whiff of specificity: Helm suffered, it said, from a difficulty of the "lower bowel." In the face of such evasions, a confused Breckinridge sent an investigating surgeon to get to the bottom of things. "I have carefully examined this officer," the surgeon reported, "and find that he has Hemorrhoids, and fissure of the anus." (In speaking of the Civil War, Shelby Foote said it best: "It wasn't all about valor.")

While recuperating, Hardin traveled to Selma. He took Aleck with him, now his aide-de-camp. The new position came with a promotion of its own — to first lieutenant. The reunion at Selma was a needed one, though the mood was dampened by Sam's death and daily news of Confederate setbacks. After Shiloh, the Union's juggernaut rolled on in the West. The Confederate army retreated to Corinth, and then abandoned the city as polluted and indefensible. Memphis fell to the Union freshwater navy; New Orleans and Baton Rouge to the Union saltwater navy. Both fleets then converged on Vicksburg, the last holdout on the river.

David, Aleck, and Hardin converged on Vicksburg too. For reasons that can only be suspected, David had quit the First Kentucky after Sam's death. Possibly his heart wasn't in it. Tom Taylor, the man who had organized the regiment, had been dead awhile. David wasn't well suited to quartermastering anyway, especially to *assistant* quartermastering. With his brother killed and his own anger rising, perhaps he really did pant for the "tented field and blood galore." Fortunately, his own residence in the city and the press's coverage of Sam's death had given him a bit of cache among New Orleanians. In May, Company A of the Twenty-second Louisiana, formerly the Perseverance Guards, elected David their captain and rechristened themselves Todd's Company. Specializing in heavy artillery, the Twenty-second Louisiana was needed at Vicksburg immediately. The city was propitiously located atop a two-hundred-foot bluff that sloped steeply down to the river. From that vantage, David's regiment could rain down on the Union navy like a wrathful God. The man in charge of that navy, Admiral David Farragut, was no fool, however. He knew that Vicksburg could not be taken in the same manner as low-lying New Orleans. Vicksburg would require a combined offensive, with the navy bombarding the city from the riverfront and infantrymen assaulting it from the rear. Hardin and Aleck were among the reinforcements who arrived later to deal with this second threat.

This first Union siege of Vicksburg lasted seventy-five days, from mid-May through the end of July. For the first time in his Confederate career, David rose to the occasion and excelled. His artillery units were repeatedly cited for exemplary service under trying circumstances. "For more than seventy-five days and nights," his superior reported, "these batteries [have] been continuously manned and ready for action at a moment's notice; during much of this time the roar of cannon has been unceasing, and there have been portions of it during which the noise of falling shot and the explosions of shells have been such as might make the stoutest heart quail." What he was describing, of course, was shell shock, a condition yet to be named. The Vicksburg bombardment was too intermittent to mount a serious assault on the men's psyches, but the cannonading was what they most remembered — the eerie and unnatural sounds, the booms of the mortars on the river, low and distant, shaking the bones, the weird shredding sound as shells ripped the air and then broke with a pop, the iron fragments, each in its own key, whistling, screaming, almost singing as they hurtled toward earth. It was, one witness recalled, a "demoralizing music," a "chorus of ruin and chaos." Men can get used to anything, however. A month into the siege some of Helm's boys devised a way to jockey wild boar in improvised pig races. Mounted quickly and steered by the ears, the animals were almost governable. One swine, spooked by a shell, ran rider and all off the bluff. The incident dampened the men's enthusiasm for a moment, but they all ate ham at the jockey's wake.

Clearly, when soldiers under fire have the time and inclination to ride pigs for sport, the military situation has stalemated. By July, the Union juggernaut was breaking on the bluffs of Vicksburg. The infantry assault had bogged down in the region's loessial soil, unable to find a convenient approach to the city. The gunboats had kept the enemy awake but not much more. With the initiative passing to the besieged, the rebels sent in their ironclad ram *Arkansas*. Like its sister the *Tennessee*, the *Arkansas* had been under construction at Memphis when the city fell. Unlike the *Tennessee*, it had escaped, though it wasn't much to look at. Ordered to "finish and equip [the] vessel without regard to expenditure of men or money," Kentuckian Isaac N. Brown searched out and found his new charge at the head of the Yazoo, four miles from dry land and farther still from anything like a naval yard. Some of the *Arkansas*'s armor was at the bottom of the river; the rest had yet to be made. Its engine was in pieces, its guns scattered, their carriages non-existent. The ship was, its new captain noted, a "mere hull." But in five weeks, Brown had the *Arkansas* in something like working order. It was still incompletely armored (though the weakness was concealed over with a little boilerplate). Its twin engines were not always in sync, meaning it would do an occasional slow doughnut in front of the enemy. And it was manned, in part, by sixty Missourians who had never served on a boat or fired a large gun in their lives. Nevertheless, the vessel constituted the whole of the Confederate navy in the sector — so off it went to lift the siege of Vicksburg.

As the *Arkansas* steamed into the elbow where the Yazoo meets the Mississippi, it was sighted by three federal patrol boats: the ironclad *Carondelet,* the wooden gunboat *Tyler,* and the ram *Star of the West.* The *Carondelet* was the most storied and the most dangerous, having participated in the campaigns against Fort Henry, Fort Donelson, and Memphis. The *Tyler,* being wooden, was vulnerable, and the *Star of the West*'s firepower was limited to whatever potshots its men could take with their rifles. All three reversed course to avoid the *Arkansas*'s bow ram, and the *Carondelet* and *Tyler* commenced firing with their aft guns. Most shots deflected harmlessly off the *Arkansas*'s angled sides, up and over Brown, who insisted on remaining topside. A shell did graze him, but he brushed it off. "I received a severe contusion on the head," he later wrote, "but this gave me no concern after I had failed to find any brains mixed with the handful of clotted blood which I drew from the wound." As the *Arkansas* closed in on the three vessels, it started to take more significant damage. A ball blasted through the pilot house and killed one of the navigators. The riflemen aboard the *Tyler* began firing in volleys at Brown, and finally caught him just above the left temple. He was sent sprawling and unconscious to the deck. When he awoke, he was being laid out below among the dead.

Things were going far worse for the federals, however. The *Arkansas*'s forward guns had sent balls ripping through the *Carondelet*'s vulnerable aft, killing or wounding thirty-five. More important, the ship's steering mechanism had been disabled. Without the protection of their ironclad, the other two federal boats steamed downriver for reinforcements. The *Arkansas,* while a little the worse for wear, made a headlong pursuit, turned a bend in the river, and met a "forest of masts and smokestacks" — the federals' entire upper fleet, more than twenty boats. Fortunately for the *Arkansas,* most of them weren't moving. Despite the sounds of an hourlong battle upriver, few of the Union vessels had worked up a full head of steam. Seizing the initiative, Brown plowed straight in among them. In such close quarters, he figured, his sides couldn't be rammed and his cannon couldn't miss. "[We fired] to every point of the circumference," he later wrote, "without the fear of hitting a friend or missing an enemy." Of course, in such close quarters Brown couldn't remain topside. Below deck, the temperature was 120 and rising. The "shock of missiles" hitting the *Arkansas*'s sides was "literally continuous." Some of them found the soft spots in the armor. Even when they didn't, shrapnel and minié balls poured in through the portholes. Brown said it was like standing in the center of an erupting volcano. Half his crew was killed or wounded, but they somehow steered the ship through.

David, Aleck, and Hardin, with most of the Confederate forces at Vicksburg, watched the *Arkansas*'s battle from the city bluffs. When finally it broke free and steamed to safety beneath their batteries, they let out an immense cheer and raced down to the river. The men that emerged from the smoldering can were, said one Orphan, "the most despicable, smoke-begrimed looking set" imaginable, but all "were elated [with] victory." Hardin's regiments took up position in the ravines near the boat and supported the crew as they made their repairs. Some of the Orphans were grudgingly pressed into naval service to replace the many casualties. Everything had to be done hastily, however. Farragut, they knew, would be back with a vengeance. That night both federal fleets, upper and lower, opened up on Vicksburg with all they had. "[It] was the most spectacular and pyrotechnical event of the war," remembered a witness. "The air was literally burdened with ascending and descending shells, [all] crossing each other in their flight Heavenward before they reached their zenith [and plummeted to] the ground." Because David's company was manning a lower battery and Hardin and Aleck's regiments were manning the ravines, the three men got to spend an odd sort of evening together. With "every color of the rainbow" arcing over their heads and "balloon shaped clouds of smoke . . . floating slowly [and] softly" by, the scene was almost "sublimely grand."

For the next week, the *Arkansas* tangled with the Union gunboats, always fighting to a draw. Finally, on July 24, David spent the night with Aleck and Hardin amid the lower bluffs to watch what promised to be another naval version of a knife fight. The federal boats had worked up some steam and launched a few desultory shells. One of them landed close enough to give Aleck and Hardin a good dusting. But these were not an opening salvo but the Yankees' parting shots. Farragut was disengaging. The *Arkansas* had enraged him, but he decided to bide his time and wait his chance. He sent the lower fleet downriver toward New Orleans, the upper fleet upriver toward St. Louis. The first siege of Vicksburg was over. The Confederacy had not been cut in two. Despite all the year's reverses, the rebels had held a two-hundred-mile stretch of river between Vicksburg and Port Hudson, which they fortified extensively.

For the western Confederacy, it was the first good news in months — and Confederate high command volunteered Breckinridge to follow it up with some more. On July 27, Breckinridge left Vicksburg with four thousand men, Hardin and Aleck among them. Their goal was to recapture the Louisiana capital of Baton Rouge. To many of them, it felt like a really bad idea. They had hardly had time to celebrate the end of the siege. They were tired, malnourished, unhealthy. "My own troops [have] suffered severely from the effects of exposure at Vicksburg," Breckinridge admitted, "from heavy rains without shelter, and from the extreme heat." There were problems with the mission itself too. Baton Rouge lay within the protection of the Yankee gunboats along the river — and infantrymen would be useless against those. Breckinridge had been impressed by the *Arkansas,* however. With the ironclad to distract the river fleet, he thought his men might have a chance at retaking the city. Confederate command assented to the plan and informed Breckinridge that the *Arkansas* would be in position to support his offensive by daylight, August 5.

From Vicksburg, the Orphans traveled by train to Jackson, then set off on foot for Baton Rouge. At the height of a Louisiana summer, the fifty-mile march quickly turned brutal. The white sand road reflected the heat and scorched the feet of the shoeless men. Searching for relief, some ducked into the woods to drink from stagnant pools, then fell out with dysentery or malaria. Of the almost 4,000 who began the march on July 30, only 2,600 were still standing five days later when they reached the Comite River. There, ten miles from the city, Breckinridge allowed the Orphans to fall out, fall down, or splash about the water. Aleck spent his time writing letters to his mother and sweetheart. He struck up an acquaintance with a local farmer named Pratt who was also a Kentuckian by birth. The man and his daughters agreed to tend him if he fell. In the evening, Aleck listened as Breckinridge dedicated speeches to his "brave, noble, ragged Kentuckians." Then the raggedy men shouldered their packs and stumbled off into the night.

The evening was an unusually dark one. The road glowed a bit in the starlight, but the woods and cane fields surrounding it were pitch black and crawling with mist. Hardin's men led the way, and as they reached the outskirts of the city, Hardin called a halt to wait for dawn and the order to attack. Asleep on their feet or staring dully into the gloom, the men were startled around four in the morning by a "terrific volley of musketry" from inside the thicket. Almost immediately they heard the sound of horses closing, and then a cavalry company burst upon them from the woods.

What happened next is not entirely clear. Breckinridge's official report is vague, saying only that some of his irregular forces (known as partisan rangers) had "leaked" forward, encountered enemy pickets, and, "galloping back, they produced some confusion, which led to rapid firing for a few moments." But this avoids the tricky question of blame: who fired on whom and why? By one news account, the rangers were entirely in the wrong and, indeed, disgraced themselves. They became "frightened at a shadow," the article reported, "and fled from the field, riding over several officers and men, and wounding them severely." When Hardin's brigade ordered the cowards to halt, they refused and, unfortunately, had to be cut down. Another version of the story sharply contradicts this one. According to it, the rangers, properly scouting in front of the main army, encountered advanced federal pickets around three-thirty in the morning. A firefight ensued; the rangers pushed the pickets back and then turned to report the enemy's position to their army's main column. As the rangers emerged from the woods, Hardin's jittery brigade got spooked and fired on them. The rangers, sure they had been ambushed, returned the fire with considerably more effectiveness.

Whatever the cause, however, the effect was pandemonium. Before he could utter an order, Hardin was on his back, his horse rearing and falling on him, shattering his left leg. Struggling upright, he pleaded with his men to lower their guns. But it was too late. Aleck was already stretched out on the ground, glassy-eyed and bleeding. Hardin was staggered. There was no last word or gesture to report to Emilie or her sisters. Aleck just lay there, slipping insensibly away.

Under the circumstances, Hardin could no longer lead his brigade. As the rest of the army went on to defeat, he stayed behind to tend to Aleck and his own wounds. Both men were carried back down the road to Pratt's farm. Somewhere between the gate and the farmhouse, Aleck died. He was buried near a plum orchard about four miles from Baton Rouge. Someone, perhaps Hardin, carved "A. H. Todd" into the

VI.

THE YEAR HAD BEEN a sobering one for the nation. A war that was supposed to be short and glorious — as the Mexican War had been — had revealed an entirely different nature. For the first time in human history, an industrialized country had picked upon itself, and the results were staggering. That both sides were only partly industrialized made it worse. The technology for inflicting damage on bodies vastly outstripped the technologies available for putting them back together. As both sides came to terms with the conflict's true nature — its probable effects and duration — the national mood began to darken. The Confederacy, its western half all but cut from the bone, lost much of its early swagger. The Union's victories, while substantial, were obscured by its disappointments — the failure to take Richmond and a devastating defeat at Fredericksburg in December. When apprised of the "butchery" that had befallen his soldiers on Marye's Heights, Lincoln seemed "heart-broken," a witness remembered, "and soon reached a state of nervous excitement bordering on insanity."

The Todds too were reeling. Sam and Aleck were dead, and Hardin was seriously wounded. Furloughed for forty days, he recovered enough by September to take post duty at Chattanooga, where Emilie joined him as aide and nurse. That winter was an unusually hard one. A soldier on duty there recalled, "Chattanooga at that time was a horror spot. It was the greatest mudhole the mind of man could conceive. The streets were cut into huge gullies by the heavy army wagons, and all the pleasures of life had fled from" the town. Hardin and Emilie made the best of it, however, and made a sort of funny pair — Hardin hobbling around on crutches, Emilie often beside him, becoming a sort of mascot of the brigade. Kitty also came to Chattanooga — though not to stay. She had decided to seize the opportunity afforded by Hardin's new post to make a dash for home. She was particularly worried about her mother, who had lost two sons in five months and had no one to comfort her. Setting off in a buggy with a few members of Hardin's old cavalry brigade, Kitty traveled by night through Union-occupied territory, finally fetching up on the hills above Uniontown, Kentucky. Hardin's detail watched as Kitty trundled down the hill and disappeared into the town below, and then took their leave. Unfortunately, from Uniontown, Kitty took a steamer upriver to Louisville, where rumors of her arrival spread quickly among the federals. Seized and detained, she was allowed to go free only after Lincoln sent a telegram informing the arresting officer that he should "attend strictly to his own duties," adding, "We are not making war on women."

Back in Selma, Elodie missed her sisters, but could take some comfort in her swelling belly. She and Nathaniel had married earlier in the year, and her pregnancy seemed a sort of symbol. The past buries the past; life goes on; who knew but that the new year might be a better one. On January 9, 1863, Elodie gave birth to a boy. She named him for the brother she had lost at Baton Rouge. Less than a week later, Nathaniel wrote to Hardin: "Our joy was [short-lived]. The little cherub died yesterday morning. . . . The body was christened & named Alex Todd."

5

1863: The Death of Absalom

I.

WHILE HARDIN HELM continued to recuperate at Chattanooga, the soldiers of his old command were taken into the battle of Murfreesboro (or Stone's River) about a hundred miles to the northwest. On January 2, John C. Breckinridge, Helm's immediate superior, made a reconnaissance of enemy positions and discovered a federal division holding a hill at his front. Beyond the hill was a river, and above the river, a bluff fortified with some fifty-seven field pieces. The Union position, he concluded, was *strong*. Nevertheless around noon, General Braxton Bragg told Breckinridge that he wanted him to take that hill. Breckinridge kept his cool and bent down to again sketch with a stick what he had seen. Bragg did not care. "Sir ... I have given the order to attack the enemy in your front," he said, "and expect it to be obeyed."

Raging, Breckinridge returned to his officers and found them even more mutinous than he was. Roger Hanson, now in command of the Orphan Brigade, was particularly incensed and offered to go back to headquarters and kill Bragg. Having railed against the stupidity, however, Breckinridge now committed himself to the sacrifice, and at four P.M., he sent his men forward. At the base of the hill, they fired up and then tore after their bullets as if they meant to beat them to the top. Once they had gained the hill, however, they were, as their general had predicted, a perfect target for the fifty-seven field pieces. All went off at once, and a spent fuse from a spherical case shot tore through Hanson's leg. Breckinridge tried to help stanch the flow of blood, but there was no use. Meanwhile, his division was still trying to move forward. A few men managed to patter across the river, where they made easier marks than they had on the hill. As the remnants of Hanson's brigade began to fall back, Breckinridge mingled among them, crying out: "My poor Orphan Brigade! They have cut it to pieces!"

Hanson's loss was Hardin's gain. On February 16, Hardin Helm became the official commander of the Orphan Brigade — the command he had always wanted. The feeling was evidently mutual. Calling him their "Gentle General," Hardin's men saw him less as a father figure than as an older brother. Deeply familiar with that role, Hardin would occasionally, when faced with the Orphans' legendary rascality, wish that he had a trifle less popularity and a trifle more authority. This quibble aside, he was elated. Having missed chances at Baton Rouge and Murfreesboro, he was by spring recovered and ready finally to lead men into battle.

II.

IN MAY, another Todd scandal erupted, this one of the Edwards variety. For two years Ninian had been Springfield's commissary commissioner — and for two years the chorus calling for his removal had swelled. The commissioner's job was to take bids and make contracts (on the government's behalf) for the provisioning of the state's soldiers and prisoners of war. Of course, such government contracts comprised a lucrative business rife with abuse — and Springfield Republicans begged Lincoln to sack Edwards, chief of the abusers.

Ninian's corruption charge capped a decade's worth of deteriorating relations between the two men. In the 1850s, as their beloved Whig Party lay on its deathbed, both had faced stalled political careers. Only Ninian had turned Judas and joined the Democrats, however, a move that quietly appalled Lincoln. In 1858, when Lincoln ran for senator under the Republican banner, Ninian had backed the Democrat Stephen A. Douglas. In 1860, when Lincoln ran for president, Ninian had again stumped for Douglas. None of this stopped him from pestering Lincoln for loans and free legal advice. And it did not stop him from sending snooty replies when he failed to get them. "Always prompt in attending to any business for my friends and especially *the members of my own family*," he wrote Lincoln in a huff, "I confess I felt hurt when you failed to answer. . . . I thought, considering the *relationship* which existed between us for years *and previous to your marriage*, that I was not properly treated."

Of course, once Lincoln was elected, Ninian changed his tone. In a masterpiece of smarm, he wrote the new president to say that he would not be able to make his interest payment that month. "I have been so *much embarrassed* as to make it necessary for me to be from my family nearly all of my time for the past two years," he confessed. Between building a house for his daughter, Julia, and helping to purchase a newspaper for his son-in-law, he was $14,000 in the hole. His neediness duly established, he moved on to patching up his politics. He differed with the Republican platform only on a single insignificant point, he claimed, and he had never objected to Lincoln personally: "I believed you honest and eminently qualified for the office & I did not hesitate to say so publicly, and I moreover said if there was a man living without faults I believed you to be that man." "I write this because it comes from the heart," Ninian claimed before signing himself "as ever your friend."

Ninian's not-so-subtle campaign for a government job was followed up by letters from associates supporting his qualifications. "He is embarrassed & needs aid," David Davis wrote to Lincoln. "It pains me to know that after he has passed the meridian of life, he finds that he is [so] troubled." Orville Browning promised Ninian he would recommend him also. "If you were, as I supposed, rich, and able to help yourself and others," Browning told him, "I would not do this. As it is, it will give me the very greatest pleasure to serve you."

Lincoln was inclined to help, as he had all the Todds, and offered Ninian the commissary commission and the rank of captain. Immediately, the cry went up from loyal Republicans. "We . . . protest against such an appointment in the most emphatic manner," wrote the Illinois state secretary, treasurer, and auditor in a combined letter. "For several years we have been ferreting out, and exposing, the most stupendous and unprecedented frauds ever perpetrated in this country, by men closely connected with Mr. Edwards. . . . If appointed we feel assured that he may be an instrument . . . in the hands of these men."

The state's most responsible money men were speaking most emphatically of Ninian's snug relations with Illinois's ex-governor Joel Aldrich Matteson. The fraud Matteson had committed, while perhaps not "unprecedented," was still impressive. While governor (1853–57), he had come across a trunk of old I&M Canal scrip. The canal project itself dated back to 1839, and most of the scrip had already been issued and redeemed by the state. (The trunk's contents were just the extras from the print run — the equivalent of blank checks.) Nevertheless, Matteson slowly began to redeem them — to the tune of $250,000 (or $5.3 million today) by the time he was caught in 1859. Outraged, the legislature called for an investigation, but Matteson had many friends and more lawyers. A grand jury indicted him — and then changed its mind amid allegations of jury tampering and bribery. Matteson's mansion was seized and sold by the state, but that only put a dent in the budget shortfall — and Matteson remained a free man. Lincoln disliked Matteson so thoroughly that he said in 1855, when both of them had tested the waters for the Senate: "[Matteson's] defeat gives me more pleasure than my own gives me pain." (And this was *before* the discovery of Matteson's "unprecedented" fraud.) Nevertheless, Lincoln ignored the warnings and appointed Ninian to the post.

The result was a political catastrophe. Ninian hadn't been in charge more than two months before Republicans cried foul. "As we predicted," they wrote Lincoln, "[Matteson] is now *in person* furnishing subsistence to the troops. . . . We again insist that this outrage against common decency be corrected, [that Edwards] be required to contract directly with honest men, and not indirectly with thieves and scoundrels." Ninian was shocked. "If Gov. Matteson has any interest in the contract *I* don't know it," he protested. He had only honored the lowest bid after advertising for sealed proposals. He was even willing to resign his post. "I certainly should have never accepted it . . . ," he wrote, "but for my very great pecuniary embarrassment — Even with it a claim was sent to a lawyer to be sued on at the next Court." In the face of such suave weaseling, Lincoln let the matter go.

By May of 1863, however, Illinois Republicans were so tired of Edwards and his cronies, they were ready to hang somebody. Ninian, they claimed, had spent two years shamelessly milking the public tit. "I heard Mr. Edwards Say before he [was appointed that] He would [be] ruined," Yates wrote to Lincoln. "His house was mortgaged and would have to be sold from over his head &c. And now I am told he brags on how much money he has made, has bought a fine Carriage & horses. And has large deposits in [the] Bank. And all from a Salary of Eighteen hundred dollars. . . . How it is That he can make all this money on his Salary, I cant conceive." Lincoln might have been tempted to dismiss such charges, except that they were also coming from Ninian's

banker: "The sums acquired are too large to have been obtained hon-
estly," the man wrote. "[These men] have not only been living off of the
General Government for the past two years but getting *rich* from the
stealings."

Grift was only part of the problem, however. In a furious petition
campaign, state Republicans charged Edwards and company with
something closer to treason. "[Edwards] has wielded his whole power
and influence against Your Administration," they informed the president. All the contracts, all the associated patronage jobs, had gone
to "Rebel Sympathizers" and "Blatant Democrats" with no interest in
prosecuting the war. Men loyal to Lincoln were being drafted and dying. Men who openly denounced the administration and the war were
safe in their sinecures, making a killing inadequately provisioning soldiers. "When you ask us to help put down treason," an exasperated
George Weber wrote Lincoln, "we are instinctively wont to commence
to put down some of your office-holders and their assistants, who are
doing more than any other class of men to render your administration obnoxious and the efforts of your friends fruitless. . . . For Liberty's
sake — for our country's sake and for God's sake, put down as you can,
as easily as you can turn your hand, this nest of Copperheads."

Lincoln turned his hand. He had had enough. When Ninian learned
what was in the wind, he wrote Lincoln another credulous protest of
innocence. He was guilty, he said, repeating himself, only of accepting
the lowest responsible bid among sealed proposals. "If any objections
are urged against me," he wrote. "I hope you will give me a hearing." Lincoln's response, sent through Ninian's son-in-law, was carefully mod-
erated but couldn't conceal his frustration and disappointment. "The
appeal [for] a hearing does not meet the case," he wrote. "The trouble
with me is of a different character — Springfield is my home, and there,
more than elsewhere, are my life-long friends. These, for now nearly
two years, have been harassing me because of Mr. E[dwards] and Mr.
B[ailhache, Edwards's cozy associate]. I think Mr. E & Mr. B., without dishonesty on the other hand, could have saved me from this, if
they had cared to do so. They have seemed to think that if they could
keep their official record dryly correct, to say the least, it was not any
difference how much they might provoke my friends, and harass me.
If this is too strong a statement of the case, still the result has been the
same to me; and, as a *misfortune* merely, I think I have already borne
a fair share of it."

For Lincoln, these were strong words. When it came to bearing a "fair share" of something, he usually shouldered the lion's share and protested only when about to buckle under the weight. Ninian seemed late to realize that his brother-in-law's patience had limits, and that the forbearance of a president was a thing better not tested. Adopting the oleaginous tones he had used to get the job in the first place, he admitted that he *had* come into some money lately—through a fortuitous sale of land. But it pained him "to think in *these trying times*" that Lincoln should be "troubled on [his] account," so he offered to leave the contracting part of the job to someone else while he controlled the purse strings from Chicago. Ninian capped his unctuous appeal with an intriguing trump card: "You speak of your life long friends in Springfield desiring a change. I would like to ask you, if when you were a young man I was not your most devoted friend in more ways than one. Let Joshua F. Speed, your own ~~conscience~~ recollection, and a letter of yours written to me in 1842 before your marriage, answer." The letter Ninian mentions is now lost, but he is clearly driving at something. A few passages later, he refers to it again: "In your present situation [as president] I do not wish to add to your embarrassment [but] I could mention some things to show that I was ready and willing, to furnish, when you were a young man, substantial evidence of my *devoted attachment to you*." We cannot *know* what Ninian is driving at, but it seems safe to translate his meaning thusly: "When we were young men I was not only a devoted friend but, more than this, I was made the confidant of an embarrassing truth—a truth documented in a letter in my possession. Make of this reference what you will." Was Ninian appealing to an old friend—or blackmailing him?

Lincoln preferred the former interpretation. "I certainly do not suppose Mr. Edwards has, at this time of his life, given up his old habits and turned dishonest," he wrote Ninian's son-in-law. "In what I may do, I shall try to so shape it, as to not seem to mean more than is really intended." Ultimately, Lincoln allowed Ninian to keep his commission (and thus his salary), though he did strip him of most of his power and transferred him to Chicago. Comparing this result to the possibility of a court-martial or a transfer to the front, Ninian was content. "I am not unmindful," he wrote Lincoln from Chicago after the scandal had blown over, "[that] I owe you for many acts kindness to me—which I shall ever remember with *heartfelt gratitude*. . . . Very truly your friend & relative, N. W. Edwards."

III.

WHILE LINCOLN WRESTLED with Ninian, Helm settled into his new command. By mid-May his Orphans were so well drilled and well oiled, he doubted "if there ever was a better army." Champing at the bit to lead them in battle, he was elated when a distress call came from a familiar quarter — Vicksburg.

The federal plan to take Vicksburg was a product of Ulysses S. Grant's own ponderous but perfect logic. The city sat on a two-hundred-foot bluff on the east side of the Mississippi River. The navy had tried to take it from the west and failed. North of the city was a massive bayou. This left only two approaches — south and east — which meant Vicksburg would have to be taken from *inside* enemy territory. To effect this, Grant proposed to march his army south along the west bank of the Mississippi, cross over, march inland, and attack the city from the rear. His closest and most able subordinate, William Tecumseh Sherman, thought it a terrible idea and said so. "[You will be] putting [yourself] in a position voluntarily which an enemy would be glad to manoeuvre a year . . . to get [you] in," Sherman told him. With his back to a river and Confederate forces above and below him, Grant would be sticking his head into a guillotine with no way to draw it back out. Grant's logic had spoken, however, and by April the finest campaign of the Civil War was under way. The federals crossed the Mississippi on April 30 and won five battles in seventeen days. By May 18, Grant and Sherman stood on the Walnut Hills outside the city. "Until this moment I never thought your expedition a success," Sherman admitted. "I never could see the end clearly till now."

To fortify their defenses, the Confederates dug in literally, creating a ring of earthworks and trenches east of the city. David Todd's brigade occupied a position along Jackson Road, the center of the Confederate line and the most prominent approach to the city. The Twenty-first Louisiana, David's actual regiment, held the right of the road from behind what was called the Great Redoubt, a massive earthwork "fort" with parapets fifteen feet high. To the left and across the road from David's regiment, the Third Louisiana held what was called the Third Louisiana Redan, a crude salient that jutted out from the rebel line.

Sure that rebel reinforcements (like Hardin's) would soon be upon him, Grant determined to o'erstorm the ramparts before he was himself attacked in the rear. A hasty charge by Sherman's men on May 19 was repulsed with heavy losses. Undaunted, Grant called for a complete reconnaissance of rebel positions, and on May 22 launched a general assault against the whole of the Confederate line. The result was a catastrophe. At the Third Louisiana Redan, federals were cut down in the narrow approach until the sheer mass of dead and dying blocked others from coming through. At the Great Redoubt, David and his men decimated all who approached. The federals who did make it to the "fort" jumped into the ditch at the front, threw up their ladders, and began to climb — only to find the ladders too short. Some panicked and ran. Others clung to the earthen wall as David's men dropped crude grenades on their heads. The federals saw 3,200 killed, wounded, or missing in the assault; the Confederates lost fewer than 500. For three days afterward an embittered Grant refused to collect the dead and dying from in front of the rebel position. David Todd was again treated to the smell of dead Yankee as Grant seemed determined to stink the rebels out of Vicksburg. Finally, on May 25, he responded to a note from the overall commander of Vicksburg's forces, John C. Pemberton, pleading "in the name of humanity" for him to recover his wounded and bury his dead. Grant acceded — and grudgingly admitted that a frontal assault would not work. "I now determined upon a regular siege," he noted later in his memoir. "[I would] 'out-camp the enemy,' as it were, and . . . incur no more losses."

It was not in Grant's nature, however, to merely sit and wait. If the Confederate redoubts could not be stormed from aboveground, he would scuttle them from below. Working night and day, in the middle of a Mississippi summer, a detail of federals dug thirteen undulating corridors, called saps, toward the rebel line. To make sure they weren't sniped from rebel parapets, the diggers worked behind mobile bulwarks called sap-rollers — large cylinders of bundled cane and dirt pushed forward by poles. Cutting channels seven feet wide by seven feet deep, federal sappers often progressed at a rate of more than a hundred feet a day. The loessial soil around Vicksburg has unusual properties. It excavates easily, and the resulting cavities hold their shape without bracing. When it rains, however, everything "melts like butter." Thus the men on both sides were hiding within a scarred landscape that constantly wanted to flatten out and expose them.

Watching the federal saps crawl toward their line, Confederates could do little but wait. A shortage of percussion caps forced them to conserve their small arms fire. They did have plenty of ordnance, and they would occasionally try to take out one of the sap-rollers. David's brigade even managed to set one on fire after shooting it with bullets wrapped in tow and turpentine. But Pemberton decided that his remaining shells were too precious to waste on sap-rollers. One day the Yankees would get close enough to climb out of their trenches and make a general charge. He would need all of his firepower to throw them back.

For the rebels, then, life under siege was oppressive. They were pounded by a continuous federal bombardment, hunkered down in their redoubts, bored, exposed, and filthy. Disease took its toll — as did hunger. Their drinking water had been befouled by animal carcasses. Yankee sharpshooters waited for their heads to peek above the parapets or their shadows to pass the gun loops cut into their earthworks, then fired. Both were good kill shots — head and torso. By June, when Yankee saps were close enough to share a wall with some rebel trenches, federal soldiers bored through with their bayonets, stuck their rifles into the hole, and fired.

All of this suited David Todd perfectly, however. This was war the way he liked it — brash and raw. Some days, he and his men swapped insults with the Yankees. Other days they traded tobacco for food or coffee. Some nights the two sides serenaded each other; sometimes they threw a live grenade back and forth. It was an almost boyish mode of fighting — deadly and disregarding of human life, but oddly playful. It squares, moreover, with a federal officer's memory of David from later in the war. The two men met aboard a steamer on the Alabama River after the siege. David was bound for Selma; the officer, a Colonel Roberts, had been taken prisoner but was given liberty of the boat. When David learned that Roberts was from Springfield, he made polite inquiries about his Illinois relatives and treated Roberts with "marked courtesy." Then as they were parting he told Roberts, "I hope you will get exchanged and we will meet on the battlefield. I'll do my best to put a bullet through you." This was David's way of war: no malice or mercy, just men trying to kill each other between drinks. And that's what he liked about Vicksburg. It was stripped down and simple, a test of manhood he enjoyed taking because he knew he could pass it. There were no marches, charges, or battle plans. A man just had to live rough, and if he got a bead on a Yankee, shoot him down like a deer. A Yankee might do likewise to David, of course. But the way he figured it, if a man lifted his head above his trench he was too stupid to need it anyway.

All good things come to an end. By June 22, the federal sappers in David's front had reached the apex of the Third Louisiana Redan. From there they sank a mine under the Confederates' feet and filled it with 2,200 pounds of black powder. The rebels could hear the Yankee miners scratching around beneath them and sank a shaft of their own to try to find them. It was a race, said one Confederate, to see "who [was] going to be the smarter and blow the other up first." The federals won. On June 25 they lit their fuses and at three-thirty P.M. an explosion blew man and earth into the sky and reduced the apex of the rebel redan to a smoldering crater. As the Yankees poured into and out of that crater, they were treated to a final surprise. With the exception of the half-dozen counterminers who had just been blown up, the Third Louisiana had pulled back from the redan and entrenched themselves in perfect position to fire on the advancing federals. The Yankees who weren't cut down scrambled back to the crater and dug in for almost twenty-six hours of the nastiest fighting at Vicksburg.

Grant hoped that if his men could hold the crater long enough, he could get his artillery into position to support a decisive breakthrough along Jackson Road. Unfortunately, fewer than a hundred federals could occupy the crater at a time. The Third Louisiana, now reinforced by David's company and others, were determined to dislodge them. From brutally close range, they fired salvo after salvo and lobbed grenades and shells with five-second fuses into the crater. The federals did their best to stamp out the fuses with their feet; they picked up the grenades and threw them back as quick as they could. One private managed to return twenty grenades before his arm was blown off and he bled to death. Despite such heroics, the federals were being mangled in a mud bowl. Listening to their groans, one Union general cried, "My God! They are killing my bravest men in that hole." Finally, after more than a day, Grant called it off. He had learned his lesson. The breach had been too narrow to exploit. He ordered all thirteen saps widened, and by June 30 he was informed that all would reach the Confederate line in a few days. He was now in position to sink thirteen mines and blow thirteen holes in the rebel line. Unless Vicksburg was reinforced, it would fall.

For months, Vicksburg's defenders had looked in vain for relief. Their most logical savior was Joseph Johnston, whose army was nearby at Canton. Johnston had evacuated Jackson prior to the federals' arrival, claiming he had too few men either to hold the town or to harry Grant. By early June, however, reinforcements — including Hardin's brigade — had swelled his numbers to 31,000. Coupled with Pemberton's men, the combined Confederate force was larger than Grant's. When the Orphans arrived, they assumed they would march on Vicksburg directly. Grant assumed so too, and he dug a ring of outward-facing entrenchments to protect his inward-facing ones. Three weeks later, however, Johnston had barely stirred, and Hardin began to get restless. "I do sincerely hope," he wrote home, "that we may be all[owed] to relieve the [Vicksburg] garrison before their strength is entirely exhausted." But that's just what Johnston was determined to do — get there too late. He had never supported Pemberton's decision to bottle his army up at Vicksburg. Better the town should fall. With the weight of an entire expectant nation on his shoulders, Johnston shrugged.

Another man who might have stormed to Vicksburg's relief was Robert E. Lee. The Army of Northern Virginia had been so successful in the east that Confederate command seriously considered shipping it fifteen hundred miles west to take on Grant. Lee, however, while conceding Vicksburg's importance, had another idea. He would draw federal pressure away from the town by marching his army north into Pennsylvania.

George Todd traveled with Lee's army on what would come to be called the Gettysburg campaign. Surgeon to Paul Jones Semmes's Brigade (McLaws's Division, Longstreet's Corps), George appears, like his brother David, to have enjoyed damning his White House connections — particularly in front of Yankees. In May, after the battle of Salem Church, he had fallen in to drink with a captured Union doctor named Daniel Holt. Holt found George "anything but a pleasing personage" but tried his best to make polite conversation. "I had the pleasure of seeing the President and [your] sister at a corps service a few days previous," he said. "Well, I don't know as I feel any the better or worse for that," George replied. "She is a poor, weak-minded woman anyhow." (Holt agreed, though he didn't say so.)

On the Gettysburg campaign, George's conduct was even more scandalous. According to Northern papers, he took a fiendish delight in pillaging Pennsylvania. In Chambersburg, he went house to house pocketing valuables until "arrested . . . in his insolence" by a woman who informed him "in rather an earnest manner that further searches . . . would result in the splitting of his head with her hatchet." Undeterred, George supposedly "took charge of the stealing operations . . . pretending to pay in rebel scrip but in fact plundering the town relentlessly." Finally, his conduct became too outrageous even for his fellow rebels, who evicted him from a seized drugstore as having "no business being there."

Perhaps George did cut an unusually wide swath of destruction through Pennsylvania. More likely, he was the only marauder Pennsylvania matrons knew by name. Of course, they knew his name because he had a tendency to drop it. In this sense, George was carrying on a Todd family tradition of helping the press to scapegoat him and his family. In damning his relations by his own conduct, he amplified his aptness to serve as the archetypal plunderer — driven not merely by greed but spite. The Northern press certainly had a winning formula in the Todds. The family seemed to have members who fit every negative stereotype of the war: David, the sadistic jailer; Ninian, the war profiteer; and now George, the looter. That they may have deserved their reputations is not the point. A single family was being made to fill all the negative roles in a national morality play.

While occasionally obnoxious, George was a fine surgeon. A talented dissector in school, he adapted more readily to trauma surgery than the family doctors who joined the corps. Even so, Gettysburg would overtax his speed, skill, and stamina. On July 1, 2, and especially 3, Lee's army inflicted a bloodletting upon itself from which it never recovered. Twenty-two thousand men, almost a third of the army, were killed, wounded, or missing. George worked tirelessly in these days, and many of the seven hundred amputations he credited to himself were performed in the aftermath of Gettysburg. But in truth, no one could put Lee's mauled army back together. On July 5, in a driving rain, Lee withdrew from Gettysburg, his train of wounded stretching out for miles behind him. "Scarcely one in a hundred had received adequate surgical aid," John Imboden admitted after riding the length of the train. "Many of them had been without food for thirty-six hours. Their ragged, bloody, and dirty clothes, all clotted and hardened with blood, were rasping the tender, inflamed lips of their gaping wounds. Very few of the wagons had even straw in them, and all were without springs. The road was rough and rocky. The jolting was enough to have killed sound, strong men." With each jolt, fresh prayers and execrations went up from the occupants: "'Oh God! Why can't I die?,'" "'My God! Will no one have mercy and kill me and end my misery?'" "It was my sad lot to pass the whole distance from the rear to the head of the column," Imboden remembered, "and no language can convey an idea of the horrors of that most horrible of all nights of our long and bloody war."

Many of the wounded couldn't get a place in the wagons and had to shamble along behind. J. C. Smith of Greencastle, Pennsylvania, watched as the caravan of Lee's miserables slunk back south. "It was an easy matter to trace their route of flight," he noted. "Dead horses, broken-down and abandoned wagons, cannons, carriages and caissons, [and] new-made graves were everywhere to be seen. It was simply a road covered with wrecks." Some of the wrecks were still moving. Soldiers shot in the arm, shoulder, neck, or face lurched along at the back of the train like an army of the undead. Whenever they made it to a pump, they descended on it, each man putting his wounded body part "under the spout while another would pump cold water on the sore. Then he would do a like service to his comrade." Smith estimated the number of wounded who passed through his town at 12,000 to 15,000.

The Gettysburg campaign had done nothing to relieve the pressure on Vicksburg. On July 3, rather than watch his line blow up in thirteen different places, Pemberton sent word that he would meet Grant on Jackson Road. The meeting went badly at first — Grant demanded unconditional surrender, and Pemberton stubbornly wanted to save face — but subordinates patched together an agreement that, after adjustments, ended the siege. On July 4, silence reigned over Vicksburg. "For so many long days and nights it had been a continuous [bombardment]," said one federal. "Now it was still, absolutely still [and the silence] was leaden. We could not bear it, it settled down so close; it hugged us with its hollow, unseen arms till we could scarcely breathe."

By Grant's decree, Pemberton's men were paroled rather than imprisoned, and all officers were allowed to keep their side arms. David considered the terms "excellent indeed" and wrote his mother that he was proud to have participated in the city's defense. "Forty-eight days is quite a long siege for modern warfare," he told her, "as poorly provision[ed] as we have been." Life under siege, moreover, hadn't left a mark on him. "I have escaped sound from scratch or blemish," he wrote home, "but I have nearly half of my poor fellows killed & wounded." Vicksburg's survivors, David included, were sent to a parole camp at Enterprise, Mississippi. There they were to stay until they were declared "exchanged" on September 12. David claimed that he "hate[d] to be idle in these times," but he nevertheless spent some of his days at the Powhatan in Richmond, again "recuperating." On his way to town he met Joseph Waddell, an old friend who seemed none too happy to see him. "Going down I fell in with Capt. D. H. Todd,"

Waddell noted. "[He] seemed rejoiced to see me, as his mother and mine were old friends. He insisted that we should take a room together at the hotel, which of course I acquiesced in, although he is not very congenial." Vicksburg's heroic stand behind him, David seemed back to his sinning old self.

IV.

NEWS OF VICKSBURG'S collapse demoralized Hardin. Militarily, it was a catastrophe — but it was a crushing blow personally too. Despite his promotions, Hardin Helm's Confederate career had been a disaster. He had been off on a recon during the battle of Shiloh; he had been crushed by a horse before the battle of Baton Rouge; he had still been in recovery during the battle of Stone's River; and now, with a brigade drilled to perfection, he had been mysteriously sidelined from Vicksburg. "As usual with me I am in a grand retreat," he noted bitterly as the Confederates evacuated Jackson. "We have had to drink [water] that you would not in ordinary times offer your horse, [and we] have hardly slept out of a swamp [once]." In 1861, Hardin, like thousands of others, had stood before the daguerreotypist with a pristine uniform and a vague idea of becoming a Confederate Washington. War, however, has a way of slimming men's egos. They dream not of fame and power but of the life they took for granted while they pursued such things. At some point, a chink began to open in Hardin's mental armor. For the first time, his letters home betrayed a desire to do something other than soldier. "I am very anxious to live quietly with my little family," he admitted to Emilie, "& want to be with the children as they grow up. . . . If I could do so without lowering myself in my own estimation, I would resign. . . . Excuse me for giving way to this little weakness; it is not often I permit such feelings to take possession of me." He needn't have apologized. By 1863, Emilie's resolve was weakening too. "War. War is the sole theme," she wrote wearily in her diary. And war wasn't enough to raise her daughters on. "[The] girls have a doll dressed as a soldier," she noted. "I offered to dress [her] as a girl, [but] they refused." It is a telling anecdote. Though Emilie had worked tirelessly for her husband's brigade — stitching up their clothing and mending their mattresses — her daughters didn't recognize her contributions, or at least not enough to want their doll to wear a dress.

In late September, Hardin took a short leave. He visited Emilie and the children for a few days in Atlanta, and then hurried back to meet his brigade near a sluggish stream called the Chickamauga. After a month and more of steady retreats, the Confederates would retake the offensive on September 18, seeking to cut the federals off from their supply base at Chattanooga. The Orphans were spared from the worst of the fighting until September 20, when it became their turn to charge the Yankees' stubborn left flank.

"Cracking jokes as usual," the Orphans were "in the finest spirits" before the charge. Some were natural pranksters. More laughed to relieve the tension. A few just sat alone with their thoughts. Every man had his own way. At nine-fifteen, Hardin "got up and mounted his horse, laughing and talking as though he were going on parade." He formed his brigade in a single line and gave the order to advance. For almost half a mile, they saw nothing of Yankees. The ground around Chickamauga, like that around Shiloh, was a tangle of trees and brush with an occasional opening. About ten o'clock, Hardin called a halt on a low ridge. Across a mossy clearing, they could see a group of federals behind a makeshift bulwark of crude logs and fence rails. One of the Union soldiers later admitted that he thought Hardin and the other officers might have made easy targets standing atop a hill giving orders — but no one fired. Instead, everything was done in relative quiet and with great deliberation. The Yankees formed in two close lines that could fire and reload alternately. Across the clearing, the Confederates planted their flags, stepped to the line, and saw to their rifles. When all was in readiness, Hardin spurred his men forward.

The Orphan Brigade's first charge literally broke on the federal breastworks. The right half missed the bulwark entirely and breezed to the side, turning not into the Union flank but away from it and racing pell-mell down the line of a crude road. This left Hardin and the left half of the brigade, about six hundred men, charging alone into four entrenched federal regiments. To make matters worse, the brigade that was supposed to be covering their left had failed to make the charge. The result, an aid later said, was a "perfect tornado of bullets" coming at them from all angles. Hardin's men faced not only fire from their front but diagonal, enfilading fire from the whole extended (and otherwise unoccupied) Union line. Falling back to the ridge, Hardin rallied the men for another go. There seems to have been no talk of waiting for the missing brigade to the left or reuniting with the missing half of their own brigade to the right. In Hardin's defense, he followed his orders to the letter.

The second charge of the Orphan Brigade was more successful than the first. Leaf litter had ignited in front of the federal entrenchment and partially screened the attack. The Orphans made it to within thirty yards, "giving & taking death blows which could last but a few minutes without utter annihilation," before they were again repulsed. Inclined to rally a third time, Hardin called out to his aid, John Pirtle. "He had just said, 'John,'" Pirtle remembered, "[when] I saw a twitching in his face and a pallor. I called: 'You are shot!' Before he could reply I dismounted, rushed to his horse, and he fell off into my arms." The bullet had ripped through Hardin's right side and mangled his liver. Behind their bulwark, the federals raised a victorious cheer. They had not only beaten back the charge but bagged a general. Worried that the cheer signaled an advance, Hardin yelled to Pirtle: "Get an ambulance, quick, for God's sake. Don't let me fall into their hands!" As the Orphans rallied themselves (and suffered a third and final repulse), Pirtle and William Wallace Herr, the man who would later marry Kitty Todd, carried Hardin's litter over the ridge and off the field.

The Orphans' losses in front of the federal breastwork had been staggering. The Second Kentucky lost half the regiment, the Ninth almost half. Hardin himself was carried a mile to the rear. The doctor looked at his wound, grimaced, and said nothing. "Is there hope?" Hardin asked. "My dear General," the doctor replied, "there is no hope." Conscious for most of the day, Hardin listened to the sounds of battle as they swelled and then fell away. He asked the doctor for the result. "Victory," the doctor said. "Victory," Hardin repeated before he slipped into unconsciousness.

That morning, Emilie had vacated her Atlanta hotel room and caught a train south to stay with a cousin. "Sick . . . discouraged and out of heart," she stood on the crowded platform, her dress partly covering "a soldier who seemed [to be] sleeping." "Something in his attitude sent an arrow to my heart," she later wrote, "and I said, 'What is the matter with that man?' [But I already knew] he was dead." Somewhere south of the city the telegram caught up with her: "Atlanta, Ga.: Mrs. General Helm is in Griffin. Find her and send her up in train today. The General is dead." "I cannot describe the return journey," Emilie later noted, "and for days and weeks after I scarcely remember at all."

V.

ON SEPTEMBER 20, as things were wrapping up at Chickamauga, Lincoln received a telegram from Rosecrans. "We have met with a serious disaster," the general admitted. "It seems that every available man was thrown against us." It was a couple days before Lincoln learned that Hardin was among those thrown. Mary was sojourning in New York, so Lincoln had to telegraph her with the report. "We now have a tolerably accurate summing up of the late battle between Rosecrans and Bragg," he said. "Of the killed, one Major Genl. and five Brigadiers, including your brother-in-law, Helm." Burying the news of Hardin's death amid other particulars, Lincoln seemed to lack sympathy, but he could hardly have lamented the passing of a Confederate general over a telegraph system devoted to Union military communiqués. The real extent of his feeling was kept private, though glimpsed by the Illinois jurist David Davis. "I never saw Mr. Lincoln more moved," Davis said, "than when he heard of the death of his young brother-in-law, Helm. . . . I called to see him about 3 o'clock on the 22d of September. I found him in the greatest grief. 'Davis,' said he, 'I feel as David of old did when he was told of the death of Absalom. Would to God I had died for thee, oh Absalom, my son, my son?'" "I saw how grief-stricken he was," Davis remembered, "so I closed the door and left him alone."

The story of David and Absalom is told in the second book of Samuel. At the book's outset, David is made king and unites the northern and southern tribes of Israel. Under his leadership, the empire expands and God promises a period without foreign interference. Unfortunately, the kingdom itself is slightly corrupt, as is David. While mostly kind and fair, he commits acts that he knows to be sins in the eyes of God. His prophet, Nathan, predicts calamity, and David tries to atone, but it is too late: sin cannot be taken back. Meanwhile, David's oldest living son, Absalom, is enjoying himself in Jerusalem. Handsome, amiable, and enormously popular, he gathers around him a rebellion to dethrone his father. David's generals wish to crush the rebellion, and David accedes, but he implores them to "deal gently for my sake with . . . Absalom." In a bloody engagement in the forests of Ephraim, 20,000 of Absalom's followers are cut down and the rebellion is broken. Absalom himself gets his head stuck in the lower-lying branches of a tree and can only dangle helplessly as a general plunges spears into his heart. Reports of the victory are carried to David, but he can only ask: "Is the young man, Absalom, safe?" Finally someone tells him the truth, and he is unmade by the news, wailing "O my son Absalom, my son, my son Absalom! would God I had died for thee, O Absalom, my son, my son!"

Lincoln was not a broad reader but a deep one. He loved a few texts, and he loved them with a perfect monogamy. A few snippets of poetry, a smattering of Shakespeare, and, especially after Willie's death, the Bible — he bore into these until he could feel the bones that structure man's world. In comparing himself to David, then, Lincoln did not do it glibly. He would long before have weighed the comparison in every particular, searching for comfort, guidance, and historical precedent. In the Israelites, he would have seen a people, humble because it was a sin not to be, chosen by God for the example they might set before the world. And in David's kingdom, Lincoln would have seen striking parallels to his own: the fissure between north and south; the period of expansion and prosperity; the sin; and the price to be paid for sin. He must particularly have been struck by the story's denouement. David's lament for his rebellious son upsets his subjects, who are inclined to vengeance against the remaining rebels. David, however, will not hear of it and rebuilds his kingdom on forgiveness. Mercy saves Israel and gives the country a second chance to fulfill the promise God had made, through it, to the founders (Abraham, Jacob, and Moses) and the world.

Lincoln's reaction to Hardin's death, then, provides a clue to his own evolving interpretation of the Civil War. Like David's Israel, Lincoln's America was born to founding fathers and chosen by God to cradle the best hope of earth. The country had sinned, however, and, threatened with self-destruction, it needed to be chastened to be reborn. Here then is a source of Lincoln's remarkable insight into the war — originating in the Bible and given personal resonance by his brother-in-law's death. Scarcely two months after Chickamauga, Lincoln was graveside at Gettysburg, beginning (as David had begun after *his* lament for Absalom) to remind his people not only why they fight but why they forgive. For what is most remarkable about the Gettysburg Address is its utter failure to distinguish between blue and gray. Standing over Confederate and federal graves, Lincoln did not say that "the brave *Northern* men ... who struggled here" had consecrated the ground "above our power to add or detract." Neither did he urge his audience to take "increased devotion to that cause for which *Union soldiers* gave the last full measure of devotion." According to Lincoln, *all* of the dead were bound up in a common experiment — to test whether democratic government would endure. And all of the soldiers were fighting not *against* each other but *for* the same thing — a chance that their common country might be reborn. In this sense, though he lived two generations after them, Abraham Lincoln is the ultimate Founding Father. The house Washington, Jefferson, and Adams had built had been too flawed to stand. Lincoln framed a new house at Gettysburg, the house we live in, the House of Abraham. It would remain for the second inaugural to explain *why* we needed a new house, a new father, a new birth. But like David before him, Lincoln knew his people would have to be coaxed into a deeper understanding. Gettysburg was just the first step.

VI.

LIKE MANY of the Orphans who fell at Chickamauga, Hardin Helm was buried in a graveyard in Atlanta. His funeral left Emilie rudderless. For two years she had followed her husband from post to post. Now he was someplace she couldn't follow. At twenty-six, she was a widowed mother of three. Looking forward, she knew only that she wanted to go home. She wanted to be with her mother. Getting back to Kentucky, however, would prove no small challenge. Other Todds had crossed the lines. Charles Kellogg had done it — under the protection of Hardin's retreating cavalry. Kitty Todd had done it — under the protection of Hardin's special detail. The man who had vouchsafed both trips was now dead. Emilie did have other friends. Indeed, she was inundated with well-meaning condolences that "intruded" on her "hour of deep affliction" to "pour some balm into [her] wounded heart." But no balm could spirit her home.

Emilie's first appeal went out to Braxton Bragg, commander of the Confederate Army of Tennessee. Happy to be of service to the "widow of [their] gallant deceased general," Bragg responded with a pass permitting Emilie and her three children to cross the line at any point she might choose. The pass was worthless, however, without the corresponding permission of a federal general. On Emilie's behalf, Bragg sent a note by flag of truce to Rosecrans's replacement at Chattanooga, George H. Thomas. The request was for "Mrs. Helm, widow of Gen'l B. H. Helm of our service, and sister of Mrs. Lincoln" to be allowed to return to "her friends" in the North. "I trusted the mention of both relations would secure the desired object," Bragg wrote Emilie, "and was greatly surprised at the answer." True to his name, the "Rock of Chickamauga" proved stony. "Inform[ed] . . . that Mrs. Helm, a sister of Mrs. President Lincoln, desired to return to her friends," noted the *Macon Daily Telegraph*, General Thomas "brutally refused." Undaunted, Bragg appealed directly to Grant. A softer touch, Grant acceded, but by then the battle of Chattanooga was heating up, and no one could pass.

Fortunately for Emilie, another avenue opened as the one through Chattanooga closed. For a month, her mother and in-laws had been trying to get in touch with her. It had taken them almost three weeks to learn definitively that Hardin was dead. Hardin's father was so inconsolable, friends feared for his sanity. Speaking for many who had lost children in the war, his mother cried, "[He was] my son, my son, my first born, my pride, my hope. . . . How can I outlive him?" Somehow she got a letter through to her daughter-in-law: "Come home to us Emilie. You shall be as a daughter & his children as my children." At the same time, Mr. Helm wrote to Emilie's mother, Betsey. "I am totally at a loss to know how to begin," he admitted. "Could you or one of your daughters write to Mrs. Lincoln and through her secure a pass?" Betsey was way ahead of him, however. Having already lost two sons and a son-in-law, she was desperate to have her babies about her. Sixty-three years old, she determined to go south to personally escort Emilie back to Kentucky. "[I must] make every exertion," she wrote Elodie, "to obtain a pass to get Emily & children . . . to return with me to this place or wherever she may wish to live. All places are alike to me. My dearest hopes are almost buried."

On October 15, Lincoln sent Betsey a pass allowing "Mrs. Robert S. Todd, widow, to go South and bring her daughter, Mrs. General B. Hardin Helm, with her children north to Kentucky." Unfortunately, the pass miscarried, and it was some weeks before Betsey learned that the president meant to give his permission. Thus it was not until November 14 that the *Richmond Dispatch* announced, "The mother of Mrs. Lincoln arrived in this city on the steamer *Schultz*." From Richmond, Betsey traveled into the Deep South, where she was finally reunited with her children — Emilie, Elodie, David, and Martha — after a separation of two years. Together they grieved the losses to their thinning family. In the company of some of her remaining children, Betsey must have realized that her "dearest hopes" were not entirely buried.

The reunion was short-lived. The *Richmond Dispatch* had informed its readers that Betsey would take up permanent residence in the South, but that was impossible. She had left too many cares and too much of herself at home. Then too, living in the South was expensive, and Emilie had too long trespassed upon the generosity of others. With the fighting in Chattanooga turning against the Confederacy, Betsey realized her only way home lay in retracing her steps. Emilie had hoped to avoid this route. The nurse of her children was a slave, freed by the Emancipation Proclamation. If taken north she could claim the liberty that for a year had been but a paper promise. Faced with two options — free the woman or leave her in the South — Emilie chose the latter.

To get out of the South, Betsey and Emilie traveled first to Richmond, where they boarded a flag-of-truce steamer bound downriver for Fort Monroe. The fort operated as a sort of federal way station at the confluence of the James River and Chesapeake Bay. If flag-of-truce boats (and their passengers) passed inspection, they would be allowed to continue up the coast to Baltimore. Upon boarding, federal officers informed Emilie that she would have to take the oath of allegiance before proceeding farther. She was staggered. She had assumed that her pass would be enough. She desperately needed to get back to her home and its resources, financial and emotional. But how could she desecrate Hardin's memory by taking an oath that pledged her allegiance to the country against which he had stood in arms, administered by men wearing the uniform of his murderers? How could she, the wife of a Confederate general with ties to the White House, take her first chance to turn her back on the country that had raised her husband so high on its shoulders? Whatever the consequences, she decided, she could not take the oath. The officers were flummoxed by this response. Mrs. Helm did not seem haughty; indeed, she was obviously anguished. Moreover, it was clear from her paperwork that her brother-in-law (the president of the United States and their commander in chief) wanted her to return to Kentucky. Finally, Emilie suggested that she be allowed to continue to Washington on parole. There she would apply to the president directly, and if he said that she needed to take the oath, she would return to the fort. Happy for a way out of the impasse, the officers telegraphed the White House with the proposal. Lincoln wired back immediately: "Send her to me." With that, the party continued on to Baltimore. Betsey and the two youngest children remained there; Emilie and her four-year-old daughter, Kate, went on to Washington.

The Lincolns' "Little Sister" arrived at the White House a pathetic figure. She had crossed over the Todds' great divide — and she looked the worse for it. "Mr. Lincoln and my sister met me with the warmest affection," Emilie confided in her diary. "We were all too grief-stricken for speech. . . . We could only embrace each other in silence and tears."

Over the next week, the sisters gave each other what comfort they could, circling around the subjects that pained them most. "We talk of old friends," Emilie confessed, "we talk of immaterial things. . . . [We] cannot open our hearts to each other as freely as we would like. This frightful war comes between us like a barrier of granite closing our lips but not our hearts, for though our tongues are tied, we weep over our dead together and express through our clasped hands the sympathy we feel for each other in our mutual grief." Grief, like water, has a way of running together to cut a common channel. Emilie had lost a husband, Mary a son, and both were keenly conscious of the damage that had been done to their once happy family. Here was their chance to do some healing, and the sisters probed each other carefully to figure out the extent of each other's injuries. "We approach any subject timidly and wonder if anything we are about to say can give the other pain," Emilie admitted. "Sister Mary's tenderness for me is very touching. She and Brother Lincoln pet me as if I were a child, and, without words, try to comfort me."

Emilie comforted the Lincolns in turn. Upon first seeing his Little Sister again, Lincoln had stepped forward to remove her bonnet. He had done it awkwardly, stooping low and fumbling with the strings, utterly out of practice with such things. But it was a sweet moment, too — endearingly personal. With all his burdens — and hers — here was the president of the United States fiddling with her headgear. Emilie was one of the few attractive women Lincoln could be so familiar with, and petting her, staring into her face, was good for him. The Lincolns' marriage had always run more smoothly when there was a Todd around to moderate it. As soon as Lincoln had Emilie alone he asked, "I feel worried about Mary, her nerves have gone to pieces. . . . What do you think?" As soon as Mary had Emilie alone she asked, "What do you think of Mr. Lincoln? . . . I really think he looks very ill." In both cases, Emilie told the truth: Brother Lincoln seemed "thinner than [she] ever saw him;" Sister Mary seemed "very nervous and excitable." "Once or twice when I have come into the room suddenly," Emilie admitted to her diary, "the frightened look in [Mary's] eyes has appalled me." "She seems to fear that other sorrows may be added to those we already have to bear," Emilie confessed to Lincoln. "I believe if anything should happen to you or Robert or Tad it would kill her." In saying these things, Emilie confirmed the Lincolns' worst fears for each other. But the Lincolns did not need someone to lie to them. They needed someone to help them admit the truth to themselves. One morning Emilie found her sister reading an article about herself in the newspaper. "Kiss me, Emilie," Mary said, dropping the paper, "and tell me that you love me! I seem to be the scape-goat for both North and South!"

Moments like these helped the two sisters open up, though on one occasion Mary opened up too much. After retiring one night, Emilie heard a soft knock at her door. "I want to tell you, Emilie," Mary said on being admitted, "that one may not be wholly without comfort when our loved ones leave us. When my noble little Willie was first taken from me, I felt that I had fallen into a deep pit of gloom and despair without a ray of light anywhere. . . . If Willie did not come to comfort me I would still be drowned in tears, and while I long inexpressibly to touch him, to hold him in my arms, and still grieve that he has no future in this world that I might watch with a proud mother's heart — he lives, Emilie! He comes to me every night, and stands at the foot of my bed with the same sweet, adorable smile he has always had; he does not always come alone; little Eddie is sometimes with him and twice he has come with our brother Alec, he tells me he loves his Uncle Alec and is with him most of the time." Mary was trying to share with her sister the deep comfort she had found in spiritualism. This was Mary at her most vulnerable, and most helpful. But here was a divide Emilie could not cross. Her bedroom, the Prince of Wales Room, was spooky enough already. The purple drapes and purple wallpaper seemed "gloomy and funereal," and as Mary talked of the ghost of the boy who had died there, she spoke with "a thrill in her voice" and her eyes grew so "wide and shining," it gave Emilie the chills. "I had a feeling of awe as if I were in the presence of the supernatural," she noted in her diary. "It *is* unnatural and abnormal, it frightens me."

This incident was exceptional. For the most part, the sisters became increasingly comfortable with each other and together transformed the White House into a sanctum sanctorum. It helped that it was winter. With the cold out and the warm within, it was easy for them to stay bundled within their own little world. Gradually, even the war began to seem approachable. One day, Tad and Katie were sitting before a fire, looking at old photographs. After showing his little cousin one of himself, Tad picked up one of his father. "This is the president," he told her proudly. Katie shook her head: "That is not the President, Mr. Davis is President." Tad would not have it. He loved being the president's son. "Hurrah for Abe Lincoln," he cried. "Hurrah for Jeff Davis," Katie replied. The whole scene was deeply amusing to Lincoln. Determined to pacify the "little belligerents," he placed one on each knee. "Well, Tad," he said, "you know who is your President, and I am your little cousin's Uncle Lincoln." Here, for a moment, was the war as everyone in the room wished it could be, a semantic argument between innocents, solved before any damage had been done to their affections or virtue.

Such regression could not be sustained forever. In the endless traffic of visitors to the White House, the war as it really was finally overtopped the sisters' careful barriers. Usually when Mary received guests, Emilie discreetly left the room. On one occasion, however, a caller asked after Emilie specifically, and contact could not be avoided. The caller was Senator Harris, who claimed to be looking for news of a mutual friend. He appears to have had another agenda, however. After making his polite inquiries, he completely changed the subject: "Well, we have whipped the rebels at Chattanooga and I hear, madam, that the scoundrels ran like scared rabbits." Harris's comments were designed to sting. Emilie could hardly have assented to such a characterization without implying that her husband, dead only a month, should also be reckoned a scoundrel or scared rabbit. Reeling under the sleight, Emilie replied through a choked throat, "It was the example, Senator Harris, that you set them at Bull Run and Manassas."

Now the air was positively crackling. Mary tried to change the subject, but the senator wheeled on her. "Why isn't Robert in the army," he asked. "He is old enough and strong enough to serve his country. He should have gone to the front some time ago." Whatever he lacked in tact, the senator more than made up for in precision. He could scarcely have notched an arrow better calculated to go straight to Mary's heart. Having recently lost one son, she clung to Robert desperately. Attempting to salvage the conversation (and get her own barb in), Mary admitted that the fault was her own, that her son was desperate to join up but that she had insisted that he stay in college a little longer since "an educated man can serve his country with more intelligent purpose than an ignoramus" — which she undoubtedly meant to serve as a portrait of Harris himself. Certainly Harris took it at that way. Rising, he said pointedly to Mary, "I have only *one* son and he is fighting for his country." Not feeling that this was quite a sufficient rejoinder, he decided to have another go at Emilie as well. "And, Madam," he said, turning on her, "if I had twenty sons they should all be fighting the rebels."

"And if I had twenty sons, General Harris," Emilie replied, "they should all be opposing yours." With that the senator took his leave and the air went out of the room. Cold and trembling, Emilie stumbled for the door, "blinded by tears," her heart "beating to suffocation." Before she could reach it, however, Mary had caught her up in her arms. Sobbing into each other's shoulders, they began to realize that in sharing their grief they would only double it.

Meanwhile, General Sickles, who had come in and been shown out with Senator Harris, decided to report the entire incident to the president. Sickles had lost a leg due to his own ineptitude at Gettysburg, and as he stumped his way back up the White House steps he became a tangle of crutches and curses. By the time he regained the landing, he was even more out of sorts than he had been when he left the parlor. The president listened politely but with mounting humor as Sickles solemnly recounted the scene. "The child has a tongue like the rest of the Todds," Lincoln joked when the general had finished. Sickles was less amused, and, slapping his hand against a nearby table, he thundered, "You should not have that rebel in your house!" Incensed by the general's tone, Lincoln was nevertheless calm: "General Sickles, my wife and I are in the habit of choosing our own guests. We do not need from our friends either advice or assistance in the matter."

Sickles was right, however. Dark clouds were already gathering over the White House, brewing scandal. "My being here is more or less an embarrassment," Emilie confessed to her diary. "They have . . . invited me to make them a long visit next summer . . . but it will not be possible." A week after she had arrived, Emilie concluded that, for everyone's sake, she needed to continue on her way to Kentucky. There was still the sticky question of the oath, however. In what may or may not be a coincidence, Lincoln had been working on a new amnesty policy immediately prior and possibly during Little Sister's stay. On December 8, he issued what he called the Proclamation of Amnesty and Reconstruction, establishing a legal framework for sectional reconciliation. The Confederacy, he claimed, was not a foreign power — the war would not end with a treaty negotiated by Congress. Rather, the rebellion was the work of individual law-breakers, and the war would end when they were pardoned by their president. This put Lincoln in the convenient position of being able to pardon his sister-in-law, who would be one of the earliest test cases of his new policy. According to his proclamation, rebels needed to do only three things to be forgiven: 1) put down their guns; 2) release their slaves; and 3) pledge their allegiance to the Union. The wrinkle, in Emilie's case, was that only one of these applied to her (the oath of allegiance) and she didn't want to take it. Bending the law a little, Lincoln presented Emilie with two documents before her departure: an oath and a pardon. The oath, apparently, he pretended she had taken and set aside. The pardon was hers to keep. It said, "Mrs. Emily T. Helm . . . having on this day taken and subscribed the oath . . . is fully relieved of all penalties and forfeitures, and . . . is to be protected and afforded facilities as a loyal person." (Among the things Lincoln specifically wanted protected was some cotton Emilie claimed to own in the South. To his amnesty, he added a specific note decreeing that when the cotton came within Union lines, it was to be protected until Emilie could come and claim it.)

The final parting between the Lincolns and Little Sister was a hard one. The moment they all stepped outside, the calm they had created within the White House collapsed behind them. Emilie was about to spiral back out into the vortex, and none of them knew when or if they would be together again. "You know Little Sister I tried to have Ben come with me," Lincoln said as they parted. "I hope you do not feel any bitterness or that I am in any way to blame for all this sorrow." Emilie assured the president that her husband had loved him but that he had followed his conscience. "For weal or woe," she said, "[we] must side with [our] own people."

6

---·---

1864–65: A Whole People

I.

B Y 1864, the Lincoln administration had suffered all kinds of embarrassment at Todd hands. David had been exposed as a desecrator of Union corpses. George had been exposed as a looter of Union homes. Sam and Aleck had literally died to see the Union unmade. Emilie, the wife of a Confederate general, had slept for a week in a White House bed. Elizabeth's husband had grown rich at the government's expense. Margaret's husband had actually committed treason. And yet all these flaps were as nothing compared to the controversy generated by a tiny article that appeared on March 2, 1864, in the *Richmond Enquirer*.

The article concerned the activities of Martha Todd White, the tenth-born of the Todds. Matt, as her family called her, was older than Emilie, younger than David. She wasn't as pretty as her younger sisters, but she had more sass. In 1850, she had married a Selma physician, Clement Billingslea White. Despite his profession, Clem was not a healthy specimen. At 107 pounds, he seemed to Elodie always "thin and feeble" and "far from well." The Confederate army, which had come to specialize in "thin and feeble," took him anyway. Over his wife's objections he joined up rather than suffer the humiliation of the draft. "I fear [he] will do no good and require constant nursing," Elodie predicted, and she was right. Ultimately, Clem proved "too delicate to stand the fatigue of camp life" and was sent home.

In the meantime, however, Matt and Elodie were left alone in Selma. Jeered by the "Anti-Whites" and grieving their "once happy family," they were thrown back on themselves for companionship and support.

"We are always together," Elodie admitted, "and are more company for each other than for anyone else." Studying her sister closely, though, Elodie realized that while they loved each other deeply, they were not all that alike. "[We] resemble each other somewhat in appearance," she admitted, "[but] I think us [as] totally unlike as any two sisters I ever saw in disposition." To be sure, both were Todds. Ticking off the blemishes of her character, Elodie noted: "I cannot govern my temper or tongue," "I am one of the most unforgiving creatures you ever knew," and "I [occasionally feel] myself more of a Todd than ever, and they are noted for their determination or as *malicious* people would [say] *obstinacy*." But in admitting these traits, Elodie kept them in check. Matt was a different case. She would never have thought to apologize for such things. She was brighter and brasher than her sister, less introspective and more outgoing. People who liked her described her as a brilliant conversationalist with "great personal charm of manner." But like Mary Lincoln, she had a tongue that could cut like a "Damascus blade." Indeed, said a witness, "in appearance, mind and manner [she was] more like [a young] Mary Lincoln than any of her sisters."

It was exactly this combination of personal qualities that got her into trouble, though what exactly she did is a matter of dispute. According to the *Enquirer*, Matt had "gone through the lines to Lexington, Kentucky, and being a sister (Todd) of Mrs. Lincoln, was permitted to go on to Washington." After a stay of some weeks, she had returned to the South in late February with a uniform that, upon inspection, proved to be of extraordinary value. Each of the buttons was made of gold, set into a wooden frame and covered in Confederate cloth. "The gold thus brought through is valued at between thirty and forty thousand dollars," the *Examiner* chuckled, and Matt's actions constituted a "remarkable instance of woman's ingenuity."

Then as now in the news business, some stories had legs and some didn't. The story of Martha Todd White and the gold buttons took off like a herd of horses — though not because it was true. Southern papers reprinted the story because it reinforced the idea that the Confederacy could not be defeated because Southern women wouldn't allow it. Northern papers reprinted the story for an entirely different, but equally simple, reason: it was an election year — Lincoln was vulnerable, and the story was embarrassing. The first paper to politicize the White matter was the *New York Tribune*. The paper's editor, Horace Greeley, was a Republican but a self-described "earnest one-term man." They way he figured it, the party could either dump Lincoln or get dumped at the polls. On March 28, under the title "Aid and Comfort for the Enemy," his paper ran a short article affirming and even expanding on the *Enquirer* story. Upon investigation, it appeared that the uniform was but the tip of a contraband iceberg. "It is stated in the best-informed circles that Mrs. J. Todd White, the sister of Mrs. Lincoln, did pass through our lines for Richmond via Fortress Monroe with three large trunks containing medicines and merchandise, so that the chuckling of the Rebel press over her safe transit with Rebel uniforms and buttons of gold was founded in truth." The *Tribune* was the widest-circulating newspaper in the free states. In verifying the allegations against Martha, it had effectively declared open season on Abraham Lincoln.

The papers that took the deadliest aim were those allied with the Copperheads, or Peace Democrats. They opposed the war and demanded an immediate settlement with the South. For years they had been vilified as venomous snakes (hence the name) who poisoned the Union war effort by unexampled treason. Here in the White story was something of revenge. Through his family connections, Lincoln himself was guilty of treason, and Copperhead papers set to drawing those connections in their blackest ink. A few retellings and embellishments later, the story was as damning as it was ridiculous. White, claimed the *New York World*, "was a rebel spy and sympathizer," who had gotten a special pass from Lincoln "enjoining upon the Federal officers not to open any of her trunks, and not to subject the bearer of the pass, her packages, parcels or trunks, to any inspection or annoyance." When approached by the provost and General Butler, the commander at Fortress Monroe, she had pulled out the pass and said "in substance, as follows: 'My trunks are filled with contraband, but I defy you to touch them. Here (pushing it under their noses), here is the positive order of your master!'" Butler and associates had no choice. Faced with an order "written and signed by [the President's] own hand," they had to allow White to pass. "To-day," claimed the paper in mock indignation, "the contents of his wife's sister's trunks are giving aid and comfort to the enemy — not least is the shock which these facts will give to the loyal hearts whose hopes and prayers and labors sustain the cause which is thus betrayed in the very White House."

The charge that Lincoln himself was guilty of treason was ridiculous — and effective. By late April the story was mushrooming out of control. Versions of it had appeared in papers in Washington, New York, Chicago, Houston, Cincinnati, Detroit, Columbus, Memphis, St. Louis, and elsewhere. More alarming, voters were beginning to respond. On April 27, the White House got a letter from O. Stewart, a soldier with the Third Michigan recuperating in a Washington hospital: "Mr President Sir. I inclose a Peice of paper taken from the *Detroit Free Press* stateing that you gave Mrs Todd Mrs Lincoln sister a pass through our lines with a Trunk of medicines and Contraband goods and valuble Papers. now if this is so will you please have the Ed of the Chronicle confirm it or Condemn it and oblige for I dont beleive our President would do that pleese Answer. yours, O. Stewart."

Clearly something needed to be done, and indeed Lincoln's associates were already working behind the scenes to stanch the political hemorrhage. A week before Stewart's letter, John Nicolay, one of Lincoln's private secretaries, had written to General Butler, enclosing a copy of the *World* article and asking him a series of questions: "Will you please inform me whether Mrs. White presented to you what purported to be anything more than the usual pass . . . ?" "Did she take with her more than ordinary baggage?" "Was or was not her baggage inspected?" "Did she use the language alleged in the above statement?"

"I am sorry that you or any body else should feel annoyed with the silly story about the conduct of Mrs. White," Butler wrote back. "If she had been any body else but a relative of the President she would have entirely escaped observation." A lawyer by training, Butler went on to address the article's assertions "point by point." Mrs. White had come through Fortress Monroe. She had "no other than the ordinary quantity of baggage." She showed "no other or different reluctance than that usual with ladies to have their baggage examined." She did not show an "autograph pass or order from" the president. She did not conduct herself with anything other than "courteous and ladylike deportment." In short, "nothing . . . had occurred which should 'give a shock' to any 'loyal hearts.'"

Using Butler's letter as a template, Nicolay then drafted an article exonerating White and enclosed it in a letter to Horace Greeley. The *Tribune*, Nicolay said, had vouched for a story that was "from the first, without truth or foundation." It was only fair that the *Tribune* now print a retraction. To his credit, Greeley agreed. Like any editor he had his political leanings, but he also had professional integrity and a moral conscience. As he told Nicolay, "I want to publish all the truth I can and as few falsehoods as possible." Then too, as a Republican,

Greeley was disgusted by the political hay the Democrats had made of the story and galled that they cited his paper as their authority, even for the stuff they made up.

On April 27, the same day Stewart had written the president, Greeley published his retraction. Few papers followed suit, and his vindication of White only helped to kill a story that was moribund anyway. Politically, Lincoln was embarrassed but not crippled by the White allegations. His reelection chances depended far more on the movements of his armies than the activities of his in-laws. Even so, an important question remains: quite apart from what Matt was *alleged* to have done, what *did* she do?

Answering that question requires asking another: how did Matt get north in the first place? In a December 19, 1863, letter to Lincoln, Matt told him how she did it. When Emilie and her mother had traveled from Richmond to Baltimore on his pass, she had gone with them. It is possible that Lincoln knew she would be hitching a ride, vaguely possible that he gave her her own pass. But the language of her letter suggests otherwise. "I took advantage of . . . fortuitous circumstances," she boldly admits, "to assist [Emilie and Mother] together with my own need for medical advice from a former physician." Having thus snuck into the North, she now asked Lincoln if she could stay longer. "Relying on your friendly relation towards us," she said, "[I hope you will allow] me to remain a sufficient length of time to recruit my health. I also request permission to replenish my wardrobe [and] take for my own use articles not now to be obtained in the South." If he wouldn't allow this, she said, "a pass to return south unmolested will be acceptable." Lincoln's reply, if any, has never surfaced. Matt remained in the North for some months. She may have spent some of that time in Kentucky visiting with her mother, Emilie, and Kitty. By March, she was ready to return home.

Like her mother before her, Matt's only way south was to retrace her steps through Fortress Monroe. This time, however, she would not be able to ride on Emilie's coattails. She would need a pass of her own. Calling at the White House, she sent her card in to Mary — and was refused an audience. She repeated the application two or three times, always with the same result. The Lincolns might have snubbed Matt for any number of reasons. She had never been as close to Mary as Emilie or Elodie or Kitty. She was more outspoken and less discreet than any of them. She had already taken advantage of the president by sneak-

ing into the North on Emilie's pass. Who knew what she might do if allowed in the door? Finally, just to get rid of her, Lincoln sent her a pass
to proceed south and hoped it would be the last he would hear of her.

It wasn't. Matt sent the pass back, requesting that he add a special clause that would exempt her trunks from search. Lincoln refused.
Matt, nothing if not persistent, settled in for a siege. According to witnesses, she made herself conspicuous by talking "secesh" and waving
her pass about in a Washington hotel. She enlisted the aid of two Kentucky representatives (Robert Mallory and Brutus Clay), who took her
requests in to the president personally. Undoubtedly suffering an acute
case of Todd-fatigue, Lincoln finally snapped. When Clay stepped into
his office to bend his ear on the same tired subject, he told the con-
gressman that "if Mrs. W. did not leave forthwith, she might expect to
find herself within twenty-four hours in the Old Capitol Prison."

Matt took the hint. She packed her trunks and boarded a flag-of-
truce boat bound for Fortress Monroe. There, like Emilie before her,
she ran into a little trouble. At eleven-thirty at night, the assistant provost demanded that she come down to his house. Matt was incensed
that she should be so "badly treated," and her "temper came out," touching off an argument. The bone of contention was her "mass of luggage,"
thirteen trunks in all, which the provost found both excessive and suspicious. He wanted them searched. Matt preferred he didn't and appealed up the chain of command, all the way to General Butler.

Benjamin F. Butler was not a friend to the South, at least by reputation. When New Orleans fell to the Union navy in 1862, his forces had
occupied the city and decisively brought it to heel. Unruly crowds were
threatened with artillery. Shopkeepers who turned away federal trade
had their stores seized and sold. A man who removed the federal flag
from the New Orleans Mint was hanged in its courtyard. And once the
city's menfolk were crushed, Butler wheeled upon its ladies. Haughty
to the last, New Orleans belles had thought they could sit atop their
pedestals and hurl insults, expectoration, and the contents of their
chamber pots down upon the heads of federal men. Butler informed
them otherwise. In his infamous General Order No. 28, he decreed,
"When any female shall by word, gesture, or movement, insult or show
contempt for any officer or private of the United States, she shall be
regarded and held liable to be treated as a woman of the town, plying
her avocation." All he meant was that if women didn't behave like ladies they wouldn't be treated like ladies; if they degraded themselves
in public, they were no better than prostitutes. To the panicked Victo-

rian ear, however, Butler had said that the city's most patriotic belles would be bedded like the whores they were. Butler's order had pressed the South's ultimate panic button, and Confederate soldiers abandoned their companies to come south and kill him. Until Sherman marched to the sea, no Union general was more loathed than Benjamin Butler.

Fortunately for Matt, Butler's reputation exceeded him. He did not hate all things Southern. At the 1860 Democratic National Convention in Charleston, he had backed Jefferson Davis through fifty-seven straight ballots. In the general election of that year, he had supported John C. Breckinridge, the candidate of the party's southern wing. After the war, he would even invite a former Confederate officer, Henry Kyd Douglas, to go deep-sea fishing with him. There, over glasses of rum and aerated water, the conversation turned to Martha Todd White.

According to Douglas, Butler still remembered the case with a wry fondness. Around March 18, an enraged provost had come to him to demand that he seize a tower of baggage. The tower's owner was Martha Todd White, a rebel sister-in-law of the president. Butler was no fool; he figured the bags contained contraband. But he quickly decided that the political cost of opening the trunks was higher than the cost of leaving them shut. "Discovery," he thought, "would have involved the detention of Mrs. White and her trunks, a public disclosure, [my] own embarrassment and the especial embarrassment of President Lincoln, who would have released her and brought on himself" a pitiless bombardment from the press. Thus, much to the provost's dismay, Matt was allowed to go.

Clearly, Butler had not been entirely honest with Nicolay. In his letter he had said nothing of Matt's "mass of luggage" or her argument with the provost; he had never alluded to his own decision to leave the lid on a Pandora's box of presidential miseries. And yet if his letter is examined again, one realizes that it contains no false statements either. Like any good lawyer, Butler had focused only on denying the most specific charges in the most general language. Did Matt have a lot of bags? Some women have more. Did Matt object to her bags being searched? Some women object more. Was Matt ever high-tempered? In *his* dealings with her, she had been a perfect lady. Indeed, Butler made only one statement that might have gotten him into trouble. Speaking of himself in the third person, he had said: "General Butler did not wish to open her trunks." In drafting his editorial for the *Tribune,* Nicolay ignored that line altogether and instead followed the logic of a line from later in the letter — "Mrs. White showed no other or different reluctance than that usual with ladies to have their baggage examined" — which strongly implied that her bags *were* searched.

So what *was* in the trunks? Though capacious enough, they probably did *not* contain the fabled Uniform of the Golden Buttons. That story, the progenitor of so much of the trouble, actually *predated* Matt's return to the South. Who wrote it and why is a mystery. Some of the trunks' contents are known, however. After Matt passed "inspection" at Fortress Monroe, she was escorted to a Richmond hotel by Henry Kyd Douglas, the man who would later reminisce with Butler over rum and soda. According to him, one trunk contained the wedding clothes of Hetty Carey, a Baltimore belle living in Richmond and widely regarded the "most beautiful woman of her day and generation." (Her wedding to General John Pegram in St. Paul's Church would be the social event of the winter season. Unfortunately, Pegram would be killed three weeks later; his funeral service would be held in the same church, pronounced by the same pastor, and attended by the same guests as his wedding.)

Another of Matt's trunks contained a keg of brandy and a keg of whiskey. Intended for the hospital, they took a quick detour when she was called upon by General John Hunt Morgan and a few of his cavalry officers. The men had recently escaped from the Ohio state penitentiary, where they had been confined for four months after their so-called Great Raid of 1863. Deducing that an air duct ran below their cell, they had carefully chipped away at the concrete floor, hiding the pieces in their furnaces and bed ticking and covering the hole with a large carpetbag. Once in the duct, they had tunneled up beneath the other cells, not breaking through until a rainy night when they knew the guard dogs would be penned up. Now back in Richmond, Morgan and company were the toast of the town, and at Matt's invitation, they were only too pleased to raise a glass (or more) to themselves.

The next day, her celebrity rising, Matt was invited to call upon Mr. and Mrs. Davis at the Confederate White House. Almost certainly she had met them three years before at the ball that inaugurated the Confederacy. The intervening years had been hard ones. The reverses at Gettysburg, Vicksburg, and Chattanooga; the transfer of Grant to the eastern theater to take on Lee; the increasing effectiveness of the Union blockade; the decreasing likelihood of European intervention — all had taken their toll on rebel morale. But in a parlor full of partisan conversation, Confederate defeat could still seem inconceivable. Basking in her notoriety and congratulated for her patriotism, Matt was in her element, among her people, in the only White House that would admit her. And perhaps, as accused, she really did tell "with great vim the story of her outwitting her too credulous 'brother Lincoln.'"

Credulity and decency are easily mistaken for each other. For his part, "brother Lincoln" could only lament his latest attempt to do right by the Todds. Matt's stunt and the news articles that followed had done only a fraction of the damage they might have. Had she been arrested, had he been forced to intervene, the political injuries in an election year might have been grave. Thanks to Benjamin Butler, Lincoln had dodged a bullet. But if the political toll had been fortuitously minimal, the personal toll was rising. On April 29, Lincoln met informally with his naval secretary, Gideon Welles, and unburdened himself of his sad and sordid dealings with Martha. "He gave the details with frankness, and without disguise," Welles related in his diary. "I will not go into them all, though they do him credit on a subject of scandal and abuse."

II.

IN SEPTEMBER, George Todd was transferred from field duty and put in charge of First South Carolina Hospital. One of seven Charleston-area medical facilities devoted to the care and comfort of soldiers, First South Carolina was the gem of the system. Its founder, Robert Kinloch, had realized early in the war that a rising tide of wounded would swamp the city. Existing hospitals had been expanded and new facilities had been opened by private citizens, but Kinloch rightly predicted that more would have to be done. What was needed, he decided, was for the Confederate States Medical Department to erect something on a grander scale. A new hospital should be located convenient to the city but sufficiently outside it to be free from crowds, noise, sanitation problems, and any potential shelling from the Union navy. Its grounds needed to be accessible but extensive enough to promote tranquility and recovery. Surveying his options, Kinloch decided upon Rikersville, a small town four miles north of Charleston, as the perfect setting. There he acquired the India Rubber Factory and the German Rifle Club and began converting their buildings into his flagship hospital. The Rifle Club's grounds swept through a scenic pine grove along the Ashley River. The rubber factory's buildings were open and ample, perfect for conversion into wards. When finished, the hospital had a kitchen and mess room, an on-site laundry and apothecary, and room enough to accommodate three hundred patients. The largest of its four wards — all named for high-ranking Confederates — was "90 by 60 feet, well warmed and ventilated, lighted by 33 windows, and ha[d] pleasant and spacious galleries on either side." "Taken together," reported the *Charleston Mercury,* the facilities and grounds made Rikersville Hospital "a spot admirably calculated for the sick and convalescent."

George's transfer to the hospital came during a period of upheaval for the entire system. In the spring, federal forces had opened their Operations Against the Defenses of Charleston campaign. Assaults on Fort Wagner on Morris Island in Charleston Harbor — including one led by Robert Gould Shaw and the Fifty-fourth Massachusetts — sent a host of prisoners and wounded, some of them African Americans, into the city's jails and hospitals. Already groaning to capacity, the system was further destabilized when the Union general Quincy Gilmore erected a two-hundred-pound Parrott gun on Morris Island and threatened an indiscriminate bombardment of Charleston if the harbor forts, Sumter and Wagner, weren't evacuated. Confederate authorities refused, and on August 21, 1863, Gilmore opened fire.

Gilmore's gun did little damage, but Charleston's exposed lower wards were gradually abandoned and hospital patients and personnel relocated to points north of Calhoun Street. During the reorganization, the city's medical department decided finally to adopt the naming convention mandated by the Confederate Congress (hence Rickersville Hospital became First South Carolina). They also decided to bring in some new blood. Several factors may have recommended George Todd. First, and indisputably, he was a skilled surgeon. Something like 70 percent of Civil War wounds were wounds to the extremities, and flesh-mangling minié balls left surgeons few options outside of amputation. Limb removal was a doctor's stock and trade — and George was a whiz with the bone saw. Indeed, after the war, it would be claimed that he had performed the first successful amputation at the hip joint.

Another factor recommending George may have been a negative one. While valuable as a medical asset, he had proved problematic in the field. He had been occasionally at odds with the men in his unit; he had not always followed orders; and, in marching through Pennsylvania, he had inflamed the local populace, which is exactly what Robert E. Lee had been keen not to do. George may have had a talent for organization and surgery, but he certainly had a talent for prickly defensiveness. Perhaps as the head of a hospital, he would feel secure enough to concentrate on the things he was really good at.

Unfortunately, his appointment had rather the opposite effect. Chafing under others' authority, George had no qualms about abusing his own. In fairness, there is no evidence that he was anything other than careful while attending the wounded Confederates in his care. Yankee casualties, however, were another matter. Since the spring, Union soldiers, black and white, had been languishing in the city's hospitals and jails. Ordinarily, such prisoners would have been exchanged long before George took over at Rikersville. The exchange system, however, had broken down over the issue of the black troops. The federal government insisted that black soldiers had the same right as white ones to be exchanged. The Confederate government disagreed, claiming that a black man caught in arms was guilty of inciting servile insurrection and could be sentenced to death. In its "leniency," the rebel government might return them to servitude, but they would certainly never exchange them. Faced with such intransigence, the federal government had little choice but to refuse to exchange any troops whatever. The results were inevitable. By 1864, the impasse had created massive overcrowding in prison systems, North and South.

To be sure, the Charleston prison would never be as notorious as Andersonville or Elmira, but it shared many of their deplorable features. Like Andersonville it was an open stockade. High brick walls enclosed a dirt yard with little in it or on it except a single privy that looked as if it had never been cleaned. "We had no shelter from sun or rain," remembered one prisoner after the war. "The sink was so illy arranged that it soon became an intolerable nuisance, productive of disease and death. The water was miserable, our ration was meal, rice, and lard in very small quantities. As the result of all this, upward of one hundred officers, who were comparatively well when taken to Charleston, died. There could be no excuse for crowding us so closely in this jail yard for there were plenty of unoccupied buildings in Charleston." Another survivor agreed, calling it "the most horrible place [he] was ever in." "We had no shelter whatever," he remembered. "For rations we had some fresh meat [and] corn meal [but] no dishes to cook this with. . . . The stench and insufficient food made many sick. Some had the yellow fever. We, of course, protested against the treatment; but they always replied, 'It was good enough for damned Yankee sons of bitches.'" Both of these men fell sick and were transferred to area hospitals, but others were not as lucky. From his hospital window, one witness could see the unfortunate wretches who had remained behind in the jail yard. "A more horrible-looking set of creatures I never saw," he admitted. "I cannot express to you how badly they looked. . . . [T]o a great extent they were naked, and a great portion of them had become idiotic. . . . They were left there to die, some of them under a few trees there, but no other shelter." Almost mercifully, the zombie-men "died off very rapidly, and seemed to have no desire to live."

With other area physicians, George was supposed to make regular rounds of the prison to tend to the wounded, minister to the sick, and remove to a hospital the direst cases if necessary. Instead, according to witnesses, he would "come around among the men and kick and abuse them without trying to benefit their condition in the least." "[Todd was] the most degraded of all the rebels we had anything to do with," said one. "A more rabid secessionist was no where to be found," remarked another. A third complained that he had "never heard a man capable of using such volleys of profane and obscene language as this surgeon, who claimed to be a brother of Mrs. Lincoln." George's treatment of the prisoners at the Charleston jail yard was mild by comparison to the wrath he visited upon some of the Yankees who were transferred to his hospital. In language reminiscent of that used to describe his brother David, George's patients remembered a man who would in "raving fits of madness . . . pound and kick" the patients and ordered the severest punishments for such mild infractions as spitting on the floor. On one occasion, a lieutenant from one of the Union Kentucky regiments actually talked back to him. George pulled the man from his bunk, "kicked him in the most brutal manner, and had him bucked and gagged for more than an hour." By the next day, the man was dead. "I am G—d d——d glad of it," George said on learning the man's fate. "I meant to kill the son of a b—h before he left here."

There are hints that George reserved his most brutal treatment for African Americans. A soldier captured at Fort Wagner was made to do menial duties around the hospital. When he stopped to talk to a (white) Union officer, George immediately ordered him to be whipped. "Soon the screams of the poor fellow convinced me the order was being executed," remembered the Union officer. Another telling incident began with two men squabbling over a wash basin. The basin had been assigned to a particular ward, and a Rikersville surgeon had told a captured black soldier to make sure it never left the premises. Later, a white Union deserter, who had also been captured, spied the basin and decided to take it for his own. The black man told the white man that the basin had to stay, but the white man only abused him, then and later. When the black soldier had finally had enough of tongue lashings he said, "You have no right to talk in that way. . . . I am a soldier in the United States Army and you are a deserter." The deserter took the case to Todd. Other (white) members of the ward sided with the black soldier and told Todd that he had only been obeying the explicit directions of one of his own surgeons. George replied that he "did not care a damn" and took the soldier outside to be punished with forty lashes. When the soldier returned, he could only say, "For God's sake, how long has this thing got to last?"

Fortunately for Mary Lincoln, George's activities at the Charleston hospital never rose to the level of scandal. After a few months, George was removed as the head of First South Carolina and reassigned to a post where he would have no interaction with enemy soldiers. Then too the prisoner of war issue was not as prominent as it had been in the war's early months, when David's conduct had shone in the national spotlight. By 1864, the issue had faded from the public's consciousness — and would not reemerge until the war was over and prisons like Andersonville, Elmira, and Charleston turned out their undead.

III.

IRONICALLY, the Todd who came nearest to being arrested in 1864 was not Martha or George but Emilie. Having left the Lincolns in December, Emilie had returned with her mother to Lexington. There she was happy to be reunited with Kitty, relieved to be done wandering, glad to be someplace where she didn't have to worry about her babies making all the noise they needed to. There too, she was finally at a place where she could make all the noise *she* needed to. She had played the brave widow for months. Returned to the hometown of her youth and again dependent on her mother, she had an eerie sense of having come full circle. She was really single again; Hardin was really gone, and grieving could properly begin.

Unfortunately, the Kentucky Emilie returned to was more divided and dangerous than the one she'd left. The state hadn't seen a major battle since 1862, but it had somehow spiraled into violence anyway. Some of the killing was "official," as when raiding parties under Nathan Bedford Forrest or John Hunt Morgan clashed with federal "occupying" forces. But increasingly, the violence was of the nastier and more partisan kind, the kind that looks less like war and more like murder. Bands of Confederate guerillas, operating outside the chain of command, marauded across the state, seizing property and harassing Union sympathizers. Some groups engaged in reprisal killings, avenging themselves for lost farms and lost brothers. Others were simply brigands, using politics as a smoke screen for sadism and greed. Union commanders loudly deplored such rebel lawlessness — and quietly admitted that their own militias weren't much better.

On July 5, Lincoln concluded that if something wasn't done Kentucky would slip into a civil war all its own. He suspended the writ of habeas corpus and proclaimed martial law in the state. The man in charge of enforcing that law and bringing Kentucky to heel was the Union general Stephen Gano Burbridge. Unfortunately, Burbridge did not have Lincoln's mix of firmness and flexibility. Before being relieved of command, he would alienate Kentucky so thoroughly that it would determine, after the war, to re-remember itself as a Confederate state.

Burbridge's policies were not merely draconian but indiscriminately so. It is one thing to insist, as he did, that any man caught blowing up a river steamer would be summarily drowned. The punishment is harsh, but it is aimed at a specific class of people. It is something else again to acquiesce, as Burbridge did, in the "Great Hog Swindle," an attempt to force all of the state's pig farmers to sell only to government-selected butchers at non-negotiable prices. Here the punishment is relatively mild (the price for the hogs was probably a fair one), but it falls on the backs of a very general population. Many of Burbridge's policies had this same "liberality." In suppressing newspapers, arresting editors, impressing horses and property, tampering with elections, and intimidating voters, he discouraged a few closet Confederates and alienated a thousand moderates.

On July 16, Burbridge issued his infamous General Order 59: any rebel sympathizer found within a five-mile radius of a guerilla incident would be deported and have his or her property turned over to the victims of the incident; and when any unarmed Union citizen was murdered, four guerillas would be taken from the local prison and publicly shot at "the most convenient place near the scene of the outrage." Burbridge's threat was not an idle one. A slew of executions followed. Two men were shot, pursuant to the order, on July 19; two more on July 27; two on July 29; four on August 12; five, including one woman, on August 15; two on August 20; four on September 4, and so on. In all, some fifty executions took place during Burbridge's tenure, and at least six occurred in or around Lexington: two men, who were rumored to be legitimate Confederate soldiers, were hanged at the Lexington fairgrounds, and four prisoners were taken from Lexington's jail and shot outside the capitol.

Given the political climate, it is perhaps not surprising that in late July a group of Burbridge men turned up with an arrest warrant for Emilie. It was exactly the sort of harassment Lincoln had expected and the reason he had given her the declaration of amnesty. Emilie produced the document. The men read it and grudgingly withdrew. But the incident branded her as disloyal and gave grist to the rumor mill. By early August, alarming accounts of her conduct, almost certainly exaggerated, had reached the president's ear. Taken aback, Lincoln fired off a telegram to Burbridge. His amnesty, he told the general, had only been intended to protect Emilie "against the mere fact of her being General Helm's widow." He did not intend to protect her "against the consequences of disloyal words or acts, spoken or done by her since her return to Kentucky." "Deal with her for current conduct," he concluded ominously, "just as you would with any other."

The incident, it should be said, came at the lowest point of Lincoln's presidency. The war seemed interminable, his reelection improbable. In the spring, Grant's Overland campaign had proved a national bloodletting: 55,000 federal casualties in May and June. And for what? Grant's army was now bogged down outside Petersburg. Sherman too seemed bogged down, outside Atlanta. Another promising spring offensive was grinding to a halt, and the country was howling. Lincoln's political prospects, never bright, seemed to be winking out. "Mr. Lincoln is already beaten," Horace Greeley claimed. "He cannot be elected. And we must have another ticket to save us from utter overthrow." Lincoln was almost inclined to agree. "Do you expect to be elected?" someone asked him. "Well," he replied, "I don't think I ever heard of any man being elected to an office unless some one was for him."

The comment was typical of Lincoln's feelings of weariness and isolation. "The springs of [my] life are wearing away," he told a friend in an unguarded moment, "and I shall not last." When another friend told him to get some sleep, Lincoln responded that he couldn't: "The tired part of me is *inside* and out of reach." When Harriet Beecher Stowe asked about his plans after the war, Lincoln laughed: "After the war? I shall not be troubled about that. The war is killing me."

Many who were close to the president agreed. Significantly lighter than when he took office, "prematurely aged by public labors and private griefs," he looked like death, or at least like one of its incarnations. He was described variously as a "ghoul," an "undertaker," and a "huge skeleton in clothes." "[His] personal appearance is the subject of daily remark among those who have known him formerly," admitted Henry Villard. "Always cadaverous, his aspect is now almost ghostly." The journalist Noah Brooks preferred the image of a zombie: "His hair is grizzled, his gait more stooping, his countenance sallow, and there is a sunken, deathly look about the large, cavernous eyes, which is saddening to those who" knew the "hearty, blithesome, genial, and wiry Abraham Lincoln of earlier days." Even Horace Greeley, no "idolator" or even "adulator" of the president, had to admit that the man appeared to be at death's door. "He has been carried further toward the grave by his four years in the White House," Greeley reported, "than he could have been by ten years of constant labor."

It is no wonder then that Lincoln turned Emilie over to Burbridge. Sleep deprived and sickly, headed for defeat, having only recently fielded a political threat from Martha Todd White, Lincoln had had it with the Todds. When he heard the rumors of Emilie's conduct, he was prepared to believe them.

So what had Emilie done? In all fairness, probably nothing. To be sure, with the exception of Levi, the Todds who remained in Lexington were conspicuously pro-Confederate. Elizabeth had had two sons killed in the rebel service and had hotly (and publicly) praised John Hunt Morgan. Emilie had just returned from the South, where she had lovingly buried her husband, a Kentucky Confederate general. These facts alone would have been enough to invite the enmity of Unionist neighbors. In addition, Emilie, Kitty, and later their visiting sister, Margaret, all quietly campaigned on behalf of various Confederate prisoners. These campaigns included occasional letters to Lincoln, though they were always respectfully written. "I hope I am not intruding too much upon your kindness and will try not to *overstep* the limits that I should keep," Emilie wrote in one such letter. "Hoping you will pardon my troubling you and much love to Sister Mary, Belive me, Truly Yours," Kitty noted in another. "Efforts to reach *you* through *me* are made weekly & almost daily by reason of our family connection," Margaret wrote in a third, "but I think I have resisted them with prudence & due consideration for you."

None of these campaigns rose to the level of a crime, even in Burbridge's Kentucky, and the attempt to arrest Emilie was never repeated. Perhaps Burbridge *had* sought to detain her for the mere fact of being Helm's widow. Perhaps the rumors had simply run their credible course.

By October, Emilie was confident enough of her standing with the Lincolns to make a second trip to the White House. The reason for the trip was purely economic. In September, Atlanta had fallen to Sherman. This had dramatically improved Lincoln's chance of reelection — and brought Emilie's cotton within Union lines. If she didn't go and get it now, she figured, it would be seized or burned. The meeting between Lincoln and Little Sister fell quickly into a familiar and profitless pattern, however. Lincoln explained that he had given his amnesty *contingent upon her taking the oath,* which she had never done. In giving her the amnesty document anyway, he had stuck his neck out as far as he could. How would it look if he now gave a permit for cotton — the most sought-after commodity in the country — to the widow of a Confederate general just before the election? Emilie's position was an equally familiar one. With the stroke of a pen her brother-in-law could save her from a lifetime of penury. And she was not *dis*loyal; she was just what a wife should be — respectful of her husband. She had taken an oath to honor him, and honor him she would. Lincoln might have pointed out that she was required to honor Hardin only until they were parted by death — but he did not. He was tired. She was tired. The former tenderness between them seemed locked away somewhere, so she left.

Emilie's trip back to Kentucky was a sad one and the news on her arrival sadder — Levi had died. By his own conduct and preference, Levi's relations with his stepmother and half siblings had long ago soured. Cut loose from the mooring of his marriage in 1859, he had drifted into depravity. He had no house, no business, no friends willing to loan him any more money. In 1861, his wife had died and his kids were sent away. By 1864, there were few left in Lexington who cared what Levi Todd did to himself. On September 12, he had sent the Lincolns a pathetic request for money. Without clothing, without "means of *substincance,*" he stood "in great need of things . . . necessary for the Winter." If the Lincolns could loan him "from $150 to $200," he would return it "without fail" and would not only vote for Lincoln in the coming election but would "bring to the polls many *new recruits.*" The town drunk rarely has a lot of pull with the electorate. In stumping for Lincoln, Levi might have gotten himself beat up, but he could never have turned the state for his brother-in-law. Levi had convinced himself that the plan was workable because it was his only hope. "With the kind assistance of those who ought to be my friends," he told Lincoln, "I will be all right. . . . Rest assured that I will be ever true to you . . . and will travel and talk for you in every crowd." The Lincolns did not respond, and a month later, shortly before Emilie's return, Levi died of "utter want and destitution." Lingering over a protracted suicide, he had finally completed his life's work of drinking himself to death.

For Emilie, her half brother's pathetic end seemed both a shock and a warning. If Levi could die of "want and destitution," so could she. Levi had been an able-bodied man. She was a widow (with three children, no money, and no job skills) whose friends and relatives stood amid the ruin of former farms and fortunes. "With such a sad, such a dreadful lesson," Emilie again wrote the Lincolns to "beg and plead" for a pass that would allow her to go South and attend to her cotton. "The last money I have in the world" is gone, she told them. "I have been a quiet citizen and request only the right which humanity and Justice always give to Widows and Orphans. I also would remind you that your Minnie bullets have made us what we are. . . . If you think I give way to excess of feeling, I beg you will make some excuse for a woman almost crazed with misfortune."

IV.

"YOUR MINNIE bullets have made us what we are. . . ." It was a tough line for a man of Lincoln's tenderness to read. His "Little Sister" held him personally responsible for the war. Was he? He almost didn't know anymore. It had all gone on too long; he was too tired. He did not answer the letter. There was no point. Another Todd was slipping away. Surveying the damage to his in-laws, Lincoln must have noticed: here in one family, his family, was the nation and the war writ small. "Crazed with misfortune," shrill with hate, collapsed in self-interest and grief, the Todds were difficult to look upon. But Lincoln would not have missed the symbolism, the ironies. He had always been attentive to what might be called the familied nature of the conflict. Both literally and figuratively, he was accustomed to think of the war in familied terms. If the Todds did not help shape his interpretation of the war, they certainly resonated with it.

Like everyone who lived through it, Lincoln experienced only a part of the war, a fraction of the whole, and drew his conclusions from his partial experience. He had very little exposure to the war the soldiers knew, for instance. His own military service had been confined to the Black Hawk War, and, by his own admission, the main enemy there had been the mosquitoes. As president, he paraded with soldiers, reviewed their ranks, and visited them in the hospital — but he had no real idea what battle was like. Nor could anyone tell him. In struggling to capture the "incommunicable experience of war," soldiers turned feebly to meteorological metaphors: bullets seemed to "fall like hail" and artillery to "roll like thunder." Such language came naturally to farm people and helped to make familiar what was deeply unnatural and unsettling about the battle experience. But in making such comparisons, soldiers were trying to get at something else. Battle was an assault on their senses. They were blinded by smoke. They were choked with dust and powder. Their eardrums were blown out by their own guns. Even if they weren't shot, they were pelted by pieces of tree, rock, animal, person. It was a "blast of hell sweeping into one's face," a "deadly wind impossible to stand against," a "hurricane of combustibles," a "murderous leaden storm." And when the storm had passed, what remained was hard to believe — a field of "loathsome earth-soiled vestiges of humanity" "kicking like a flock of dead partridges."

This was not the war Lincoln saw. His vantage was a different one. He saw not the dead men but their kin — the ones with the gaping holes in their lives, not their bodies. Widows and orphans, mothers, fathers, and sisters all sobbed their daily way to the White House and begged him to minister to their miseries. And minister he did. "Some of my generals complain that I impair discipline by my frequent pardons and reprieves," Lincoln admitted upon commuting one deserter's death sentence, "but it rests me after a day's hard work, that I can find some excuse for saving some poor fellow's life, and I shall go to bed happy to-night as I think how joyous the signing of this name will make himself, his family and friends." Lincoln's commutations are legendary, of course, but for each one of them he made a dozen quieter adjustments — transferring brothers so they could be in the same regiment, furloughing men to attend to family business, sending a pair of orthopedic boots to a soldier whose sister said he would be a permanent cripple without them. "[Lincoln] did merciful things as stealthily as others committed crimes," Robert G. Ingersoll remembered. "Men and women were continually coming to him with their sorrows," recalled one of Lincoln's assistants. "Now it was a mother asking for her sick or wounded son, that she might take him home with her and nurse him back to health. Then it was another mother, who had given four of her sons to her country and three had fallen in battle and but one was left, and she wanted him. Then it was a group of anxious men and women pleading for the forfeited life of some deserters, or for the establishment of a hospital, or for some other mitigation of the horrors of the war." And Lincoln, more than any other cabinet member, more than any other man in America, gave them a hearing. Perhaps he was a long way from the physical horrors of the battlefield, but the emotional toll of the war literally came home to him, almost every day. As a result, he saw a war the generals didn't — a war that was not a sequence of battles but a vast mosaic of family crises.

If the war was *literally* a family affair for Lincoln, it was also one *figuratively*. Even before the war, he had couched his politics in familial language. With most men of the era, he had routinely referred to "Founding Fathers" and "sister states." Slaveholders were "our Southern brethren," and the discord over slavery threatened our "national feeling of brotherhood." Grown accustomed to such metaphors, Lincoln quite naturally couched the Civil War in familial terms too. "[The United States is the] home of one national family," he reminded Congress in 1862. "We are all of the same family, same sort," he said of Northerners and Southerners in 1863. The rebellion was "this unhappy fraternal war."

In making such statements, it may be argued, Lincoln was only following prevailing practice. In referring to the legislative process as "national housekeeping" or the Mississippi River as the "Father of Waters," he was just being poetical. Lincoln's use of such terms went beyond the poetical and beyond prevailing practice, however. The idea of an American family — its reciprocal obligations and allegiances — lay at the core of his attempt to define the war's meaning. Certainly, he did not ladle on the pap the way the sentimentalists did. His touch was a lighter one — as any good writer's should be. Lincoln did not use familial imagery more often than other politicians — he just used it more effectively.

In the years before the war, for instance, Southern magazines had followed the end logic of their own racial preoccupation and run articles attempting to convince readers that Yankees and Southerners constituted different *races*. The implication was obvious: separation, South from North, made simple ethnic sense. Lincoln, by contrast, believed that Americans were "one national family . . . one united people." He used such language not merely because it sounded good but because nothing else conveyed his meaning. Except that of family, there is, after all, no other relation that *cannot be severed*. Lincoln's union, then, was not just legally but *morally* permanent. There was no President Davis, no rebel government, no such thing as a Confederate — each was what he called a "moral impossibility." He was the president of all the states and all the people within them: "one national family . . . one united people."

Of course, Lincoln's most famous domestic metaphor — the concept of a "house divided" — backfired. In accepting the Republican nomination for Senate in 1858, he had said that "a house divided against itself cannot stand" — a reference to Matthew 12:25: "And Jesus knew their thoughts, and said unto them, Every kingdom divided against itself is brought to desolation; and every city or house divided against itself shall not stand." When Lincoln made the speech, he had no idea that a civil war was coming. He had brought up the sectional divide only to heal it, to remind Americans that they descended from one house and possessed but one house. If they would only put slavery back on the road to ultimate extinction, peace would again reign under their Fathers' roof. Unfortunately, Lincoln's remarks, intended to defuse fratricidal impulses, instead channeled them into politics. By 1861, Southern papers reprinted the parts of the speech that made it seem as if Lincoln thought a civil war inevitable. He had after all strongly implied that a divided people couldn't coexist without destroying each other — they *cannot stand.* How different was that from William Henry Seward's notion that free and slave labor were locked in an "irrepressible conflict"? Lincoln had given his listeners two sons and one house — nature's ultimate recipe for disaster.

The willful misinterpretation of his "House Divided" speech frustrated Lincoln, but it also schooled him. The use of familial imagery, he learned, could cut both ways. It could alleviate tension by drawing on natural allegiances and affections, or it could exacerbate tension by drawing on equally natural rivalries and jealousies. Once he was in office, Lincoln's use of the domestic metaphor became extremely careful. In his Gettysburg Address, he painted with a very fine brush, saying only that "four score and seven years ago our fathers brought forth" (gave birth to) one nation, "conceived in liberty." Here was not one house for two brothers to squabble over. Here was a family that could not fight at all because there was only one member, a single nation, an only child.

Lincoln's affection for the familial metaphor is perhaps most evident in his reading. Given the legal and constitutional crisis secession represented, he might have spent his time perusing Locke, Rousseau, or the Federalist Papers — but he didn't. He walked around with his nose in his Shakespeare, which he often read aloud to those who tarried too long beside him. He had three particular favorites: *Richard III, Hamlet,* and, above all, *Macbeth.* All three are tragedies. (*Richard III* is classified as a history, but it certainly fits the tragic mold.) All three are set in grieving, war-torn countries: Hamlet's Denmark is "contracted in one brow of woe"; Richard's England "hath long been mad, and scarr'd herself"; Macbeth's Scotland is a "down-fall'n birthdom" where "each new morn / New widows howl, new orphans cry, new sorrows / Strike heaven on the face." And in all three cases, the country's wounds are self-inflicted; a division in the ruling family has rent the kingdom and touched off a civil war. Why would Lincoln, who lived such miseries, want to read about them? Because sometimes misery must be fed if it is to build and break. In his favorite plays, Lincoln crawled into a world where houses fall, families divide, and countries bleed in language so beautiful it has to be true. Shakespeare reflected back to Lincoln his own feelings, and allowed him to feel the pain he already felt more intensely, and thus more cathartically. "Let us seek out some desolate shade," the Bard beckoned, "and there / Weep our sad bosoms empty."

There is a final symmetry to the three plays: in each, the plot, as well as the violence, is set in motion by a single act of fratricidal ambition. Richard murders his brother; Claudius (Hamlet's uncle) murders his brother; and Macbeth murders his cousin, all to gain the throne. Lincoln, it has been suggested, perversely identified with these characters. He too had seized a throne and set a country to scarring itself, and his guilty conscience found its echo in these plays' long monologues about the consequences to a man (and his country) when his desire to be great trumps his desire to be good. This may be (very) partly true. Maybe Lincoln did see his ugly face reflected in Richard's. Perhaps he and his wife were as "plotty" as the Macbeths. But surely their country was suffering out of all literary proportion to their crimes. Indulge his guilt as he might, Lincoln knew that he was not, like Richard, "determined to prove a villain." He knew that he could not, as Macbeth did, order the massacre of a rival's family. No, something *was* rotten in Denmark — its offense *was* rank and it did stink to heaven, but it wasn't the Lincolns' ambition.

Precisely what stank about America, Lincoln outlined in his second inaugural address. For 250 years, the country had enriched itself, and debased itself, by enslaving, brutalizing, and raping other human beings. Northerners *and* Southerners had profited by slavery and acquiesced in slavery until finally God Himself had come down to remove it. "I tremble for my country," Jefferson had said, "when I reflect that God is just, that his justice cannot sleep forever." By Lincoln's reckoning, God's justice had awoken, and He intended to mete it out Old Testament–style — fortune was to be repaid by misfortune, and all debts were to be sunk in blood.

Not an inspiring address, when one thinks about it. Lincoln was telling his audience that they were suffering because they deserved to, and, if they went on suffering, well, they had it coming. Never before or since has an American president said such a thing to his people. Never has an American war been conducted with so little righteousness and so much acceptance of blame.

The point of Lincoln's address was not to assign blame, however. Quite the opposite. He was trying to establish a national mood for Reconstruction. Blood had been spilled, he granted, but no revenge could be taken. Northerners had not killed Southerners or vice versa. God had killed them all — and for good reason. The nation's attitude, then, should be that of any other sinner whom God seeketh to chasten: it should submit, and then move more humbly forward: "With malice toward none, with charity for all, with firmness in the right as God gives us to see the right, let us strive on to finish the work we are in, to bind up the nation's wounds, to care for him who shall have borne the battle and for his widow and his orphan, to do all which may achieve and cherish a just and lasting peace among ourselves and with all nations."

It was a message to the thousands of families, like the Todds, united by blood, divided by bloodshed. And it was an answer to Emilie's letter, in its way. They were not his minié balls. He had not made the Todds what they were. They were all in this together, all atoning for 250 years of sin. It might seem unfair that they were paying off dead men's debts, but the wounds the past inflicts on the present are often the most severe. And besides, Lincoln was beginning to suspect that a conflict that seemed to be tearing the country apart was in fact condensing it. "The awful calamity of civil war, which now desolates the land, may be but a punishment, inflicted upon us, for our presumptuous sins," he speculated, but who knew but that it might serve "the needful end of our national reformation as a whole People?"

V.

A MONTH AFTER his inauguration, Lincoln was at Ford's Theatre, laughing at a play he'd already seen, when an actor slipped in behind him, raised a gun to the back of his head, and pulled the trigger. Lincoln's unconscious body was carried to a boarding house across the street; his ghost, not tethered by much, departed the next morning, on April 15, 1865. Historians with an eye for the trivial have noted that at his death Lincoln's pockets contained two pairs of spectacles and a lens polisher, a pocketknife, a watch fob, a linen handkerchief, and a brown leather wallet containing press clippings and a Confederate five-dollar bill. Many have wondered why he would carry the bill on his person, but there is no real mystery. It symbolized his curiosity about, and his commitment to, the other half of his national family.

As news of the assassination rippled out, a distracted nation looked up from its varied pursuits and focused for a single collective moment on a shared spectacle. A president had never been assassinated before, and there were no emotional precedents. In the South the mood was strangely somber. Many had long wanted something bad to happen to Abraham Lincoln, but this was perhaps too bad. And in the little hamlets among the North's common people, where the rail-splitter was a folk hero, the sorrow was palpable. A friend of Lincoln's, John Kasson, was struck by one such scene. His stage had stopped to change horses in the middle of the night, in the middle of nowhere, and he noticed a small telegraph office illuminated in the darkness. A crowd of "villagers and working-men stood half-dressed, many in shirt-sleeves, around the open window [and] as the words were spelled out slowly, one after the other, the operator repeated them, rehearsing with painful distinctness the assassin's shot, the leap on the stage floor, the falling head of the great patriot and martyr, the oozing wound, [and] the escape of the guilty." Scanning the emotions of the crowd, Kasson was struck by the rage and sorrow that, warring to a standoff, had left everyone perfectly still. "There were only . . . gloomy eyes and . . . firm-set teeth," he said, and the "click-click-click" of the telegraph seemed like "the heart of the people throbbing with the pulsations of the passing vitality of their hero, in the deep darkness and silence of the night."

In ways Lincoln would have appreciated, his death, superadded to the war's others, did condense the nation. He passed from life to legend and from legend to myth, becoming the kind of story Americans wanted to tell about themselves. Walt Whitman, long a fan of the president's, was among the first to see the potential of the Lincoln myth. "As I dwell on what I myself heard or saw of the mighty Westerner," he noted, "and blend it with the history and literature of my age, and of what I can get of all ages, and conclude it with his death, it seems like some tragic play, superior to all else I know, vaster and fierier and more convulsive, for this America of ours, than Eschylus or Shakespeare ever drew for Athens or for England." Horace Greeley agreed. If the Civil War was a national tragedy, Lincoln was the "indispensable hero of the great drama."

But casting Lincoln as the hero of a great drama has made it harder for us to see him for what he was. His message of reconciliation was not born of his greatness of heart but of the uniqueness of his circumstances. In 1864, when he told a friend, "I have not suffered by the South . . . [but] with the South," he meant it literally. The Todds were a complicated swirl of affection and obligation, embarrassment and endurance. But they were, for better and often worse, Lincoln's family. In reporting on the president's final interment, a witness noted that in scanning the crowd "no blood relatives of Mr. Lincoln were to be found . . . none answering to his name could be discovered." "Mrs. Lincoln's relatives," however, "were present . . . in some force."

Epilogue

THE TODDS did not die with Lincoln, though the country (and history) lost interest in them as quickly as if they had. Having introduced the Todds in the order in which they were born, it only seems right to part with them in the order in which they exited the stage:

David (1871)

A WEEK BEFORE the war ended, David Todd married a well-off widow, Susie Williamson. Paroled from the army shortly after, he settled in Huntsville, where he operated as a merchant and lived comfortably on his wife's inheritance. In 1869, Congress opened an inquiry into prison abuses, and David Todd's name came up more than once. Though he had served as their commandant for only two months at the very beginning of the war, former inmates of the Richmond prison system singled him out as uniquely nasty. One prisoner testified that Todd "deserved hanging as richly as did Wirtz." Another corrected him — Todd deserved it more: "Had Todd been at Andersonville, with Wirz's opportunities, he would, I believe have killed more men than his pupil did. Wirz killed to please his superiors; Todd, from personal delight in human blood and suffering."

David's health declined rapidly after the war, though the exact circumstances have been confused over the years. An issue of *Flake's Bulletin* (Galveston) was the first to muddy the waters when it claimed in 1867 that David had been "killed toward the end of the war" — despite the fact that he was still alive. According to Emilie, her brother "was wounded by a bullet in his lungs, lingered for a few years and died after the close of the war." In another statement, she said that by the time she went to the White House in 1863, two of her brothers had been killed: "one at Corinth, the other at Baton Rouge, and the third one was slowly dying from a wound received at Vicksburg." Following her mother's lead, Katherine Helm noted in her 1928 book, *Mary, Wife of Lincoln,* that her uncle David "lay mortally wounded after the battle of Vicksburg." Deliberately or otherwise, these and other sources have contributed to the myth that, though he did not actually die until 1871, David was somehow a casualty of the war. Given his instinct for self-promotion, David may have originated the claim himself, and he certainly would have appreciated so many historians repeating it.

But the better evidence contradicts the claim. First, David himself wrote to his mother that he had escaped Vicksburg without a scratch. Second, in 1861, before he had ever been in combat, David was seen in a Richmond hotel vomiting up blood like a harpooned whale. Third, short obituary notices appearing in 1871 in the *Galveston Tri-Weekly News* and the *Philadelphia Inquirer* list David's cause of death as "consumption." Finally, according to a few friends, David *was* shot through the lungs — before the war in a "whore-house brawl" — and this had more to do with his "early demise" than any "Yankee Minie."

A likely casualty, then, of the whorehouse and not the battlefield, David Todd took his last ragged breath on July 30, 1871, at the age of thirty-nine. Shortly after he heard the news, the Union surgeon Charles Gray, who had attended to David in 1861, reopened his prison diary. Next to where he had penned David's claim that "he was not born to die in his bed," Gray added a note: "He *did* die in his bed, or some one else's bed, after all, but waited altogether too long before doing it."

Betsey (1874)

AS GUNS FELL SILENT and mail traffic opened back up, Southern friends wrote to Betsey to assure her that they had followed her "peculiar situation during the terrible war" and had condoled with her during her "sad bereavements." She didn't say much in return. Instead, she waited until after her death to make a definitive statement, when she had erected on her gravesite a monument not to herself but her sons.

The twelve-foot obelisk is inscribed "In memory of my boys, Samuel B. Todd, David H. Todd and Alexander H. Todd, all Confederate soldiers." On a nearby marker for Sam and Aleck, Betsey had written, "By their deeds ye shall know them." She might as well have said, "By their deeds ye shall know *me*."

Martha (1868), Kitty (1875), and Elodie (1877)

MARTHA'S HUSBAND, the "thin and feeble" Clement White, somehow survived the war by more than thirty years. Martha, despite her reputation for vivacity, survived it by only three. She died of undisclosed causes in Anna, Illinois, in 1868 at the age of thirty-five.

Kitty also made an early departure. In 1866, she married William Wallace Herr, the man who had helped bear Hardin's body from the field at Chickamauga. Like her mother, Kitty was nothing if not fertile, but she didn't have her mother's luck. In 1875, ten days after giving birth to her fifth child, she died at the age of thirty-three.

Elodie too had a checkered pregnancy history. After losing Alex in infancy, she gave birth to a healthy baby boy, Henry, in 1864. While he could not replace the brothers lost or sisters scattered by the war, he came pretty close. As a cousin put it, the boy's laugh helped to "drown the troubles of the times."

In 1869, Elodie added another boy to the household, Lawrence Percy Dawson, who would go on to marry his first cousin, a daughter of the Kelloggs'. Unfortunately, Elodie's health declined after Percy was born. Having lost his first two wives to the birthing couch, Nathaniel did not want to lose another. But he was not careful enough. In 1877, Elodie became pregnant a fourth time, and she had a vague sense that her luck was running out. "I try to console myself," she wrote Emilie, "that my health can scarcely be worse than for the past year without being a permanent invalid or dying."

By late summer Elodie was bedridden with piles (which we call hemorrhoids) and neuralgia (a nerve pain that often follows an outbreak of shingles). Both can be brought on by pregnancy; neither is life-threatening. Unfortunately, Elodie's doctor treated her with morphine and heavy doses of chloroform, which, over the course of months, certainly killed her pain and probably killed her baby. The doses were eventually discontinued, but on the morning of November 14, Elodie "became restless & complained so much" that the doctor gave her another shot of morphine. This one put her down permanently. The next afternoon, Elodie "could not be aroused" and gave "birth to a still-born male suddenly (*in a moment*) and without evidences of pain or consciousness." Devastated, Nathaniel sent for another doctor, but it was too late. "I found [Mrs. D.] impossible to arouse," the doctor noted, "with high fever, pulse so rapid that I could not count it & breathing rapidly & laboriously. Nothing [we] could do availed anything, and she breathed her last at 7:35 P.M." Elodie was thirty-seven.

Mary (1882)

FOR WEEKS AFTER the assassination, Mary lolled inconsolably in a White House bedroom while servants and interlopers looted the downstairs and Andrew Johnson, the new president, worked out of a tiny office at the Treasury. When finally she did pack up and leave, the city and the nation seemed glad to be rid of her. In truth, they had never liked her and not even for Lincoln's sake were they were going to start now. Though she had been holding her husband's hand when he was shot in the head, she would always remain to a merciless nation a pathetic, but never a pitiable, figure.

Why? Her sister Elizabeth said it best: "Mary has had much to bear though she don't bear it well; She has acted foolishly — unwisely and made the world hate her." No biography of Mary Lincoln has ever explained it better. She did have much to bear. All that might have made her content with herself — her boys, her husband, her "advancement" — were stripped from her. She ascended to the White House only to have a son die and a husband murdered; Lincoln became a martyr to the Civil War while she became a scapegoat. Neither was her "baptism of sorrow" complete in 1865. In 1871, at the age of eighteen, Tad came down with pleurisy and wheezed his way out of the world strapped upright for a month in a sleeping chair. In 1875, Mary's only remaining son, Robert had her committed, betraying her so completely that she would refer to him as a "monster of mankind." The entirety of her life had unfolded like the final scene of a Shakespearean tragedy. Mother dead early, father dead early, extended family shattered, nuclear family eradicated, she was left alone on the stage, alone on the planet.

Given her disappointments, it is sad that Mary's contemporaries expected her to "bear it well." But they did. A widow, they believed, ought to mourn with decorum. She would be pitied only to the extent that she refused to pity herself and stoically accepted God's plan. Mary did none of these things. Her suffering, she claimed, was not merely inconsolable but incomparable. "No *such sorrow* was ever visited upon a people or a family," she said, as if it were a contest. And to make sure that people knew she was winning the contest, she *always* wore black, *always* wrote on black-bordered stationery. And self-pity dripped from her as she wrote. "Marked out by fate for sorrow," she endured a "daily crucifixion" that would end only at the grave. Her contemporaries, however, refused to see a woman who might be redeemed by suffering; they saw instead a diva of grief whose histrionic performances seemed an unwelcome encore to a life of indulgence and aggrandizement.

Many thought she was just plain crazy — including her son Robert, who in 1875 had her committed to Bellevue Place, an insane asylum in Batavia, Illinois. In truth, though, Mary's was a disordered but not a deranged mind. Her spiritualism, coupled with her medications, made her see strange things and say strange things, but her hovering dead did no one any harm and were one of her few remaining consolations. "I would not care to live a day," she wrote a friend, without "the beautiful & consoling belief that our beloved ones, whose home is in Heaven can, unseen by us, enter into our midst, witness the anguish we suffer [and] console us by their invisible presence."

More problematic than her ghosts was her monomania on the subject of money. Mary was a sort of financial bulimic. The control of money, not food, alternately stabilized and destabilized her psyche. She horded and spent in an endless cycle of indulgence and regret. Having refigured her personal vulnerability and personal insecurity as financial vulnerability and financial insecurity, she stitched bonds into her dress, haggled with clerks, became paranoid that people were out to steal from her, tackily sold off her dresses, petitioned Congress for cash, and complained of penury — all in the face of the irrefutable fact that Lincoln's estate had left her relatively well off. She did not want the money for itself, however; money had come to represent love, and justice — and no one can have enough of those. When the Grants were given a house, when the widow Garfield was given a larger pension, when the public failed to pay enough for her dresses — Mary took it personally because she was not being properly *valued*. In revenge, she revalued herself in occasional binges of purchasing. Curtains she'd never need or gloves in numbers she could never use — the items themselves didn't matter. Shopping made her feel important and pampered;

pretty things distracted her from ugly realities. None of this made her crazy, but it did make her embarrassing — especially to Robert — who finally convinced himself that confining his mother was the only way to control her.

Ultimately, it was Elizabeth who helped to rescue Mary from Bellevue. The sisters had been estranged since the war, but when her doctor (and jailer) asked Mary if she had any option to confinement, she did not hesitate. "It is the most natural thing in the world to live with my sister," she told him. "She raised me and I regard her as a sort of mother." Elizabeth agreed, and gently reconciled Robert to the idea of restoring Mary's freedom to embarrass him. He groused a little about his "Aunt Lizzie's interference with [his] painful duty," but Robert eventually acceded, and Mary was returned to the Edwardses. There, on the top floor, her cataracts having all but claimed her eyesight, she turned ever-tighter circles until the lights went out on July 16, 1882.

Elizabeth (1888), Ann (1891), and Frances (1899)

IN ADDITION to Elizabeth, Ann and Frances remained in Springfield for some years after the war. The Edwardses continued to live in the house on the hill, though it was a quieter place than it had been during what Elizabeth called "the happy era of my existence." In 1865, Ninian retired from his various professions and shifts; Elizabeth retired as a hostess. "We are both unusually feeble," she admitted. "I do not think that any other persons ever grew old so rapidly." The postwar period she called her "somber years." Mostly she just felt tired. She had been a mother too long — to her sisters, her children, her grandchildren. Mary plagued her and paced her ceiling. But there were problems too with her eldest daughter, Julia. Beautiful, the girl also proved flighty, flirtatious, and risqué. In a letter to Robert Todd Lincoln, Elizabeth admitted, "Insanity appeared . . . in the case of my own daughter, at the early age of thirteen." Married at eighteen, Julia was not mentally responsible enough for monogamy. A "wayward girl" for much of her life, she was susceptible to sexual predators, and in 1872, her behavior became so scandalous that she and her husband had to escape to Argentina. It was a blow Elizabeth "never recovered from." "The disappointments and sorrows of life have touched me most keenly," she admitted to Emilie. "[Only] a lingering desire to promote the pleasure of others [can] draw me out of the seclusion I certainly most enjoy." Elizabeth found the ultimate seclusion, and her final rest, on February 22, 1888, at the age of seventy-four.

Ann and Frances fared a little better in the postwar period. Though remembered as "the most quick tempered and vituperative . . . of all the sisters" (no mean claim), Ann buried herself in her fancy work (needle-point) and traveled occasionally to Cincinnati to buy new patterns and material. She and Clark sold their store sometime after 1870, and Ann, at least, moved out west, where she died in California in 1891.

Frances almost immediately became a widow after the war. Her husband, William Wallace, supposedly died "from exposure in the service," though that seems a broad interpretation. As an army paymaster, Wallace might have been exposed to camp diseases or the elements. But his physician, Charles Ryan, was quite specific about his symptoms. Wallace, he said, suffered from suppurating "fistulous openings" in his urinary tract that caused him to leak like a dicky garden hose. The source of the infection could have been venereal, or perhaps staphylococcal, given the accompanying fever. The openings were cauterized with silver nitrate, and Wallace tried to catheterize himself regularly, but he found the procedure difficult and frustrating. When he passed in 1867, he was probably quite relieved. Frances was then only forty-nine. She waited until the kids were grown and then "sweetly situated" herself in a "cozy cottage." She had been described in childhood as "taciturn . . . cold & reserved," so she may rather have enjoyed being on her own. She died in 1899 at the age of eighty-four.

George (1902)

IN 1861, Elodie and Martha had been the "toast of Southerners" at the Davises' inaugural ball. Just as there were Todds present at the Confederate birth, there was a Todd present at its death. When Richmond fell in 1865, the rebel cabinet fled south by train. Optimistic if not delusional, Davis believed his government-on-wheels could reassemble somewhere farther south and continue the fight. Most of those with him admired his gumption and despaired at his density. The fight now was to save him from hanging. Despite the need for speed and secrecy, however, Davis and the entourage ambled slowly southward through towns that seemed to expect them. Followed with a different kind of intensity was the progress of the Confederate treasury cars. A mountain of gold and silver was rolling past famished civilians, and paroled soldiers rightly groused that they had never been properly paid.

George intercepted the fugitive government somewhere in South Carolina. It is hard to know what attracted him to the scene or why he felt entitled to play a part in it. In picking his way to the front of the column, he fell in with some Virginia and Kentucky soldiers who thought the treasury should be divided up among the men. The Yankees, they felt, would certainly fall upon it if it remained all together — better that it should be distributed among its rightful owners, the Southern people, or at least a select group of them. Having convinced themselves of the soundness of their logic, they meant either to "have some of the money or have blood."

When George reached the cabinet he told Breckinridge, now secretary of war, that if there wasn't a general paying out "there might be rioting and bloodshed." Breckinridge was quietly appalled, but he had heard similar rumblings from others. Desperate to ensure that the Confederacy, which had begun as a "magnificent epic," did not "terminate in a farce," he agreed to dole out the silver. Somehow, George was not only present at the payout but received a share. Afterward, he and some of the other officers exchanged their silver for a part of the gold reserves they were carrying for the Richmond Bank at what they all agreed was a "rough estimate" of the market price. Though Davis's capture a few days later may fairly be regarded as the death knell of the Confederacy, this moment of supreme selfishness, in which George amply participated, can be seen as the moment when the Confederacy's last defenders turned from sacrificing for their government to scavenging it.

Now with a jingle in his pocket, George married Martha Lyles, whom he had met during a short stint at the Wayside Hospital in Camden, South Carolina. Martha was sixteen years George's junior. Perhaps the dramatic reduction in eligible men her own age had left her desperate. Perhaps she just loved George. In 1870, she gave birth to a son, George Jr., and the couple sold their house in Camden and moved a hundred miles south to Barnwell.

George had a long and successful medical practice in Barnwell, and he was described by local papers as a "prominent physician" and a "surgeon of no mean repute." In 1892, however, he ran into some legal trouble after a coroner's inquest found him responsible for the deaths of a "young white woman" and her baby. According to newspapers, the girl had been "led astray by the overtures of a young railroad contractor from the West" and had died as a result of "an abortion committed by Dr. G.R.C. Todd." George was subsequently arrested, indicted for "malpractice" and performance of a "criminal operation," and held on $1,500 bail pending his appearance at the Court of General Sessions. Community opinion was "about evenly divided" on the criminality of George's actions, and the case may never have gone to trial. But the Todd name had been raised again, and not in a favorable light. Under titles such as "A South Carolina Sensation" and "A Shocking Affair," the articles did not fail to mention that George was not only an abortionist but the "brother-in-law of Abraham Lincoln."

Martha died in 1889. George Jr. left home then or before. He and his father had been consistent disappointments to each other. His wife dead, his son fled, George withdrew into bitterness. According to his lawyer, he "lived alone, and was given to moods of deep melancholy." As a last act of spite, he deeded his house to a neighbor rather than see it go to his son. He died at home, purposely or not, from an overdose of self-administered chloroform. George Jr. then crept back into town. The neighbor, who hadn't the old doctor's spite, happily deeded the house back to him. He sold it as quickly as he could and again disappeared.

Margaret (1904)

MARGARET TODD KELLOGG lived the rest of her life in and around Cincinnati with her three single daughters. In 1900, the eldest, Minnie, was thirty-seven, still unmarried, and a stenographer. The youngest, Alice, did eventually marry—her first cousin Percy Dawson. The middle daughter, Anita, however, was probably the most interesting. She toured the country in the 1890s as "a lecturer upon English literature, an elocutionist and a linguist." The handbill advertising her dramatic readings includes a hilariously cool endorsement from Oliver Wendell Holmes — "So far as I have looked through your poems, they struck me quite favorably" — but also a warmer one — "well worthy of the highest approbation" — from her uncle N.H.R. Dawson.

Margaret's husband, Charles, died in Tampa, Florida, in 1892. Margaret also went there to die. She expired in a Daytona Beach hotel room in 1904 at the age of seventy-five.

Emilie (1930)

EMILIE LIVED the longest. She survived her husband by almost seventy years; her mother by sixty; her younger sisters by more than fifty; Mary Lincoln by more than forty. She never remarried. She lived as the widow of General Benjamin Hardin Helm for the better part of seven decades. And, unlike Mary, she did it with perfect propriety. As an 1867 magazine article reminded her, names like Breckinridge, Buckner, Hanson, and Helm would "live as long as ... [Kentucky's] fair daughters can preserve green by grateful tears the dearest, and most brilliant memories of their hearts."

This, then, was Emilie's job, her job for life — to preserve green by *grateful* tears, to cry happily forever. As a sort of professional widow, she organized for the UDC, clipped clippings, researched Todd family genealogy, and puffed up proxies of her husband in long written paeans to Braxton Bragg and John Hunt Morgan. It was as if her diary entry had been a prediction for her life, not a lament: "War. War the sole theme."

Emilie was not an embittered ex-Confederate, however. She helped her daughter write an early biography of Mary Lincoln that downplayed the Todds' division and upheld national reconciliation. Practicing what she preached, she maintained warm relations with the Northern wing of the family and grew especially close to Robert Todd Lincoln. Though she was technically his aunt, Emilie and Robert are better understood as coevals. They had "romped around" together as children, and Emilie had spent six months in Springfield, where Robert remembered her as a "very pretty girl." After the war the two became close friends. The affinity between them was partly emotional, partly circumstantial. Both had been estranged from Mary but had always loved her. Both had the odd sense of being the ones whom God had left to stand. (Robert survived his father by seventy years; his brothers by more than fifty; his mother by almost forty.) And both were understood by the public as simultaneously less and more than what they really were — Emilie would always be Helm's widow, Robert would always be Lincoln's son. Both groomed the men they stood behind, and did so without resentment, but both were happy to escape such things with each other. In sending Emilie money enough to visit him in Vermont, Robert said that she simply must accept it. "You must not think ill [of] a nephew who loves you as much as I do."

On February 20, 1930, Emilie had a heart attack. Knowing she was running out of time, she took her wartime diary out to the backyard and burned it. Seeing the fire, her daughter came running: "Mother, why would you burn your diary?" "[Because]," Emilie responded, "there's too much bitterness in it." By her own writing and through her daughter's writing, Emilie had done more than anyone to remove the bitterness from the Todds. Now she had some unwriting to do. One version of the past needed to be buried that another might live. She died later that day, at the age of ninety-three.

What was Emilie trying to hide from posterity? Some of her secrets were undoubtedly personal: details about herself and her marriage, moments when raw emotion lashed uncharitably out at the world. Others of her secrets were probably familial. For her children's sake, if not for her own, she wanted to bequeath to history a certain version of the Todds; she wanted them remembered as she remembered them, as a family of Bluegrass patriots who had seen their duty and done it, however tragic the consequences.

But the truth is, the Todds were not a tragic but rather a sad family. Of fourteen children, six died before the age of forty. Sam was shot in the back while retreating. Aleck was shot by his own men. David was shot in a brothel. Levi was a drunk, George an abortionist. And yet it is this version of the Todds, the one Emilie wanted to hide, that Lincoln learned the most from. Sadly, the most vital lesson he learned from the Todds he never got a chance to teach them: People, like families and nations, must own their flaws if they are to move forward.

Acknowledgments

THIS BOOK BEGAN five years ago when Susan Ferber, an editor at Oxford University Press, called me a bonehead. She did not use that term *exactly*, but whatever gentle word she did use translated to "bonehead" in Susan-ese. She had just finished reading a draft of my first book, *All That Makes a Man*, and had run across a footnote in which I suggested that somebody really needed to write the remarkable story of the Todds. "Here," I said, "is the first family of the United States, divided by the Civil War and redeemed by Abraham Lincoln (sort of). Somebody needs to write this!" "Take that note out," Susan told me, "and write *The Todds* yourself."

Five years later, I am glad Susan called me a bonehead. Her insight and her friendship over the years have made this book possible, and I am deeply grateful.

I began this project in excited disbelief: No biography of the Todds had been written. No study had examined Lincoln's interactions with the Todds. No one had juxtaposed Lincoln's attempt to save the national family with his attempt to save his own family. No book had examined the degree to which the Todds may have helped to shape Lincoln's emotional experience (and unique interpretation) of the Civil War. Indeed, the only books that had treated the Todds in any sustained way were seriously old: W. A. Evans's *Mrs. Abraham Lincoln* (1932); William H. Townsend's *Lincoln and His Wife's Hometown* (1929); and Katherine Helm's *The True Story of Mary, Wife of Lincoln* (1928).

How could this be? I wondered. How could such an important subject have been neglected for so long?

The answer came readily: the records that might support the Todds' story were thin and scattered across the country. Being a bonehead, I staggered on anyway, and two things saved my bacon: new technologies and the host of scholars and archivists I met along the way. About the new technologies, I'll only say what every historian already knows: this is a great time to be practicing our craft. With the click of a few keys, I scanned millions of pages of dead newspapers for every instance of the word "Todd." I browsed the census in my bathrobe and read the collected works of Abraham Lincoln while munching Doritos. Technology has revolutionized what we do.

But much of what we do, thank goodness, is still conducted in the old way — amid stacks of letters and diaries with cotton content so high, the pages feel like fabric. I logged a lot of miles tracking Todds to their burrows in the nation's various archives, and I discovered that the road can be a rugged and lonely place. Boiling the last packet of a case of Ramen Pride noodles on a hot plate in a Super 8, listening to a drunken Kentucky knife fight go down in the parking lot, I had to ask myself what I was doing so far from my family. But always in the morning, I would walk into a place of entombed secrets and whispering ghosts, and the archivist would meet me with a ready smile and a readier brain, and I would feel nothing but gratitude.

In particular, I want to thank: Ken Williams, Lynne Hollingsworth, Tom Stephens, and Charlene Smith at the Kentucky Historical Society; Mark Wetherington and Jim Holmberg at the Filson Historical Society; Bill Marshall and Jason Frahardy at the University of Kentucky; Jim Prichard at the Kentucky Department of Libraries and Archives; Cindy VanHorn at the Lincoln Museum in Fort Wayne; Cheryl Schnirring, Glenna Schroeder-Lein, and Debbie Hamm at the Abraham Lincoln Presidential Library; Ana Ramirez-Luhrs and Jody Cary at the Gilder Lehrman Collection; B. J. Gooch at Transylvania University; Michael Lynch and Steven Wilson at Lincoln Memorial University; Mary Lou Eichhorn at the Historic New Orleans Collection; Steve Tuttle at the South Carolina Department of Archives and History; and Gwen Thompson at the Mary Todd Lincoln House. I am also grateful to the scholars Michael Burlingame, Wayne C. Temple, Richard McMurtry, Jason Emerson, and Randolph Hollingsworth for their generosity in sharing their own research. The Kentucky Historical Society, Filson Historical Society, Gilder Lehrman Institute, and National Endowment for the Humanities each funded different phases of this project, and I deeply appreciate their support.

On the writing side of things, Eamon Dolan, Sasheem Silkiss-Hero, and Alison Kerr Miller at Houghton Mifflin labored tirelessly to make this a better book and endured with good spirit many an authorial idiosyncrasy.

I want finally to acknowledge some personal debts. My agent, Andrew Wylie, has my undying gratitude for his advice and support. Gavin Campbell inspired me by his friendship, his wizardry with words, and the swift boot he applied to my backside whenever I threatened to do something beneath myself. His father, Colonel William Campbell, took over my field operations in Lexington and served so ably, I shall promote him to four-star historian. Others contributed in less direct but no less important ways: my parents; my brother, Pat, and my sister, Margaret; my "brothers" Clay Riley and Stephen Rosbough; and my colleagues at Pembroke, most especially Mark and Lucinda Thompson, Margaret Crites, Bruce DeHart, Scott Billingsley and Robert Brown. My wife (and best friend), Frances, has my undying love, and my boy, Will, contributed copious amounts of drool to the final product and every day proves himself a (suspiciously odiferous) miracle. I love him so.

Notes

Abbreviations and Short Titles Used in Notes

ALPL — Abraham Lincoln Presidential Library, Springfield, Illinois
CHS — Chicago Historical Society
CW — *Collected Works of Abraham Lincoln*, ed. Roy P. Basler (New Bruswick, N.J.: Rutgers University Press, 1953)
Filson — Filson Historical Society, Louisville, Kentucky
GLC — Gilder Lehrman Collection, New York Historical Society
HI — *Herndon's Informants: Letters, Interviews and Statements about Abraham Lincoln*, ed. Douglas L. Wilson and Rodney O. Davis (Urbana: University of Illinois Press, 1998)
KDLA — Kentucky Department of Libraries and Archives, Frankfort, Kentucky
KHS — Kentucky Historical Society, Frankfort, Kentucky
LM — The Lincoln Museum, Fort Wayne, Indiana
LMU — Lincoln Memorial University, Harrogate, Tennessee
LOC — Library of Congress
OR — *Official Records of the War of the Rebellion*
SHC — Southern Historical Collection, University of North Carolina at Chapel Hill
T&T — *Mary Todd Lincoln: Her Life and Letters*, eds. Justin G. Turner and Linda Levitt Turner (New York: Knopf, 1972)
UKY — Margaret I. King Library, University of Kentucky, Lexington

PAGE **Introduction**

vii "The division of 'house against house'": Quoted in James C. Klotter, *The Breckinridges of Kentucky, 1790–1981* (Lexington: University Press of Kentucky, 1986), p. 80.

From the house on Eighth and Jackson: J. Duane Squires, "Lincoln's Todd In-Laws," *Lincoln Lore* (1968) includes the line "At every emergency, and there were many, the cry went from the White House to the Todd in-laws, 'Come.' And they always did." I am indebted to Squires for the language and the concept of a family that, whatever their difficulties, mobilized to meet true crises.

viii "In the scramble for jobs": Jean H. Baker, *Mary Todd Lincoln: A Biography* (New York: W. W. Norton, 1987), p. 203.

"villainous aspersions": Mary Lincoln to Abram Wakeman, September 23, 1864, T&T, p. 180. Mary was reacting to another charge of favoritism to presidential relatives that had appeared in the *New York World,* September 22, 1864.

If the Todds weren't Lincoln's family, then who was?: Mark E. Neely, Jr., and Harold Holzer put it this way: "[W]hen Abraham Lincoln married Mary Todd, he divorced his family for hers." Neely and Holzer, *The Lincoln Family Album* (New York: Doubleday, 1990), p. 7. Lincoln himself reflected on the fact that he was bereft of family: "The present subject has no brother or sister of the whole or half blood. He had a sister, older than himself, who was grown and married, but died many years ago, leaving no child. Also a brother, younger than himself, who died in infancy." Paul M. Zall, ed., *Lincoln on Lincoln* (Lexington: University Press of Kentucky, 1999), p. 8.

ix malicious, miserable: Mary Lincoln to Elizabeth Todd Grimsley, September 29, 1861, T&T, p. 105.

"Mary was writing": W. A. Evans, *Mrs. Abraham Lincoln: A Study of Her Personality and Her Influence on Lincoln* (New York: Knopf, 1932), p. 47.

"I am a *Todd*": Elodie Todd to Nathaniel Dawson, May 23, 1861, Dawson Papers, SHC.

"One 'd' was good enough for God": Like most of his gags, Lincoln used this one in various forms, making an authoritative version impossible. According to one source, Lincoln acquired the gag from the politician David Tod, governor of Ohio, during the Civil War: "One evening when Tod was in town Lincoln invited him over to the White House. They had a long chat together, when Lincoln finally said: 'Look here, Tod, how is it that you spell your name with only one d?' . . . Old Tod looked at Lincoln for a moment . . . then replied: 'Mr. President, God spells his name with only one d, and what is good enough for God is good enough for me.' Lincoln used to repeat this story to some of his more intimate friends, and every time he did so he would laugh until the tears ran down over that furrowed but grand face." According to another "family tradition," relayed by a Todd relative, Lincoln used a variation of the line on his father-in-law in the 1840s: "After Lincoln had been married for some time, and had written several letters to his wife's folks, the old man Todd, Mrs. Lincoln's father, came for a visit. After the customary greetings had taken place between father-in-law and son-in-law, Mr. Todd said 'Abe, you are always bragging on your abilities as a speller; how does it come that you always address me with the surname spelled with a single "d," T-o-d?' Abe's reply came quick and to the point; 'Well, dad, ever since I can remember God has been spelling his name with a single "d," and he is certainly of a family equally as prominent as any of the Todds.'" Both "origin" stories have their problems (the idea of Lincoln calling his father-in-law "dad," for instance), and they cannot both be right. The truth is probably this: the gag has existed for as long as there have been Todds and Tods. Given his appetite for such things, and his panache for working them into conversation, Lincoln undoubtedly picked the gag up and made it his own in a variety of contexts and phrasings. See "Why Mr. Tod Scorned the Double D," *Boston Traveler*, August 6, 1886, and "The Byes and Todds," *Knoxville (Iowa) Journal*, February 12, 1909, clippings at the Lincoln Museum, Fort Wayne.

xi biographies of Mary mention the irony of her Confederate connections but nothing more: Jean H. Baker's *Mary Todd Lincoln* is an exception. She does not treat the Southern Todds in depth, but she does recognize (and demonstrate) their impact on Mary's life.

xiii "Feuds which exist": *Congressional Globe*, 36th Cong., 1st sess., new series . . . no. 35, Wednesday, January 25, 1860, p. 546.

"We are divorced": C. Van Woodward, ed., *Mary Chesnut's Civil War* (New Haven: Yale University Press, 1981), p. 25.

1. Bluegrass Beginnings

2 The Kentucky militia would be mustered: My account of the battle of the Blue Licks is drawn primarily from "The Life of Colo. John Todd," Draper Manuscripts 5C51 (pp. 51.1–51.19), Wisconsin Historical Society. Boone's activities during the battle are best documented in Michael A. Lofaro, *Daniel Boone: An American Life* (Lexington: University Press of Kentucky, 2003), pp. 125–29, and John Mack Faragher, *Daniel Boone: The Life and Legend of an American Pioneer* (New York: Henry Holt, 1992), pp. 217–24.

Boone had eventually escaped . . . his men were not as lucky: See Ted Franklin Belue, "Terror in the Canelands: The Fate of Daniel Boone's Salt Boilers," *Filson Club Quarterly* 68, no. 1 (1994): pp. 3–34; William Dodd Brown, ed., "The Capture of Daniel Boone's Saltmakers: Fresh Perspectives from Primary Sources," *Register of the Kentucky Historical Society* 83, no. 1 (1985): pp. 1–18.

3 There was nothing Todd could do: See Michael C. C. Adams, "An Appraisal of the Blue Licks Battle," *Filson Club Historical Quarterly* 75, no. 2 (2001): pp. 181–203.

5 Recriminations followed directly upon grief: See Lofaro, *Daniel Boone*, p. 130; Faragher, *Daniel Boone*, pp. 222–23.

Such finger-pointing did not last long: See Lofaro, *Daniel Boone*, p. 129.

6 John Todd was not ridiculed: See Jean H. Baker, *Mary Todd Lincoln: A Biography* (New York: Norton, 1987), p. 7.

John Todd's massacre . . . was a great legacy to his family: Eventually public opinion began to turn against John Todd, and his descendants took steps to protect his memory. Two of Levi's sons, for instance, discussed placing documents in the Kentucky Historical Society that would put the entire stink on McGary. See David Todd to Robert Todd, January 6, 1848, in Pirtle and Rogers Family Papers, Filson. On the Todds' declension, see the sometimes ludicrously uncharitable W. A. Evans, *Mrs. Abraham Lincoln*, pp. 31–64.

The Todd family now lived at Ellerslie: See Baker, *Mary Todd Lincoln*, pp. 7–8.

7 Robert Todd had . . . a sorrier war record: See ibid., pp. 12–13. His record could not have been too sorry, however, because in 1855 Robert's wife was given a land grant of 160 acres as compensation for his service.

8   "Doctors are gentlemen": Caroline M. De Costa, "The Contagiousness of Childbed Fever: A Short History of Puerperal Sepsis and Its Treatment," *Medical Journal of Australia* 77 (2002): pp. 668–71. See also Sherwin B. Nuland, *The Doctors' Plague: Germs, Childbed Fever, and the Strange Story of Ignac Semmelweis* (New York: W. W. Norton, 2003), and Irvine Loudon, *The Tragedy of Childbed Fever* (New York: Oxford University Press, 2000).

10 "To have the promise of your hand": Robert S. Todd to Elizabeth Humphreys, December 24, 1825, William Henry Townsend Collection, hereafter Townsend Collection, UKY.

11 "My ideas of the felicity": Robert S. Todd to Elizabeth Humphreys, February 15, 1826, Townsend Collection, UKY.
    "I must beg leave to remind you": Robert S. Todd to Elizabeth Humphreys, October 9, 1826, Townsend Collection, UKY.
    "I am sure if you knew my situation": Robert S. Todd to Elizabeth Humphreys, October 23, 1826, Townsend Collection, UKY.
    "I am anxious for that period": Robert S. Todd to Elizabeth Humphreys, January 7, 1826, Townsend Collection, UKY.
    "I think I have some little cause": Robert S. Todd to Elizabeth Humphreys, February 15, 1826, Townsend Collection, UKY.
    "I fully expected to have heard from you": Robert S. Todd to Elizabeth Humphreys, October 23, 1826, Townsend Collection, UKY.

12 "a large family of boys and girls": Elizabeth L. Norris to Emily Todd Helm, September 28, 1895, William H. Townsend Papers, hereafter Townsend Papers, ALPL.

13 "very thin & badly": Henrietta M. Brown to Louisa V. Rucks, September 27, 1829, Joseph Adger Stuart Papers, Filson.
    "Sally was a jewel": Quoted in Katherine Helm, *Mary, Wife of Lincoln* (New York: Harper, 1928), p. 23.

14 "[Sally] preach[ed] the gospel" and "Mammy . . . Do you think you could have dreamed": Ibid., pp. 23–26. See also William H. Townsend, *Lincoln and the Bluegrass: Slavery and Civil War in Kentucky* (Lexington: University Press of Kentucky, 1955), pp. 72–73.
    The town of Lexington: On early music in Lexington, see Joy Carden, *Music in Lexington Before 1840* (Cincinnati: C. J. Krehbiel Company, 1980), p. 50. On Lexington as "the Great Hat Market," see Frances L. S. Dugan and Jacqueline P. Bull, eds., *Bluegrass Craftsman: Being the Reminiscences of Ebenezer Hiram Stedman, Papermaker, 1808–1885* (Lexington: University of Kentucky Press, 1959), p. 61.

15 Lexington's veneer of respectability: See Carden, *Music in Lexington,* p. v.
    "If you go into the Northern states": Robert M. Ireland, "Homicide in Nineteenth Century Kentucky," *Register of the Kentucky Historical Society* 81, no. 2 (1983): pp. 134–53; quotation, pp. 136–37.

16 "A Man might Get Drunk": Dugan and Bull, *Bluegrass Craftsman,* p. 23.
    "Them days the Bank officers": Ibid., p. 181.
    the governor's own son killed the man: See Hal Morris, ed., "Murder, Banking, and Kentucky Politics, 1824," *Jacksonian Miscellanies* 39 (November 1997).

17 "I think I never saw": William Preston to S. Preston, February 2, 1837, Preston Family Papers, Filson.

17 Charles Wickliffe shot the editor: See Ireland, "Homicide in Nineteenth Century Kentucky," pp. 152–53.
"no man in Kentucky": Ibid., p. 147.
The town's essential moderation: On slavery in Lexington, see Townsend, *Lincoln and the Bluegrass,* pp. 70–119.

18 But Caroline Turner had a dark cast of mind: On Caroline Turner, see ibid., pp. 74–75, and Randolph Paul Runyon, *Delia Webster and the Underground Railroad* (Lexington: University Press of Kentucky, 1999), pp. 26–27.
"unwarrantable cruelties": Orlando Brown to Orlando Brown, Jr., December 24, 1856, Orlando Brown Papers, Filson.

19 Lewis Robards's infamous slave pens: See Townsend, *Lincoln and the Bluegrass,* pp. 185–87.
"The parent storms [while] the child looks on": Thomas Jefferson, *Notes on the State of Virginia* (New York: Palgrave, 2002), p. 195.
The town's final problem was that it was dying: See J. Winston Coleman, Jr., *Lexington, Athens of the West* (Lexington: Winburn Press, 1981), p. 21.
"I don't like the idea": Eliza Kinkead to Ellen S. Bodley, December 10, 1850, Bodley Family Papers, Filson.

20 "all a disgrace": John Spalding Gatton, "'Mr. Clay & I Got Stung': Harriet Martineau in Lexington," *Kentucky Review* 1, no. 1 (Autumn 1979): p. 52. See also S. J. Yandell to mother, Sarah Wendell, October 13, 1831, in Yandell Family Papers, Filson.
holding Aleck's infant body upside down: Elizabeth L. Norris to Emilie Todd Helm, July 18, 1895, Elizabeth L. Norris Collection, hereafter Norris Collection, ALPL.
"[We] had few privileges": Elizabeth L. Norris to Emilie Todd Helm, September 28, 1895, Norris Collection, ALPL.

21 "The ladies of Lexington": Quoted in Baker, *Mary Todd Lincoln,* p. 61.
sewing willow branches into her hemline: See Elizabeth L. Norris to Emilie Todd Helm, September 28, 1895, Norris Collection, ALPL.
"A small white pony": For this and other quotations in this paragraph, see Helm, *Mary, Wife of Lincoln,* pp. 1–5. On Henry Clay as husbandman, see Wade Hall, "Henry Clay, Livestock Breeder: An Unpublished Letter," *Filson Club History Quarterly* 59, no. 2 (1985): pp. 251–57.

2. Scattered

25 "a very — very pretty woman": *HI,* p. 623.
"one of the loveliest youth": Matilda to Ninian Edwards, October 10, 1829, Ninian W. Edwards Family Papers, hereafter Edwards Papers, ALPL.

26 "The next year [will] push me so hard": Ninian Edwards to Ninian Wirt Edwards, November 18, 1831, Edwards Papers, ALPL.
a move from Kentucky . . . to Illinois: On Springfield's early history, see Paul M. Angle, *"Here I Have Lived": A History of Lincoln's Springfield, 1821–1865* (Springfield, Ill.: Abraham Lincoln Association, 1935), pp. 3–4.

27 mud problem was amplified by the "hog nuisance": See ibid., pp. 90–2.
When he first arrived in Springfield, John Hay, later Lincoln's secretary,

said: "I am stranded at last, like a weather-beaten hulk, on the dreary wastes of Springfield — a city combining the meanness of the North with the barbarism of the South." See Paul M. Angle, "John Hay's Springfield," *Journal of the Illinois State Historical Society* 38 (1945): p. 108.

"mighty Rough": *HI*, p. 446.

"pour[ing] oil over troubled waters": Quoted in Douglas L. Wilson, *Honor's Voice: The Transformation of Abraham Lincoln* (New York: Random House, 1998), p. 157.

"The gentleman has alluded to my being a young man": Quoted in ibid., p. 158. See also David Donald, *Lincoln* (New York: Simon & Schuster, 1996), p. 60.

28   Lincoln and Edwards were both elected: See Angle, *"Here I Have Lived,"* pp. 83–89; Donald, *Lincoln*, pp. 63–64.

"Well, Speed, I'm moved!": On the relationship between Lincoln and Speed, see David Herbert Donald: *"We Are Lincoln Men": Abraham Lincoln and His Friends* (New York: Simon & Schuster, 2003), pp. 29–64; quotation, p. 30.

29   Trying to console his friend: See Wilson, *Honor's Voice*, p. 211.

"Well it is hard to say just why": Michael Burlingame, ed., *An Oral History of Abraham Lincoln: John G. Nicolay's Interviews and Essays* (Carbondale: Southern Illinois University Press, 1996), p. 20.

Frances . . . demanded that he bring the man by: Interview with Frances J. (Todd) Wallace, *Chicago Sunday Times-Herald*, August 25, 1895, p. 25.

"Yes, he took me out once or twice": For this and other quotations in paragraph, see ibid.

a local doctor named William Smith Wallace: See Wayne C. Temple, "Loafing with Lincoln," *Lincoln Herald* 63, no. 2 (Summer 1961): pp. 55–63. For more on William Wallace, see "Recollections of a Springfield Doctor," *Journal of the Illinois State Historical Society* 47 (1954): pp. 57–63.

30   "company quite a while" and "quite prosperous": Interview with Frances J. (Todd) Wallace, *Chicago Sunday Times-Herald*, August 25, 1895, p. 25.

"a vacancy in [their] family": *HI*, p. 443.

31   "spread on a long table": "Mrs. Helen K. Dodge Edwards," *Journal of the Illinois State Historical Society* 2, no. 1 (1909): p. 35.

"To say that he is ugly": Quoted in Robert S. Harper, *Lincoln and the Press* (New York: McGraw-Hill, 1951), p. 93. Looking at photographs of Lincoln today, it is hard to understand his coevals' reaction to his face. In pictures, his features are perhaps not handsome, but they are certainly striking. The key to the mystery may lie in the opinion of Walt Whitman, who said that the president's face was like that of "a Hoosier Michelangelo — so awful ugly it becomes beautiful, with its strange mouth, its deep cut, criss-cross lines, and its doughnut complexion" (Walt Whitman, *Walt Whitman's Civil War* [New York: Knopf, 1961]). Whitman was unusual in his ability to find the beauty in the common man; he had a weakness for faces that were rugged and redeemed by a life of labor. Most of Lincoln's comtemporaries were less forgiving. To them, Lincoln simply looked, as he was, lower class. Then too, when they were abstracted, the life drained from Lincoln's face and eyes and he looked vaguely like a man who'd been kicked in the head by a horse, which he had been. With only photographs and a different aesthetic sensibility, we simply cannot see Lincoln as his contemporaries saw him.

32 "I leave it to you": Quoted in Bob Blaisdell, ed., *The Wit & the Wisdom of Abraham Lincoln* (New York: Gramercy, 1999), p. 145.

"Sir . . . you are the most unattractive man I have ever seen": The story is variously told. See Donald, *Lincoln,* p. 190.

"plain and simple": See ibid., p. 19.

"want of teeth": Abraham Lincoln to Mrs. Orville H. Browning, April 1, 1838, *CW,* vol. 1, p. 118.

"plain [and] plodding": Quoted in Donald, *Lincoln,* p. 22.

33 built just like Henry Clay: Others commented on the likeness. See, for instance, William D. Kelley in Allen Thorndike Rice, *Reminiscences of Abraham Lincoln by Distinguished Men of His Time* (New York: North American Publishing, 1888), p. 258: "As I contemplated his [Lincoln's] tall, spare figure, I remembered that of Henry Clay, to whom I noticed more than passing resemblance."

"One who witnessed the Presidential campaign": Quoted in Wilson, *Honor's Voice,* p. 203.

"improve[d] astonishingly": Quoted in ibid., p. 221.

"fair match for Falstaff": Abraham Lincoln to Eliza Browning, April 1, 1838, *CW,* vol. 1, p. 117.

"Mrs. Glenn [and] old Father Lambert": Quoted in Wilson, *Honor's Voice,* p. 221. Lambert is twice cited for exemplary fatness in the historical record. Apparently, he was the standard that set the standard. See John Brown to Orlando Brown, August 3, 1849, Orlando Brown Papers, Filson: "I hardly know how to begin a letter to you but I will try what I can do. The boys are very well and Judge is as fat as David Lambert himself."

"glitter Show & pomp & power": *HI,* p. 443.

34 "Damascus blade": Elizabeth L. Norris to Emilie Todd Helm, September 28, 1895, Norris Collection, ALPL.

With a rising sense of panic: Much has been written of Lincoln's collapse in 1840–41. Throughout, I have followed the argumentative line established by Douglas L. Wilson. See Wilson, *Honor's Voice,* pp. 195–232.

he told Mary that he actually *hated* her: See *HI,* p. 444.

35 Apparently she had met a man: Matilda Edwards married Newton D. Strong in 1844. Newton, at thirty-four, was twelve years her senior. When later asked why she had married "such an old dried up husband — such a withered up old Buck," she replied "He had lots of houses & gold." See *HI,* p. 444.

"the most miserable man living": Abraham Lincoln to John T. Stuart, January 23, 1841, *CW,* vol. 1, p. 229.

severest — and most productive — confrontation: Two authors, at least, have seen Lincoln's January 1841 depression as a turning point in his life. See Wilson, *Honor's Voice,* and Joshua Wolf Shenk, *Lincoln's Melancholy: How Depression Challenged a President and Fueled His Greatness* (Boston: Houghton Mifflin, 2005), pp. 43–67.

"To remain as I am": Abraham Lincoln to John T. Stuart, January 23, 1841, *CW,* vol. 1, p. 229.

"It seems to me I should": Abraham Lincoln to Joshua Speed, March 27, 1842, *CW,* vol. 1, p. 282.

"Mrs. Butler, it would just kill me": Quoted in Wilson, *Honor's Voice,* p. 236.

36 "look[ing] and act[ing]" and "To Hell": Quoted in ibid., pp. 289 and 292.

So why did he do it?: There is speculation among Lincoln scholars that the Lincolns' rush to the altar was precipitated by their having slept together. While the theory explains a lot, and fits the little available evidence, it is still too early to call it anything other than a hunch.

"I want in all cases to do right": Abraham Lincoln to Mary Owens, August 16, 1837, *CW,* vol. 1, p. 94.

"if you make a bad bargain": Abraham Lincoln to Joshua Speed, February 25, 1842, *CW,* vol. 1, p. 280.

37 "I doubtless trespassed": Mary Lincoln to Josiah G. Holland, December 4, 1865, T&T, p. 293.

Mary was chasing her husband around with a knife: See Michael Burlingame, *The Inner World of Abraham Lincoln* (Urbana: University of Illinois Press, 1994), p. 331.

"engine that knew no rest": Ibid., p. 236.

A year after the Lincolns' marriage: See Baker, *Mary Todd Lincoln,* p. 103.

38 "Aunt Betsey": For this and other quotations in paragraph, see Helm, *Mary, Wife of Lincoln,* pp. 101–2.

"Mary came in first": For this and other quotations in paragraph, see ibid., p. 100.

"This is no war of defense": Henry Clay, "Speech on the Mexican-American War" (1847).

39 "melancholy drip[ping] from him": Quoted in Burlingame, *The Inner World of Abraham Lincoln,* p. 93.

"rough diamond": Helm, *Mary, Wife of Lincoln,* p. 81.

he would always regard Ninian as the finest: Shortly after meeting Lincoln, Robert wrote to Ninian: "I feel more than gratified that my daughters have all married *gentlemen whom I respect and esteem* and I should be pleased if it could ever be in my power to give them a more substantial evidence of my feelings than in mere words or professions. Whether it will ever be in my power I cannot say & perhaps it matters little. I will be satisfied if they discharge all their duties and make as good wives as I think they have good husbands. To none am I so much indebted as yourself, in all respects." Robert S. Todd to Ninian W. Edwards, December 1, 1846, Townsend Papers, ALPL.

"jovial" spirit, "all soul, all fun, and all fire": "Mrs. Lincoln's Brother," *New York Times,* July 30, 1882, p. 2.

he [Sam] came home to roughhouse with his new nephews: Helm, *Mary, Wife of Lincoln,* pp. 100–101.

40 "were considered good people": Elizabeth L. Norris to Emilie Todd Helm, March 7, 1895, Norris Collection, ALPL.

Emilie also made a deep impression on the Lincolns' son Bob: Helm, *Mary, Wife of Lincoln,* p. 101.

one Todd whom the Lincolns conspicuously did *not* meet: According to

Pension File WC-4894, David was enrolled September 28, 1847; mustered into service on October 5, 1847; served in Company C, Third Kentucky Infantry Regiment; and was honorably discharged at Louisville, Kentucky, on July 21, 1848.

40   "I am . . . what may be called": Quoted in Townsend, *Lincoln and the Bluegrass*, p. 157.

41   chasing he-didn't-know-what anymore: Speaking of her father's political life, Elodie Todd noted: "I know my father's life was embittered, after the selection of a political life was made by his friends for him and he accepted it, and after all the sacrifises he made for them and to acquire for himself fame and name which lived only a few years after he slumbered in his grave, and it was well he did not live longer to plunge deeper in, for every other life had lost its charm and there was but the one that added, he thought, to his happiness." Elodie Todd to Nathaniel Dawson, June 12, 1861, Dawson Papers, SHC.

      he [Robert] collapsed with the chills and died nine days later: On Robert Todd's death, see *Lexington Observer & Reporter,* Wednesday, July 18, 1849; Townsend, *Lincoln and the Bluegrass,* pp. 157–73; John Brown to uncle, Orlando Brown, August 3, 1849, Orlando Brown Papers, Filson. According to the Levi O. Todd family bible: "Robert S. Todd died on July 17th, 1849 at 1 o'clock A.M. at night at his farm in Franklin County, Ky in his 59th year."

42   "inferior looking": Daniel M. Holt, *A Surgeon's Civil War: The Letters and Diary of Daniel M. Holt* (Kent, Ohio: Kent State University Press, 1994), p. 98. For other descriptions of George Todd, see Evans, *Mrs. Abraham Lincoln,* pp. 49–50.

      The legal wrangling would go on for years: The case hadn't been fully settled even by the time Lincoln was president. See Robert S. Todd's Admx Complainants in chancery against Robert S. Todd's Heirs &c., defendents, March 2, 1860, KDLA.

      She [Betsey] and her children moved into Buena Vista: Buena Vista was located on the Leestown Pike in Franklin County, Kentucky, near the Woodford County line. Betsey is listed as living in Franklin County in the 1850 census. In the 1860 census, she is listed as living in Woodford County, very near her brother David C. Humphreys, a large slaveholder. Betsey herself had nine slaves in 1860. By 1860 the only children living with her were Aleck, Elodie, and Kitty.

      George was the first to go: See H. M. Bracken, *William Bracken of New Castle County Delaware and His Descendants* (privately printed, 1982), p. 290. The 1850 census lists George as living with a gunsmith, William B. Glave. In 1861, Glave and Anne's father, Roland Curry, were arrested for their pro-Confederate sympathies. Glave was then sheriff, Curry a county judge. See *OR,* ser. 2, vol. 1, pp. 544–46.

43   He [Brown] is also famous for blabbing . . . about New Orleans's quadroon concubine system: Brown and de Tocqueville's conversation took place in Philadelphia on October 28, 1831: "We spoke of New Orleans, where he lived for twenty years. He said to me: There is in New Orleans a class of women dedicated to concubinage, the women of colour. Immorality is for them, as it were, a profession carried on with fidelity. A coloured girl is des-

tined from her birth to become the mistress of a white. When she becomes marriageable, her mother takes care to provide for her. It's a sort of temporary marriage. It lasts ordinarily for several years, during which it is very rare that the girl so joined can be reproached with infidelity. In this fashion they pass from hand to hand until, having acquired a certain competence, they marry for good with a man of their own condition and introduce their daughters into the same life. There's an order of things truly contrary to nature, said I; it must be the cause of considerable disturbance in society. Not so much as you might believe, replied Mr. Brown. The rich young men are very dissolute, but their immorality is restricted to the field of coloured women. White women of French or American blood have very pure morals. They are virtuous, first, I imagine, because virtue pleases them, and next because the women of colour are not; to have a lover is to join their class." See George Wilson Pierson, *Tocqueville in America* (Baltimore: Johns Hopkins University Press, 1996), pp. 486–87.

Louisianans had been growing sugar: On Louisiana's sugar plantations and families, see Philip Chadwick Foster Smith and G. Gouverneur Meredith S. Smith, *Cane, Cotton, and Crevasses: Some Antebellum Louisiana Sugar Plantations of the Minor, Kenner, Hooke, and Shepherd Families* (Bath, Me.: Renfrew Group, 1992).

44   a parade of nephews: The first of those nephews was Joseph Alexander Humphreys, David Carlisle Humphreys's oldest son. In 1853, Joseph married Sarah Gibson, daughter of Tobias Gibson, a large sugar planter in Terrebonne Parish. In 1850, Tobias had 148 slaves on his Louisiana plantation.

living with the Royers and working as a clerk: See the 1860 census.

Yolo County farmhand in the 1850 census: David is *also* listed in the 1850 census as living with his mother in Franklin County, Kentucky. It is vaguely possible that the nineteen-year-old, Kentucky-born David H. Todd listed in the Yolo County census is another man. More likely, David had his census taken twice, once in Kentucky before he moved and once in California after.

he [David] made sure to send a few trinkets home: See Catherine Langley to Kate Helm, May 21, 1928, Townsend Collection, UKY.

David shipped out as a freebooter: See Townsend, *Lincoln and the Bluegrass*, pp. 317–18.

what historians now call the First Succession Revolution: Chile had freed itself from Spanish control in 1818 but remained politically unstable. In 1850 the wave of revolution that began in Europe in 1848 crashed on its shore, and students, artisans, and provincials rose up against the central government in Santiago. Officially, the U.S. government sided with the centrists. "This country is treading the downward road of all the other Spanish American states," noted one member of the U.S. legation. "The civil war which has been raging here for nearly three months is daily growing more fearful in its character. They are murdering, robbing, ravishing & wantonly destroying property." Balie Peyton, Legation of the United States, Santiago, Chile, to Logan Hunton, November 23, 1851, Logan Hunton Papers, Filson.

45   he [David] was working for W. W. Crane: The *Atlantic Democrat* (New Jersey), May 25, 1861, p. 8, notes: "D. H. Todd, of New Orleans, brother of Mrs.

President Lincoln, has been appointed a First Lieutenant in the army of the Confederates. W. W. Crane & Co., in whose employ Mr. Todd has been for the last five years, have given him an outfit, and consented to continue his salary as long as the war last."

45 "complete assortment of Carriages": See ad in the *Galveston Weekly Journal*, November 5, 1852, p. 1.

At twenty-one, he [Aleck] was still living at home: See the 1860 census.

"furnished very fine" and "attended by negro servants": See Catherine Langley to Kate Helm, May 21, 1928, Townsend Collection, UKY.

Instead, he [Levi] clung to his father's final vision: "Embittered" by politics, "unfit for a merchant," and "low-spirited," Robert had been involved in many suits and countersuits involving one estate in particular, Mary Owen Todd Russell's. Russell, the daughter of John Todd, slain at the Blue Licks, was possibly the richest woman in Kentucky. To an acquaintance, Robert had confessed that "he had very little doubt his partner had ruined him but that he would very shortly be rich. That Mrs. Russell (weakly) could not live long and would give him her whole estate." The widow Russell did not intend to leave her estate to Robert, however, but to her second husband, Robert Wickliffe. See *Todd Heirs v. Wickliffe*, box 36, folder 1, p. 112, Wickliffe-Preston Family Papers, UKY; Townsend, *Lincoln and the Bluegrass*, pp. 179–83.

Levi found himself . . . repeatedly hauled into court for debts: See for instance *William O'Marra v. Levi O. Todd* (1858) and *John L. Keyes v. Levi O. Todd* (1856), KDLA. There are many other cases in which Levi O. Todd is listed as defendant, but they appear to have gone missing from the archive.

"unfortunate habits" and "confirmed habit of drunkenness": Quoted in Evans, *Mrs. Abraham Lincoln*, pp. 49–50.

46 "enjoin & restrain the Def't": Fayette Circuit Court Summons, July 13, 1859, Townsend Collection, UKY.

"sprightly and pretty" and "There seems no bounds": Mrs. John T. Stuart to Elizabeth J. Stuart, January 21 and January 28, 1855, in Harry E. Pratt, *The Personal Finances of Abraham Lincoln* (Abraham Lincoln Association, 1943), p. 95.

"When L. came home": *HI*, p. 266.

47 "family decision": Quoted in Baker, *Mary Todd Lincoln*, p. 148.

"The People of Sangamon": *HI*, p. 266.

merely a prelude to that winter's greater political humiliation: See Baker, *Mary Todd Lincoln*, pp. 148–49.

"[I] could bear defeat": Quoted in Donald, *Lincoln*, p. 184.

Trumbull was elected senator: See ibid., pp. 183–85; Burlingame, *An Oral History of Abraham Lincoln*, pp. 39–40.

"not *too* disappointed": Quoted in Donald, *Lincoln*, p. 185.

Mary was less graceful in defeat: See Baker, *Mary Todd Lincoln*, pp. 149–51.

48 The larger purpose of the trip: See R. Gerald McMurtry, *Ben Hardin Helm: "Rebel" Brother-in-Law of Abraham Lincoln, with a Biographical Sketch of His Wife and an Account of the Todd Family of Kentucky* (Elizabethtown, Ky.: Hardin County Historical Society, 1999), pp. 5–7.

The 1850s was a bad time to be in the army: See James R. Arnold, *Jeff Da-*

vis's Own: Cavalry, Comanches, and the Battle for the Texas Frontier (New York: John Wiley and Sons, 2000), pp. 9–11.

49 Helm's post was about a two-day ride west of San Antonio: See Cornelia and Garland Crook, "Fort Lincoln, Texas," *Texas Military History* 4 (Fall 1964). Helm had been in Texas for only six months . . . health problems: See Mc-Murtry, *Ben Hardin Helm*, pp. 7–8.

50 "Study hard and make yourself a smart woman": Hardin Helm to Lucinda Helm, November 12, 1855, Emilie Todd Helm Papers, hereafter Helm Papers, KHS.
"Ours is a profession": Hardin Helm to George Helm, December 9, 1855, Helm Papers, KHS.
"Tell your mother not to let you eat green apples": Hardin Helm to Emilie Todd Helm, July 7, 1857, Helm Papers, KHS.
"We are slayed": Quoted in Michael Holt, *The Rise and Fall of the American Whig Party: Jacksonian Politics and the Onset of the Civil War* (New York: Oxford University Press, 2003), p. 673.
"[I] have just finished another *whaling* Fillmore speech": Hardin Helm to Emilie Todd Helm, June 20, 1856, Helm Papers, KHS.

51 "[What] a terrible Catholic *hole!*": Hardin Helm to Emilie Todd Helm, July 4, 1856, Helm Papers, KHS.
"The excitement of speaking": Hardin Helm to Emilie Todd Helm, June 18, 1856, Helm Papers, KHS.
"I *can't* keep your image out of my mind": Hardin Helm to Emilie Todd Helm, June 20, 1856, Helm Papers, KHS.
"Your presence is essentially necessary": Hardin Helm to Emilie Todd Helm, July 12, 1856, Helm Papers, KHS.
"Altho' Mr L- is, or was, a *Fremont* man": Mary Lincoln to Emilie Todd Helm, November 23, 1856, T&T, p. 46.

52 Lincoln and Helm . . . arguing over means rather than ends: See McMurtry, *Ben Hardin Helm*, pp. 12–14; Helm, *Mary, Wife of Lincoln*, pp. 126–28.
"I have often wished": Mary Lincoln to Emilie Todd Helm, February 16, 1857, T&T, p. 49.

3. 1861: Divided We Fall

53 "I would willingly": Quoted in Allen C. Guelzo, *Abraham Lincoln: Redeemer President* (Grand Rapids, Mich.: Eerdman's, 1999), p. 261.
"the people . . . [would] set all right": Abraham Lincoln to Peter H. Silvester, December 22, 1860, *CW*, vol. 4, p. 160. Full quotation: "the people, under Providence, will set all right."

54 Clark Smith . . . offered a solution: Harry E. Pratt, "Memorabilia," *Journal of the Illinois State Historical Society* 46 (1953): pp. 397–99.

55 "Best Ladies Goods": Quoted in Baker, *Mary Todd Lincoln*, p. 165.
For Mary, shopping also satisfied deeper psychological needs: On Mary and the psychology of shopping, see ibid., pp. 118–19, 156–57.
"greatest little man [he] ever met": Ruth Painter Randall, *Colonel Elmer Ellsworth: A Biography of Lincoln's Friend and First Hero of the Civil War* (Boston: Little, Brown, 1960), p. 7. For more on Lincoln and Ellsworth's

"attraction," see C. A. Tripp, *The Intimate World of Abraham Lincoln* (New York: Simon & Schuster, 2005), pp. 109–24.

56   Kitty was smitten: Coincidentally, Ellsworth's fiancée was also nicknamed Kitty.

"nothing had ever happened": William Henry Herndon and Jesse William Weik, *Herndon's Life of Lincoln* (New York: Da Capo, 1983), p. 390.

"face was pale": Quoted in Donald, *Lincoln*, p. 273.

"almost all of whom I could recognize": Abraham Lincoln, "Speech at Lafayette, Indiana," *CW*, vol. 4, p. 192.

"No one . . . can appreciate my feeling": Abraham Lincoln, "Farewell Address at Springfield, Illinois," February 11, 1861, *CW*, vol. 4, p. 190.

57   In seeing the American people: Abraham Lincoln, "Remarks at Plainesville, Ohio," February 16, 1861, *CW*, vol. 4, p. 218.

"I hold myself without mock modesty": Abraham Lincoln, "Address to the Legislature at Albany, New York," February 18, 1861, *CW*, vol. 4, p. 226.

"I am [a man] without a name": Abraham Lincoln, "Address to the Ohio Legislature, Columbus, Ohio," February 13, 1861, *CW*, vol. 4, p. 204.

"but an accidental instrument": Abraham Lincoln, "Reply to Oliver P. Morton at Indianapolis, Indiana," February 11, 1861, *CW*, vol. 4, p. 194.

"No great harm": Abraham Lincoln, "Speech at Steubenville, Ohio," February 14, 1861, *CW*, vol. 4, p. 207.

"You need only to maintain your composure": Abraham Lincoln, "Speech at Buffalo, New York," February 16, 1861, *CW*, vol. 4, p. 221.

"If you, the PEOPLE": Abraham Lincoln, "Remarks at Lawrenceburg, Indiana," February 12, 1861, *CW*, vol. 4, p. 197.

"then why shall we not": Abraham Lincoln, "Speech at Cincinnati, Ohio," February 12, 1861, *CW*, vol. 4, p. 199.

a sea of fluttering white handkerchiefs: I am indebted to William C. Davis for the image. See William C. Davis, *A Government of Our Own: The Making of the Confederacy* (New York: Free Press, 1994), p. 166.

"united at heart": William J. Cooper, ed., *Jefferson Davis: The Essential Writings* (New York: Random House, 2003), p. 202.

"A government is formed for the South": Virginia K. Jones, ed., "A Contemporary Account of the Inauguration of Jefferson Davis," *Alabama Historical Quarterly* 23 (1961): p. 273.

58   the Confederacy's first gala event: For a description, see Davis, *A Government of Our Own*, p. 166.

"every house, little and big": Jones, "Inauguration of Jefferson Davis," p. 275.

She had met and married an Alabamian, Clement White: Clement Billingslea White was born in 1829 in Dallas County, Alabama, the son of Thomas Osborne White and Sophia R. Byrd. The Whites lived at what is now called White-Force Cottage, next to Sturdivant Hall in Selma. In the 1860 census, a Clement White is listed as a warehouse keeper living with his wife, M. T. White, and (presumably) his six-year-old son, William T. White. The Whites lived in the household of a minister, Robert Keith.

"Of course they attract considerable attention": "Lincoln's Sister-in-Law," *Daily Missouri Democrat*, February 21, 1861 p. 1, reprinted from *Columbus (Ga.) Times*.

"I made up my mind": Nathaniel Dawson to Elodie Todd, June 26, 1861, Dawson Papers, SHC.

59 "What man is there here": Albert D. Kirwan, *John J. Crittenden: The Struggle for the Union* (Lexington: University of Kentucky Press, 1962), p. 416.

"The tug has to come": Abraham Lincoln to Lyman Trumbull, December 10, 1860, *CW,* vol. 4, p. 150.

"hold firm, as with a chain of steel": Abraham Lincoln to Elihu B. Washburne, December 13, 1860, *CW,* vol. 4, p. 151.

"with all the dignity": Elizabeth Todd Grimsley, "Six Months in the White House," *Journal of the Illinois State Historical Society* 19, nos. 3–4 (1926–27): p. 46. Of the Todds present at the inaugural, Grimsley said: "Our family, in addition to Mr. And Mrs. Lincoln, and their three sons, consisted of Mrs. Ninian Wirt Edwards (Elizabeth Todd), Mrs. Charles Kellogg (Margaret Todd) sisters of Mrs. Lincoln, Mr. Charles Kellogg, Mr. And Mrs. E. L. Baker, Miss Elizabeth Edwards (Mrs. Eugene Clover) niece, myself (Mrs. Grimsley), a cousin, who was to remain six months with them" (p. 48). A later article corrects errors in and omissions to Grimsley's text. See "Six Months in the White House," *Journal of the Illinois State Historical Society* 47 (1954): pp. 310–12.

60 "I close": Garry Wills, *Lincoln at Gettysburg: The Words That Remade America* (New York: Simon & Schuster, 1992), p. 158.

61 "Suppose you go to war": Abraham Lincoln, "First Inaugural," *CW,* vol. 4, p. 269.

"Wretchedly botched," "One of the most awkwardly constructed," "loose, disjointed, rambling affair," and "death-knell of peace": "Lincoln's First Inaugural — Pro and Con," *Lincoln Lore,* no. 1243, February 1953.

62 Congratulated them for it: See "Worthy of Notice," *Richmond Dispatch,* April 19, 1861.

Sam had to sign on as a private: See *Dallas Morning News,* May 29, 1892, p. 2; and *Flake's Bulletin* (Galveston), November 8, 1867, p. 2.

"promptly and completely befuddled": Townsend, *Lincoln and the Bluegrass,* p. 318.

63 He had secured a first lieutenancy: David's lieutenancy was announced in Northern papers. See *Atlantic Democrat* (N.J.), May 25, 1861, p. 8; and *Philadelphia Inquirer,* June 3, 1861, p. 8.

"without a dissenting voice," "Tho' the step," and "My own home": Nathaniel Dawson to Joel Matthews, April 11, April 26, and May 30, 1861, N.H.R. Dawson Papers, Special Collections Library, Duke University.

"cold, not unfeeling": Elodie Todd to Nathaniel Dawson, August 4, 1861, Dawson Papers, SHC.

64 "Ever since I can remember" and "committing a sin": Elodie Todd to Nathaniel Dawson, May 9, 1861, Dawson Papers, SHC.

"We are speeding on our way": Nathaniel Dawson to Elodie Todd, April 26, 1861, Dawson Papers, SHC.

"almost strangers": Elodie Todd to Nathaniel Dawson, July 31, 1861, Dawson Papers, SHC.

"You say we hardly know each other": Nathaniel Dawson to Elodie Todd, August 21, 1861, Dawson Papers, SHC.

64   "Had I not been a volunteer": Nathaniel Dawson to Elodie Todd, May 17, 1861, Dawson Papers, SHC.
"[By the time] we are joined in the holy bonds" and "Do you not think": Nathaniel Dawson to Elodie Todd, May 20, 1861, Dawson Papers, SHC.

65   "Eastern idolatry": Nathaniel Dawson to Elodie Todd, June 2, 1861, Dawson Papers, SHC.
"sacred writing": Nathaniel Dawson to Elodie Todd, July 14, 1861, Dawson Papers, SHC.
"I am disposed to be romantic" and "I can see the men aboard plainly": Nathaniel Dawson to Elodie Todd, October 12, 1861, Dawson Papers, SHC.
"You have [from here]": Nathaniel Dawson to Elodie Todd, May 18, 1861, Dawson Papers, SHC.
"I see your image": Nathaniel Dawson to Elodie Todd, June 17, 1861, Dawson Papers, SHC.
"If fortune favors our love": Nathaniel Dawson to Elodie Todd, May 18, 1861, Dawson Papers, SHC.

66   "Sister Mary . . . receives the news" and "Your captain . . . has filled your head": Elodie Todd to Nathaniel Dawson, May 26, 1861, Dawson Papers, SHC.
"I intend writing to him": Elodie Todd to Nathaniel Dawson, July 3, 1861, Dawson Papers, SHC.
"circumstances have made me love you": Nathaniel Dawson to Elodie Todd, June 19, 1861, Dawson Papers, SHC.
"perfectly fabulous": Nathaniel Dawson to Elodie Todd, May 15, 1861, Dawson Papers, SHC.
flatterer and insincere: Elodie Todd to Nathaniel Dawson, August 19, 1861, Dawson Papers, SHC.
"lover-like": Elodie Todd to Nathaniel Dawson, December 15, 1861, Dawson Papers, SHC.
"I am sorry to hear that you are *battling*": Elodie Todd to Nathaniel Dawson, May 15, 1861, Dawson Papers, SHC.

67   "I will miss her so much": Elodie Todd to Nathaniel Dawson, June 27, 1861, Dawson Papers, SHC.
"What is to be the fate of home?": Elodie Todd to Nathaniel Dawson, May 2, 1861, Dawson Papers, SHC.
"the dusky sons of Ham": William Thomson, Jr., to William Thomson, Sr., February 2, 1861, William Sydnor Thomson Papers, Emory University.
"domestic pandemonium": Quoted in Amy Murrell Taylor, *The Divided Family in Civil War America* (Chapel Hill: University of North Carolina Press, 2006), p. 36.

68   "Kentucky has not seceded": John Crittenden to George Crittenden, April 30, 1861, John J. Crittenden Papers, Filson.
"the strongest and sturdiest champion": For this and other quotations to end of paragraph, see Klotter, *The Breckinridges of Kentucky*, pp. 80–81. Robert's political alienation from his children also alienated him from his grandchildren. See Robert J. Breckinridge to W.C.P. Breckinridge, September 1, 1864, Townsend Papers, ALPL: "These are painful things. But, as I may never see you more I am forced to say them. I have occasionally seen

your child, by accident, in the streets; and each time took it into my arms and blessed it — which God, I trust, will ratify. One more word: in case of your death, if you will provide that in the case of your wife's death, the child shall come to me, you may die assured that I will treat it as I did you. . . . And now my son, if anything befalls you, wherein a loving father may be of use to you personally, in life or death — let me know. I look my fate calmly in the face. I have written this almost without tears. What then is too hard for your loving father?"

"[Secession] has divided States [and] Counties": Samuel Haycraft Journal, October 10, 1862, Filson.

69   "Fifteen hundred Kentuckians": Harry Dixon to Richard Dixon, May 5, 1861, Harry St. John Dixon Papers, SHC.

"I think to lose Kentucky": Abraham Lincoln to Orville H. Browning, September 22, 1861, *CW*, vol. 4, p. 532.

summoned Hardin to the White House: It is not clear exactly when or how long Hardin visited with the Lincolns. According to Lincoln's secretary, John Hay, Hardin "spent some time with the family here." Burlingame, *Inside Lincoln's White House*, p. 85.

70   "100 Todds . . . all wanting offices": Elizabeth Grimsley to Cousin John Todd Stuart, March 20, 1861, Elizabeth Grimsley Papers, ALPL.

"Will it do for me": Abraham Lincoln to John Todd Stuart, March 30, 1861, *CW*, vol. 4, p. 303. Lincoln had also appointed William Wallace to the Paymaster Department. "Dr. Wallace, you know, is needy," he told Stuart, "and looks to me; and I personally owe him much" (ibid.). Why he felt he owed Wallace particularly is unclear. Certainly, as their family physician, Wallace had been an intimate in the Lincoln home. Then too the Lincolns had named their third son after him, an indicator of a close bond. One might also guess that Lincoln had taken Wallace into his confidence regarding his own medical issues.

"The position you offer me" and "You have been kind and generous": McMurtry, *Ben Hardin Helm*, p. 19.

"the beginning of sorrows" and "I am one of those dull creatures": Quoted in Douglas Southall Freeman, *Lee* (New York: Scribner, 1961), p. 111.

"With all my devotion to the Union": quoted in Emory M. Thomas, *Robert E. Lee: A Biography* (New York: Norton, 1995), p. 188.

Don't be on the side opposite your people: According to the *Dallas Morning News*, July 27, 1893, p. 6, Lee was too distracted to give Helm any real advice, saying, "I cannot help you . . . for within the last hour I have given up my own career. I have left the United States army. My own mind is too much disturbed to advise you. But do what conscience and honor bid."

"five hundred [Kentucky] troops": Elizabeth Barbour Helm Bruce to sister Mary, April 26, 1861, Helm Bruce Papers, Filson.

71   "I had a bitter struggle with myself": The exact wording of this quotation is variously given in recollections written after the war. All agree that Hardin said it, or something very like it, to "a friend, who was afterwards a member of his staff." See *Sunday Herald*, December 5, 1886, p. 2; Marie Louise Pointe, "Abraham Lincoln's True Love Story," an article from the *New Orleans Picayune* among the clippings in the Helm Papers, KHS.

71 Kitty and Betsey had arrived: Elodie Todd to Nathaniel Dawson, May 9, 1861, Dawson Papers, SHC.

Mary ... had invited her [Betsey] to the White House: "Mother-in-law of Lincoln," *Richmond Dispatch*, May 13, 1861.

she found herself attending Union prayer meetings: Elodie Todd to Nathaniel Dawson, May 27, 1861, Dawson Papers, SHC.

72 "I think [Kitty] is perfectly willing": Elodie Todd to Nathaniel Dawson, May 27, 1861, Dawson Papers, SHC.

"Kitty says if you take her beau": Elodie Todd to Nathaniel Dawson, May 15, 1861, Dawson Papers, SHC.

"Tell Miss Kitty you will claim her": Nathaniel Dawson to Elodie Todd, May 22, 1861, Dawson Papers, SHC.

"Tell [Miss Kate]": Nathaniel Dawson to Elodie Todd, May 24, 1861, Dawson Papers, SHC.

Ellsworth died the same day: See Charles A. Ingraham, *Elmer E. Ellsworth and the Zouaves of '61.* (Chicago: University of Chicago Press, 1925), pp. 142–45.

Ellsworth's troops landed just as dawn broke: Ibid., pp. 145–51; Randall, *Colonel Elmer Ellsworth*, pp. 254–63. For a largely corroborative account, see C. M. Butler to wife, May 27, 1861, C. M. Butler Papers, ALPL.

73 The detachment made for the Marshall House: Ingraham, *Elmer E. Ellsworth*, pp. 151–55; Randall, *Colonel Elmer Ellsworth*, pp. 254–63. Ellsworth's body would then be secreted out so as not to alert the other Zouaves, who, it was feared, would sack Alexandria in response.

74 "Perhaps in a manner we cannot understand" and "We needed just such a sacrifice": Quoted in Randall, *Colonel Elmer Ellsworth*, pp. 273–74.

"He did not move": Quoted in ibid., p. 261. On Lincoln's grief, see ibid., pp. 261–64; Ingraham, *Elmer E. Ellsworth*, pp. 156–63; Tripp, *The Intimate World of Abraham Lincoln*, pp. 120–24.

75 "It was his personal realization": John N. Kasson in Rice, *Reminiscences of Abraham Lincoln*, p. 378.

"This is only the beginning": Elizabeth Grimsley to John Todd Grimsley, May 24, 1861, Elizabeth Grimsley Papers, ALPL. See also Elizabeth Todd Grimsley, "Six Months in the White House," p. 56: "A real sorrow was brought into the White House, with the body of Col. E. E. Ellsworth, who fell a martyr to his rash zeal in hauling down a confederate flag, at Alexandria. He had been a member of the family ever since we went to Washington, having gone on with Mr. Lincoln from Springfield, and was much beloved."

"excellent friends": Elodie Todd to Nathaniel Dawson, June 2, 1861, Dawson Papers, SHC.

"Providence seems to have cut him off": Nathaniel Dawson to Elodie Todd, May 25, 1861, Dawson Papers, SHC.

"I am anxious for your sake": Nathaniel Dawson to Elodie Todd, May 22, 1861, Dawson Papers, SHC.

76 "How singular": Nathaniel Dawson to Elodie Todd, May 16, 1861, Dawson Papers, SHC.

"Pray do you think": Elodie Todd to Nathaniel Dawson, May 23, 1861, Dawson Papers, SHC.

P.G.T. Beauregard: Beauregard did not use his first initial during the war, but as it is commonly used today, I include it to avoid confusion.

77 "Seven of the ten captains": Nathaniel Dawson to Elodie Todd, May 29, 1861, Dawson Papers, SHC.

78 "Having heard some gentlemen conversing": Elodie Todd to Nathaniel Dawson, June 16, 1861, Dawson Papers, SHC.

he [Col. Jones] would show them what he was made of: For more on Jones and the Fourth Alabama, see Jeffrey D. Stocker, ed., *From Huntsville to Appomattox: R. T. Coles's History of 4th Regiment, Alabama Volunteer Infantry, C.S.A., Army of Northern Virginia* (Knoxville: University of Tennessee Press, 1996), p. 27; Kenneth W. Jones, "The Fourth Alabama Infantry: First Blood," *Alabama Historical Quarterly* 36 (Spring 1974): p. 37; J. Gary Laine and Morris M. Penny, *Law's Alabama Brigade in the War Between the Union and the Confederacy* (Shippensburg, Pa.: White Mane Publishing, 1996), pp. 4–5.

"Up Alabamians!": Gregory J. Starbuck, "'Up Alabamians!' The Fourth Alabama Infantry At First Manassas," *Military Images Magazine* (July/August, 1986): pp. 24–29; quotation, p. 27.

"My first thought was": quoted in William C. Davis, *Battle at Bull Run: A History of the First Major Campaign of the Civil War* (Garden City, N.Y.: Doubleday, 1977), p. 178.

"[I] watched him as he fired": Nathaniel Dawson to Elodie Todd, July 30, 1861, Dawson Papers, SHC.

79 "I waited until I saw him good": Quoted in David Detzer, *Donnybrook: The Battle of Bull Run, 1861* (New York: Harcourt, 2004), p. 313.

"conspicuously on his horse": Jones, "First Blood," p. 45.

"[We] retreated under a shower of bullets": Quoted in Davis, *Battle at Bull Run,* p. 181.

"Don't run boys": According to another source, Jones said: "Men, don't run." See Starbuck, "Up Alabamians!," p. 28.

"opened a murderous fire": Jones, "First Blood," p. 45.

80 "Everything was in great confusion": Nathaniel Dawson to Elodie Todd, August 29, 1861, Dawson Papers, SHC.

all they had accomplished: See Detzer, *Donnybrook,* p. 294; Jones, "First Blood," p. 48; Stocker, *From Huntsville to Appomattox,* pp. 24–29. It should be noted that while the Fourth Alabama sustained the second highest *number* of casualties, their casualty *rate* (killed, wounded, and missing), expressed as a percentage of those engaged, was the highest for the battle at 40 percent.

"so fatigued and lame" and "cut to pieces": Nathaniel Dawson to Elodie Todd, August 29, 1861, Dawson Papers, SHC.

"The scene presented was horrible": Nathaniel Dawson to Elodie Todd, July 24, 1861, Dawson Papers, SHC.

81 "During the fight": Nathaniel Dawson to Elodie Todd, July 25, 1861, Dawson Papers, SHC.

"You are the idol of my heart": Nathaniel Dawson to Elodie Todd, July 24, 1861, Dawson Papers, SHC.

"As much as I thought I loved you": Elodie Todd to Nathaniel Dawson, July 23, 1861, Dawson Papers, SHC.

81   "it was contrary to Army Regulations": *HI,* p. 207.

      "Would that . . . this glorious victory": Elodie Todd to Nathaniel Dawson,
      July 23, 1861, Dawson Papers, SHC.

      "I look straight forward": Elodie Todd to Nathaniel Dawson, July 28, 1861,
      Dawson Papers, SHC.

82   "engaged in writing": Nathaniel Dawson to Elodie Todd, July 28, 1861, Daw-
      son Papers, SHC.

      Nathaniel was beset by more embarrassing problems: On the charge of
      cowardice, see G. Ward Hubbs, ed., *Voices from Company D: Diaries by the
      Greensboro Guards, Fifth Alabama Infantry Regiment, Army of Northern
      Virginia* (Athens: University of Georgia Press, 2003), p. 32: "It is reported
      that Cap't Dawson, Magnolia Cadets, 4th Ala Reg't will be tried for cow-
      ardice." Nathaniel would later come to believe that the charges had been
      circulated by a man who wanted Elodie for his own: "I rec'd a letter from
      a friend, in Marengo, an influential public man, this week, in which he as-
      sures me that he has never met a man, who gave credence to the slanders at
      Manassas. He says it is currently reported, and credited, that I am engaged
      to be married, at the end of my term of service, to a lady in Selma, and that
      this report was circulated and encouraged in order to supplant me. Is such
      a thing credible? Would any man, who aspired to your hand, stoop to such
      baseness?" Nathaniel Dawson to Elodie Todd, November 27, 1861, Dawson
      Papers, SHC.

83   "I am willing to lay down my life for you": Nathaniel Dawson to Elodie
      Todd, August 21, 1861, Dawson Papers, SHC.

      "I have never felt so anxious": Nathaniel Dawson to Elodie Todd, December
      8, 1861, Dawson Papers, SHC.

      "You tell me that you have made up your mind": Nathaniel Dawson to Elo-
      die Todd, January 8, 1862, Dawson Papers, SHC.

      "I am not a Roman": Nathaniel Dawson to Elodie Todd, August 21, 1861,
      Dawson Papers, SHC.

      he [David] and a fellow Kentuckian, the poet Theodore O'Hara: *OR,* ser. 2,
      vol. 3, p. 687; see also Arch Fredric Blakey, *General John H. Winder, C.S.A.*
      (Gainesville: University Press of Florida, 1990).

84   "Revil[ed] prominent leaders": *Richmond Dispatch,* July 23, 1861. The *Dis-
      patch* printed a notice of George's release the next day. George's arrest also
      made the papers in the North. See the *Pittsfield (Mass.) Sun,* August 15,
      1861, p. 1. The letter in George's pocket had been franked by Lincoln in the
      1840s when he was a member of Congress.

      "[I] hope they will yet make friends": Elodie Todd to Nathaniel Dawson,
      August 4, 1861, Dawson Papers, SHC.

      "the picture-gallery of the town": *Charleston Courier,* August 19, 1861, re-
      printed as "What Our Prisoners Are Doing at Richmond," *New York Times,*
      September 2, 1861, p. 3.

      "The square was for weeks": William C. Harris, *Prison-Life in the Tobacco
      Warehouse at Richmond by a Ball's Bluff Prisoner* (1862), p. 32.

      "Behold how they multiply": *Richmond Whig,* December 28, 1861.

85   "One would think live Yankees": *Richmond Dispatch,* July 15, 1861, p. 2. One
      Northerner commented on the phenomenon as well: "A 'Yankee' seemed to

be as much of an object of curiosity to them as a live hippopotamus would have been." William H. Jeffrey, *Richmond Prisons 1861–1862, Compiled from the Original Records Kept by the Confederate Government* (St. Johnsbury, Vt.: Republican Press, 1893), p. 107.

"the newspapers proposed": Jeffrey, *Richmond Prisons*, p. 15. See also Lonnie R. Speer, *Portals to Hell: The Military Prisons of the Civil War* (Mechanicsburg, Pa.: Stackpole Books, 1997), pp. 19–25.

"pretend[ed] that the duty": Charles Carroll Gray Diary, August 18, 1861, SHC.

"personal delight in human blood" and "I think Wirz": *Report on the Treatment of Prisoners of War, by the Rebel Authorities, During the War of the Rebellion* (Washington, D.C.: Government Printing Office, 1869), pp. 1065–66.

"There was something in Todd's voice": Jeffrey, *Richmond Prisons*, p. 14.

"foul and scurrilous abuse": Harris, *Prison-Life in the Tobacco Warehouse*, p. 129.

"invariably" and "he struck an invalid": William Howard Merrell, *Five Months in Rebeldom; or, Notes from the Diary of a Bull Run Prisoner* (Rochester, N.Y.: Adams and Dabney, 1862), p. 29.

86 "paroxysm": *Report on the Treatment of Prisoners of War*, p. 1065.

David had just stabbed the first man he saw: Jeffrey, *Richmond Prisons*, p. 111.

lunged into the crowd: Harris, *Prison-Life in the Tobacco Warehouse*, p. 129.

"drunk during nearly the entire period" and "one of daily indignity and hardship": Ibid.

"The floor of the rooms," "became insane," and "from twelve to twenty-five feet long": Jeffrey, *Richmond Prisons*, p. 112. The source continues: "Money was very scarce among us, but I have known twenty-five cents to be offered and refused for a position in the line near the door. It seemed to us that this was a wanton and unnecessary cruelty."

"sold one article after another": Ibid., p. 129.

87 "Some of the prisoners are very saucy": "Prisoner Shot At," *Richmond Whig*, July 31, 1861.

"A Yankee prisoner named Gleason": Merrell, *Five Months in Rebeldom*, p. 30. According to Merrell, the article appeared in the *Richmond Dispatch* under the title "Sudden Death."

no witness puts David Todd at the scene of any of the shootings: One inmate allowed that David was being partly scapegoated: "I believe that some of the prisoners attribute to Todd the crime of shooting some of our comrades; or, at least, believe that the shooting was done by his orders. To give the d—l his due, I must admit there was no satisfactory evidence of this; and conclude that such acts were voluntary upon the part of the sentinels. Whenever approaching the window, we were threateningly warned by the guard below, to stand back, etc.; but the curiosity of some of our poor fellows, hungering and thirsting for a glimpse of the outer world, sometimes overcame their apprehension of danger, and they suffered according." Merrell, *Five Months in Rebeldom*, p. 29. Most prisoners, however, were equally sure the original order came from and was fully condoned by Todd: "Privates Gleason, Buck, and Tibbetts were killed, and others wounded, in consequence of Todd's order; none of them were leaning out of windows, although Gleason was near one, unsuspiciously looking out. Todd exonerated the murderer from blame. The press noticed these episodes as 'retributive justice,' or, flippantly, as 'accidents.' In those days we impaneled our own juries, and treasured verdicts for future publication." *Report on the Treatment of Prisoners of War*, pp. 1065–66.

87   "furnished a convenient excuse": *Report on the Treatment of Prisoners of War*, pp. 1065–66.

88   "The mortality among the Abolition prisoners": *Richmond Dispatch*, August 9, 1861, p. 2; Jeffrey, *Richmond Prisons*, 131.
"the bodies [had begun] to putrefy": *Charleston Mercury*, August 10, 1861.
"Negro graveyards": Jeffrey, *Richmond Prisons*, p. 22. See also Merrell, *Five Months in Rebeldom*, p. 30.
"so exasperated . . . kicked the body": Jeffrey, *Richmond Prisons*, p. 131.
"for having acted contrary": *Charleston Mercury*, August 10, 1861.

89   "A favorite expression of his": Jeffrey, *Richmond Prisons*, p. 112.

90   "spouting blood like a harpooned whale": Charles Carroll Gray Diary, August 18, 1861, SHC. Charles W. Le Boutillier, surgeon in the Ninth Minnesota, was eventually paroled but died of typhoid fever in April 1863. Charles Carroll Gray (1838–1884) of New York was also eventually paroled. He served as a U.S. Army surgeon until 1879.
"humbug Todd was": Charles Carroll Gray Diary, August 31, 1861, SHC.

91   "We received a letter from my brother": Elodie Todd to Nathaniel Dawson, September 1, 1861, Dawson Papers, SHC.

92   "This news concerning Todd": The *Herald* article was reprinted as "Captain Todd and the New York Press," *Richmond Dispatch*, October 16, 1861.
"Cousin Lizzie, have you taken leave": Grimsley, "Six Months in the White House," p. 69.
To avert suspicion: See William O. Stoddard, *Abraham Lincoln: The True Story of a Great Life* (New York, 1885), pp. 375–76.
"by no word or act of hers": Elodie Todd to Nathaniel Dawson, July 23, 1861, Dawson Papers, SHC.
"I do not believe she ever said it": Ibid.

93   "love & respect" and "there is not one of us": "A View of Lincoln from a House Divided (Cont.)," *Lincoln Lore*, no. 1652 (October 1975): p. 1.
"I never go in Public" and "We would be devoid of all feeling": Elodie Todd to Nathaniel Dawson, August 4, 1861, Dawson Papers, SHC.
"It seems strange to me": Elodie Todd to Nathaniel Dawson, September 29, 1861, Dawson Papers, SHC.

94   "That is a privilege I allow myself": Elodie Todd to Nathaniel Dawson, August 4, 1861, Dawson Papers, SHC.
"caught & hung": Elodie Todd to Nathaniel Dawson, December 22, 1861, Dawson Papers, SHC.
"I must confess" and "You do not know all": Elodie Todd to Nathaniel Dawson, December 22, 1861, Dawson Papers, SHC.
"Society [here] has undergone a change" and "There has been a *war here*": Elodie Todd to Nathaniel Dawson, January 5, 1862, Dawson Papers, SHC.

95 "if my family did not": Elodie Todd to Nathaniel Dawson, October 13, 1861, Dawson Papers, SHC.

"You see I am sad": Elodie Todd to Nathaniel Dawson, September 22, 1861, Dawson Papers, SHC.

"Surely there is no other family": Elodie Todd to Nathaniel Dawson, September 1, 1861, Dawson Papers, SHC.

"This separation I sincerely hope": Benjamin Hardin Helm to Emilie Todd Helm, October 10, 1861, Helm Papers, KHS.

96 Aleck too had made his decision: See Catherine Langley to Kate Helm, May 21, 1928, in Townsend Papers, UKY.

"You do not know how strangely": Elodie Todd to Nathaniel Dawson, October 13, 1861, Dawson Papers, SHC.

4. 1862: "Blood Galore"

97 "The treatment of our brave boys": This and other quotations in paragraph from "Important from the South, Interesting Testimony of an Exchanged Prisoner," *New York Herald*, January 18, 1862. In October 1861 there had been a little chatter in the Northern press about the Todd charges after a group of wounded Union soldiers had been released. The story only rose to a crescendo, however, after the bulk of those captured at Manassas were exchanged and began to tell their stories. See also "Late Northern News — The Wounded Prisoners Recently Released from Richmond," *Richmond Dispatch*, October 17, 1861.

Other Northern papers quickly followed suit: See for instance, the *Philadelphia Inquirer*, January 20, 1862, p. 1. The *Inquirer*'s informants claimed that some of the prison abuse stories had been exaggerated — but not the ones involving David Todd: "It is proper here to state that these prisoners do not complain of harsh treatment. They say that all the sick and wounded were uniformly well treated and well taken care of. . . . Captain Brewer, who was six months in the hands of the Rebels, and was finally released from Tuscaloosa, also states that accounts of bad treatment have been greatly exaggerated. He says that those who recognized their condition as prisoners were all well treated by the officers in charge. The released prisoners, however, all join in denunciation of Lieutenant Todd, brother-in-law of President Lincoln, whose unfeeling brutality appeared to make no exceptions."

98 "From all sides": "Prison Life in Richmond," *New York Times*, February 27, 1862, p. 8.

"The notorious Lieut. Todd": Merrell, *Five Months in Rebeldom*, p. 29.

"his taste better than any other": Elodie Todd to Nathaniel Dawson, January 5, 1862, Dawson Papers, SHC.

"look[ed] more like a dowdy washerwoman": Sarah McNair Vosmeier, "Maria Child in Her Letters: 'How *Much* Leaven It Will Take to Leaven the Cold Dough of This Nation,'" *Lincoln Lore*, no. 1795 (September 1988): p. 3.

99 "The President is the best of us": Quoted in Donald, *Lincoln*, p. 301.

"With all his deficiencies": Vosmeier, "Maria Child in Her Letters," p. 4.

99   "a cool head": Burlingame, *Lincoln Observed*, p. 87.
"half-crazy," "part-insane," "demented," and "deranged": Quoted in Burlingame, *The Inner World of Abraham Lincoln*, p. 297.
narcissistic personality disorder: See Baker, *Mary Todd Lincoln*, pp. 330, 407.
hot coffee: The incident is described in Burlingame, *The Inner World of Abraham Lincoln*, p. 277.

100 "her own milking apparatus": Quoted in Baker, *Mary Todd Lincoln*, p. 196.
"I wonder if the women": Quoted in Burlingame, *The Inner World of Abraham Lincoln*, p. 300.
"brilliant," "dashing," "dangerous": Robert V. Bruce, *Lincoln and the Tools of War* (Champaign: University of Illinois Press, 1989), p. 231.
"one of the bigger bubbles": Stephen W. Sears, *Controversies and Commanders: Dispatches from the Army of the Potomac* (Boston: Mariner, 2000), p. 198.

101 "majordomo in general" and "He has seen more of the world": Quoted in Burlingame, *The Inner World of Abraham Lincoln*, p. 305.
"one of the least creditable volumes": *Scribners Monthly*, 20, no. 6 (October 1880): p. 945.
P. T. Barnum credited Wikoff with teaching him . . . hokum: When Barnum was still "at the foot of the ladder," he traveled to New Orleans, where he marveled at the "spectacular" who had the dancer Fanny Elssler "in charge." He was particular impressed with Wikoff's ability as a promoter, and Elssler became the model for his own later success with Jenny Lind. See Richard H. Brodhead, "Veiled Ladies: Toward a History of Antebellum Entertainment," *American Literary History* 1, no. 2 (Summer 1989): p. 280. See also P. T. Barnum, *Struggles and Triumphs; or, Forty Years Recollections of P. T. Barnum*, part 1 (Kessinger, 2003), p. 108: "Fanny Ellsler was also in New Orleans, and when I saw seats in the dress circle sold at an average of four dollars and one-half, I gave her agent, Chevalier Henry Wyckoff, great credit for exciting public enthusiasm to the highest pitch and I thought the prices enormous. I did not dream then that within twelve years, I should be selling tickets in the same city for full five times that sum."
"terrible libertine": This and other quotations in Burlingame, *The Inner World of Abraham Lincoln*, pp. 305–6.
"most bare-faced flattery": Henry Villard, *Lincoln on the Eve of '61: A Journalist's Story* (Westport, Conn.: Greenwood, 1971), p. 103.
Scoundrels held another attraction: See Burlingame, *The Inner World of Abraham Lincoln*, pp. 268–326.

102 "scandal of [his] wife and Wood": Quoted in Ibid., p. 291.
"Hell is to pay": Michael Burlingame, ed., *At Lincoln's Side: John Hay's Civil War Correspondence and Selected Writings* (Carbondale: Southern Illinois University Press, 2006), p. 14.
In February 1862 the whisper became a roar: See "John Watt" at Mr. Lincoln's White House, Lincoln Institute, the Gilder Lehrman Institute of American History, www.mrlincolnswhitehouse.org/inside.asp?ID=68&subjectID=2; accessed December 26, 2006.

103 "Not a few bitter tongues": William O. Stoddard, *Abraham Lincoln: The True Story of a Great Life* (New York, 1885), pp. 375–76.

104 "a wild flower transplanted from the prairie": This and other quotations from Elizabeth Keckley, *Behind the Scenes: Thirty Years a Slave and Four Years in the White House* (Champaign: University of Illinois Press, 2001), pp. 76–78.

In early February, Willie had fallen ill: See Baker, *Mary Todd Lincoln*, pp. 208–12. News of Willie's death reached the Southern half of the Todd clan via newspaper: "I send my loved Elodie two Dispatches," Nathaniel wrote home. "One of them will inform her of the death of Willie Lincoln, and give her the melancholy particulars." Nathaniel Dawson to Elodie Todd Dawson, March 8, 1862, Dawson Papers, SHC.

"[Today] I persuaded": Elizabeth Edwards to Julia Baker, March 2, 1862, Elizabeth Edwards Papers, ALPL.

105 "such language sounds harsh" and "a serious crush": Elizabeth Edwards to Julia Baker, March [undated], 1862, Elizabeth Edwards Papers, ALPL.

In Willie, Lincoln found a kindred spirit: Lincoln called Willie's loss simply "the hardest trial of my life." See Burlingame, *The Inner World of Abraham Lincoln*, p. 103.

"[Here] the world is represented by flowers": *Herndon's Life of Lincoln* (New York: Da Capo, 1983), pp. 411–12.

"Beneath what the world saw" and "Do stay with me": *HI*, pp. 444–45.

106 "exertion of dressing": Elizabeth Edwards to Julia Baker, April 17, 1862, Elizabeth Edwards Papers, ALPL.

"be careful to refrain": Elizabeth Edwards to Julia Baker, March [undated], 1862, Elizabeth Edwards Papers, ALPL.

"The Mississippi is the backbone": William L. Shea and Terrence J. Winschel, *Vicksburg Is the Key: The Struggle for the Mississippi River* (Lincoln: University of Nebraska Press, 2003), p. 1.

107 "Richmond is very quiet": Nathaniel Dawson to Elodie Todd, March 21, 1862, Dawson Papers, SHC.

"wretched place — the capital of a swamp": Ambrose Bierce, "What I Saw of Shiloh," in William McCann, ed., *Ambrose Bierce's Civil War* (New York: Random House, 1996), p. 12.

"the 'Grand Point'": Quoted in Larry J. Daniel, *Shiloh: The Battle That Changed the Civil War* (New York: Touchstone, 1997), p. 93.

108 "Death to Yankees!": Alexander Todd Diary, UKY.

"hastily abandoned": On the First Kentucky at Dranesville, see E. D. Neill, ed., *Glimpses of the Nation's Struggle*, 3rd. series, Papers Read Before the Minnesota Commandery of the Military Order of the Loyal Legion of the United States, 1889–1892 (St. Paul: Merrill Company, 1893), p. 57.

"He looks badly": For David's movements, see Elodie Todd to Nathaniel Dawson, January 1, 1862; January 5, 1862; January 17, 1862; March 16, 1862; and April 1, 1862, Dawson Papers, SHC.

drew compliments from his commanders: Seth Field to David Todd, April 22, 1862, Helm Papers, KHS.

109 "A fine set of soldiers" and "They don't expect anything of this kind": Quoted in Daniel, *Shiloh*, p. 124.

110 "Gentlemen, we shall attack": Ibid, p. 128.

"deaf to duty and dead to shame" and "pushed by scores into the water": McCann, *Ambrose Bierce's Civil War*, p. 16.

111   "Not having any rations": "The Battle of Shiloh," *New Orleans Crescent,* April 17, 1862, p. 1.

And there they sat: Details gleaned from Daniel, *Shiloh,* p. 173.

"Balls and bomb shells": "The Battle of Shiloh," *New Orleans Crescent,* April 17, 1862, p. 1.

112   The ensuing skirmish: Anderson's description of the Crescents' charge against the right wing of the Hornets' Nest appears in *OR,* ser. 1, vol. 10, ch. 22, pp. 497–99. See also Daniel, *Shiloh,* p. 214.

After their charge, Leonidas Polk . . . offered them another option: Leonidas Polk's account of the Crescents' flanking action appears in *OR,* ser. 1, vol. 10, ch. 22, p. 410. See also Daniel, *Shiloh,* pp. 230–37.

113   "black-dark": This and other quotations in paragraph from McCann, *Ambrose Bierce's Civil War,* pp. 18–23.

114   "I can't describe it": For this and other quotations in paragraph, see ibid., pp. 23–24.

"From the time the woods was entered": *OR,* ser. 1, vol. 10, ch. 22, p. 172.

"breathed hard, as if throttled": McCann, *Ambrose Bierce's Civil War,* p. 20.

115   "For God's sake, boys": Daniel, *Shiloh,* p. 271.

"under the most murderous fire": Seth Field to David Todd, April 22, 1862, Helm Papers, KHS.

"Ah, Lieut., I believe they have got me": Seth Field to David Todd, April 22, 1862, Helm Papers, KHS. In presenting the circumstances of Sam's death, I have deferred to this source — an eyewitness account written days after the events it describes. A very different account appears in Katherine Helm's *Mary, Wife of Lincoln* (and elsewhere) and can be traced to an article that appeared first in the *Richmond State* and then in the *New York Times* in 1882. The writer, an acquaintance of Sam's and a veteran of Shiloh, remembered that "Sam Todd's regiment was thrown to the front promptly [on April 7], soon followed by ours, when almost the first object that met us as we passed over the field was the lifeless body of poor Sam, Mrs. Lincoln's brother, with a bullet hole in his forehead!" The writer for the *State* also remembered the circumstances of Sam's burial differently: "Driven back and still back, our dead were all left on the disastrous field for Grant to bury; and among those who shared these grim and hasty funeral rites there was no better man or more devoted soldier of the Confederacy than this gallant young brother of the 'Lady of the White House.'" This account cannot be easily squared with that of Lieutenant Field. It is vaguely possible that the people who claimed to have buried Sam did not but instead dumped his body from the wagon when he expired, that his lifeless corpse was then struck in the forehead during the Union advance, that the man who wrote the story then encountered the body as he claimed. But it seems more likely that a man who did not know Sam well, who may have seen *something* in 1862, lied, embellished, or misremembered the particulars when he wrote them down twenty years later. "Mrs. Lincoln's Brother, His Tragic Death at the Battle of Shiloh," *New York Times,* July 30, 1882, p.2.

He died en route to the hospital: See G. W. Stoddard to David Todd, April 21, 1862, Helm Papers, KHS. It is unclear whether Sam saw any action with the Chasseurs à Pied in 1861. Enrolled in April, he fell ill and was "discharged for sickness at Richmond in October," according to the *Flake's Bulletin* (Galveston), November 8, 1867, p. 2.

116   people figured Sam might have been captured: As late as April 12, a correspondent for the *New Orleans Crescent* would write: "I do not send you any list of the killed and wounded, as it is impossible yet to hear correct reports, and it would be cruel as well as foolish, to create false alarms." See "The Great Battle," *New Orleans Crescent*, April 12, 1862, p. 2.

"Really these battles and rumored battles": Elodie Todd to Nathaniel Dawson, April 15, 1862, Dawson Papers, SHC.

"It is my sad task": David Todd to Emilie Todd Helm, April 15, 1862, Helm Papers, KHS.

Once confirmed, news of Sam's death rippled out: See *Chambersburg Semi-Weekly Dispatch*, May 2, 1862; *Davenport Daily Gazette*, May 1, 1862; *Amherst (N.H.) Farmer's Cabinet*, May 1, 1862, p. 3. None of these papers, it should be pointed out, and only a few Southern ones, bothered to note that David, Sam, and Aleck were Mary's *half* brothers. An exception was the *Richmond Dispatch*, which ran an article, possibly at George's behest, clarifying family matters: "Relatives of Mrs. Lincoln — Having seen numerous paragraphs in various papers, and having even copied them ourselves through mistake, to the effect that Samuel B. Todd, who was killed at Shiloh, Alexander H. Todd, killed recently at Baton Rouge, and Capt. D. H. Todd, how commanding the lower water battery at Vicksburg, are brothers, and only brothers of Mrs. Lincoln, we beg to state, from authority, that Mrs. L has only two brothers — one at present in the Medical corps, CSA, the other beyond military age and in feeble health, but represented in our service by his son. These above spoken of are merely half brothers. The parties at whose instance we write do not plume themselves upon their fortuitous relation with a person of such unenviable notoriety, but simply dislike to have their existence ignored and denied. *Richmond Dispatch.*" Reprinted in the *Columbus Ledger-Enquirer*, September 3, 1862, p. 2, and in the *Macon Weekly Telegraph*, September 5, 1862, p. 1.

"died in defense of his country": *Macon Daily Telegraph*, April 24, 1862, p. 2.

"it must be a pleasant reflection": The *Delta* story was reprinted in the *Columbus Ledger-Enquirer*, April 25, 1862, p. 2.

"The 'Lady of the White House' . . . holds high revelry": H. C. Clarke, *Diary of the War for Separation, a Daily Chronicle of the Principal Events and History of the Present Revolution, to Which is Added Notes and Descriptions of All the Great Battles, Including Walker's Narrative of the Battle of Shiloh* (Augusta, Ga.: Steam Press of Chronicle & Sentinel, 1862), p. 154.

117   "unusually heavy beard": "From the West," *Charleston Daily Courier*, March 15, 1861, p. 1.

"While he was an inmate of your house": Caleb Smith to Abraham Lincoln, October 6, 1861, Lincoln Papers, LOC.

Lincoln held up the appointment: Charles appears to have overreached in requesting a foreign post. In a letter to Lizzie, Mary noted: "Yet really it is amusing, in how many forms, human nature can appear before us — *Nicolay* told me, that Caleb Smith, said to him, a few days since that he had just received a letter from Kellogg — of Cin — that he did not know why he had *not* received his appointment as *Consul* — Is not the idea preposterous?" Mary Lincoln to Elizabeth Todd Grimsley, September 29, 1861, T&T, p. 106. Kellogg never did get the job. Lincoln did appoint a Charles *C.* Kellogg to an army post on February 19, 1863, but this is a different man.

117   "Dear Caleb": For this and other quotations in paragraph, see Charles H. Kellogg to Caleb Smith, October 2, 1861, Lincoln Papers, LOC. Prior to moving to Indiana in the 1850s, Caleb Blood Smith (1808–1864) had studied and practiced law in Cincinnati, which is probably where Kellogg met him.

118   "been [temporarily] compelled": Elodie Todd to Nathaniel Dawson, May 15, 1861, Dawson Papers, SHC.

       "resident of Cincinnati": For this and other quotations in paragraph, see "From the West," *Charleston Daily Courier,* March 15, 1861, p. 1.

       "introduces Mr. Kellogg": Nathaniel Dawson to Elodie Todd, March 16, 1861, Dawson Papers, SHC.

119   "produced evidence to him" and "on the field during the whole time": Charles H. Kellogg to Judah P. Benjamin, April 18, 1862, reproduced in Mark E. Neely, Jr., "The Secret Treason of Abraham Lincoln's Brother-in-Law," *Journal of the Abraham Lincoln Association* 17, no. 1 (Summer 1996): pp. 39–44. "I am greatly distressed": Elodie Todd to Nathaniel Dawson, April 16, 1862, Dawson Papers, SHC.

       "There is evidently some great mistake": Charles H. Kellogg to Judah P. Benjamin, April 18, 1862, reproduced in Neely, "The Secret Treason."

120   "political object": Ibid. See also A. T. Bledsoe, Assistant Secretary of War, to John H. Winder, May 13, 1862, *OR,* ser. 2, vol. 2, pp. 1424–25: "Sir: You will dispose of the prisoners named as follows. . . . C. H. Kellogg, to be placed on his parole not to give information of any kind of anything he may see here, to be permitted the liberty of the city under police surveillance."

       The Kelloggs have always been classed with the loyal wing of the family: The Kelloggs' claims to loyalty rest on the following facts: Charles was born in New York, resided and worked in Ohio, applied for a federal job, and protested his loyalty to the secretary of the interior. In addition, he and his wife had celebrated the Lincolns' ascension to the presidency in Springfield and attended the inaugural in Washington afterward. (The historian William H. Townsend also mentions that "a series of recently discovered letters written by Margaret Todd Kellogg to Lizzie Fleming during the war, formerly owned by Mrs. William C. Goodloe of Lexington, shows her to have been a stanch Unionist." *Lincoln and the Bluegrass,* p. 380.) But other facts portray the Kelloggs as (at best) neutrals: Charles traveled with the Confederate army; the position he agitated for was consul (perhaps because he hoped to avoid the complications of the war altogether); Margaret, and probably Charles, spent some time during the war in Europe with Charles's brother, Minor Kellogg, an artist who lived in Rome; and Margaret spent some of her time in Lexington with her increasingly pro-Confederate mother and wrote to Lincoln to secure the release of a Confederate prisoner. See Elizabeth Todd to Elodie Todd Dawson, October 6, 1863, Helm Papers, KHS; Margaret Todd Kellogg to Abraham Lincoln, September 5, 1864, Lincoln Papers, LOC.

"I want to identify my destiny": Benjamin Hardin Helm to Emilie Todd Helm, April 20, 1862, Helm Papers, KHS. Helm was promoted to brigadier general on April 17, but the order was backdated to take effect on March 14.

"inability to perform" and "I have carefully examined": William C. Davis, *The Orphan Brigade: The Kentucky Confederates Who Couldn't Go Home* (New York: Doubleday, 1980), p. 105.

121 elected David their captain: See Arthur W. Bergeron, Jr., *Guide to Louisiana Confederate Military Units, 1861–1865* (Baton Rouge: Louisiana State University Press, 1989), pp. 125–26.

122 "For more than seventy-five days": *OR*, ser. 1, vol. 15, pp. 6–12.

"chorus of ruin": Lot D. Young, *Reminiscences of a Soldier of the Orphan Brigade* (Louisville: Courier-Journal Job Printing Company, 1918), p. 38.

improvised pig races: See Davis, *The Orphan Brigade*, pp. 111, 112–13.

"finish and equip [the] vessel": For this and other quotations in paragraph, see "The Confederate Gun-Boat 'Arkansas'" by Her Commander, Isaac N. Brown, Captain, C.S.N.," in *Battles and Leaders of the Civil War*, vol. 3 (New York: Century, 1887–88), pp. 572–79.

123 "I received a severe contusion": Ibid.

"forest of masts and smokestacks": Ibid.

124 "[It] was the most spectacular": Young, *Reminiscences of a Soldier of the Orphan Brigade*, p. 38.

on July 24, David spent the night with Aleck and Hardin: Alexander Todd Diary, UKY.

125 "My own troops [have] suffered severely": *OR*, ser. 1, vol. 15, chap. 27, p. 76.

the Orphans traveled by train to Jackson, then set off on foot: On the march from Camp Moore to Baton Rouge, see John B. Pirtle, "Defense of Vicksburg in 1862 — The Battle of Baton Rouge," *Southern Historical Society Papers* 8 (June–July 1880): p. 328; quotation, "brave, noble, ragged Kentuckians," on same page. See also Davis, *The Orphan Brigade*, p. 115.

126 "terrific volley of musketry": "An Unfortunate and Fatal Mistake," *Philadelphia Inquirer*, August 21, 1862, p. 2.

"galloping back, they produced some confusion": *OR*, ser. 1, vol. 15, chap. 27, p. 77.

"frightened at a shadow": *Richmond Dispatch*, August 25, 1862. Another version of the story sharply contradicts this one. For various reports of the incident, see Davis, *The Orphan Brigade*, pp. 116–17; William A. Spedale, *The Battle of Baton Rouge, 1862* (Baton Rouge: Land and Land, 1985), pp. 22–23.

the effect was pandemonium: Again, there are various reports of how exactly Aleck died. According to some primary sources (and most secondary accounts) he fell instantly dead on the road to Baton Rouge. This ignores the evidence of people on Pratt's farm who distinctly remember him being brought to what became a makeshift hospital. No one, however, remembers him as conscious or alert or capable of speech, which probably means that he was rendered insensible on the road but did not actually die until the gate at Pratt's farm. See Charles D. Brandenburg to Emilie Todd Helm, June 3, June 17, June 19, June 24, June 26, and July 9, 1892, Townsend Papers,

UKY; "A Sketch of General Ben Hardin Helm, Whose Remains will be Interred at the Helm Place to-day," undated clipping in Helm Papers, KHS.

127   "Dear Wife. Aleck was killed": Telegram, B. H. Helm to Mrs. B. H. Helm or Mrs. Capt. Dawson, August 8, 1862, Helm Papers, KHS.

"Last night I dreamed": Elodie Todd to Nathaniel Dawson, December 1, 1861, Dawson Papers, SHC.

"B. H. Helm was knocked over": *OR*, ser. 1, vol. 17, pt. 2, p. 181.

Death notices appeared in town papers: See the *Philadelphia Inquirer*, August 21, 1862, p. 2; *Pittsfield (Mass.) Sun*, August 28, 1862, p. 3, itself a reprint from *Albany Argus*; *Salt Lake City Deseret News*, August 27, 1862, p. 69; *Columbus Ledger-Enquirer*, August 16, 1862, p. 3; *Macon Daily Telegraph*, first mentioned on August 12, 1862, p. 2, and elaborated upon on August 30, 1862; *Houston Tri-Weekly Telegraph*, August 25, 1862, p. 1; and *Richmond Dispatch*, August 20, 1862.

"Another brother of Mrs. Lincoln [has been] killed": *Pittsfield (Mass.) Sun*, August 28, 1862, p. 3; reprinted from the *Albany Argus*.

"with apparent unconcern," "I also heard the same, Mrs. Lincoln," and "You need not hesitate": Keckley, *Behind the Scenes*, p. 97.

128   "I am one of the most unforgiving": Elodie Todd to Nathaniel Dawson, June 12, 1861, Dawson Papers, SHC.

"Are they not against *me?*": Ibid. Emphasis added.

"A dispatch of yesterday": Abraham Lincoln to Andrew Johnson, January 8, 1863, *CW*, vol. 6, p. 48. See also Andrew Johnson to Abraham Lincoln, January 9, 1863, Lincoln Papers, LOC; and Abraham Lincoln to Andrew Johnson, January 10, 1863, *CW*, vol. 6, p. 53.

129   Lincoln seemed "heart-broken": Quoted in William K. Goolrick, *Rebels Resurgent* (Alexandria, Va.: Time-Life Books, 1985), pp. 92–93.

"Chattanooga at that time": "Glowing Tribute Paid to Memory of Gen. Helm," undated clipping in "History of the Helm Family" scrapbook, miscellaneous writings, Box 9, Helm Papers, KHS.

130   "attend strictly to his own duties": "An Incident of the War, in which a Sister-in-law of Abe Lincoln Figured," *Uniontown Telegram*, April 20, 1895; McMurtry, *Ben Hardin Helm*, p. 37.

"Our joy was [short-lived]": Nathaniel Dawson to Hardin Helm, January 14, 1863, Helm Papers, KHS.

5. 1863: The Death of Absalom

131   "Sir . . . I have given the order": Davis, *The Orphan Brigade*, p. 155.

132   "My poor Orphan Brigade!": For a description of the battle, see ibid., pp. 155–60; quotation on p. 160.

"Always prompt in attending": Ninian Edwards to Abraham Lincoln, August 10, 1860, Lincoln Papers, LOC; on Lincoln's loans to Edwards, see Pratt, *The Personal Finances of Abraham Lincoln*, pp. 75–76, 80.

133   "I have been *so much embarrassed*" and "I believed you honest": Ninian W. Edwards to Abraham Lincoln, December 26, 1860, Lincoln Papers, LOC.

"He is embarrassed": David Davis to Abraham Lincoln, July 26, 1861, Lincoln Papers, LOC.

"If you were, as I supposed, rich": Orville H. Browning to Ninian W. Edwards, August 8, 1861, Lincoln Papers, LOC.

"For several years we have been ferreting out": Ozias M. Hatch, William Bulter, and Jesse K. Dubois to Abraham Lincoln, July 22, 1861, Lincoln Papers, LOC.

134   "[Matteson's] defeat gives me more pleasure": Abraham Lincoln to Elihu B. Washburne, February 9, 1855, *CW*, vol. 2, p. 306.

"As we predicted": Jesse K. Dubois, William Butler, and Ozias M. Hatch to Abraham Lincoln, October 21, 1861, Lincoln Papers, LOC.

"If Gov. Matteson has any interest" and "I certainly should have never accepted it": Ninian W. Edwards to Abraham Lincoln, October 27, 1861, Lincoln Papers, LOC.

"I heard Mr. Edwards Say": William Yates to Abraham Lincoln, May 22, 1863, Lincoln Papers, LOC.

135   "The sums acquired are too large": Jacob Bunn to Abraham Lincoln, May 25, 1863, Lincoln Papers, LOC.

"[Edwards] has wielded his whole power," "Rebel Sympathizers," and "Blatant Democrats": William Yates to Abraham Lincoln, May 22, 1863, Lincoln Papers, LOC.

"When you ask us": George R. Weber to Abraham Lincoln, August 25, 1863, Lincoln Papers, LOC.

"If any objections": Ninian W. Edwards to Abraham Lincoln, June 10, 1863, Lincoln Papers, LOC.

"The appeal [for] a hearing": Abraham Lincoln to Edward L. Baker, June 15, 1863, Lincoln Papers, LOC. William Bailhache was the business partner of Edward L. Baker, Ninian's son-in-law. Bailhache's wife, Ada, and Baker's wife (Ninian's daughter), Julia, were close friends. On Lincoln's attempt to be firm but fair with Edwards, see also J. T. Taylor to N. W. Edwards, June 22, 1863, in Ninian Wirt Edwards Collection, CHS: "Dear Captain, I have just seen the President and talked over your case with him. The President does not doubt you in any manner or shape but is embarrassed by circumstances should you remaining at Springfield, therefore, I have or will today direct Lt. Colonel Killburn to locate you in Chicago, which will be very agreeable to the President, and under the existing circumstances, I hope will be agreeable to you. The President would very much regret should you resign and I also would much regret to lose you from the Com'y Dept."

136   "to think in *these trying times*": Ninian W. Edwards to Edward Bates, June 18, 1863, Lincoln Papers, LOC.

"You speak of your life long friends": Ninian W. Edwards to Abraham Lincoln, June 18, 1863, Lincoln Papers, LOC.

"I certainly do not suppose": Abraham Lincoln to Edward L. Baker, June 15, 1863, Lincoln Papers, LOC.

"I am not unmindful": Ninian W. Edwards to Abraham Lincoln, September 16, 1864, Lincoln Papers, LOC.

137   "if there ever was a better army": Benjamin Hardin Helm to Emilie Todd Helm, April 12, 1863, Helm Papers, KHS.

from a familiar quarter: See Davis, *The Orphan Brigade*, p. 171.

"[You will be] putting [yourself]": The exact quote: "Sherman then expressed his alarm at the move I had ordered, saying that I was putting myself in a position voluntarily which an enemy would be glad to manoeuvre a year — or a long time — to get me in." Grant, *Memoirs and Selected Letters* (New York: Library of America, 1990), pp. 364–65.

137 "Until this moment": Quoted in Shea and Winschel, *Vicksburg Is the Key*, p. 143. It was a lesson Sherman would never forget. Before the campaign he had regarded it "an axiom in war that when any great body of troops moved against an enemy they should do so from a base of supplies, which they would guard as they would the apple of the eye." In some small way, the March to the Sea was born May 18, 1863, on the Walnut Hills. Quotation from Grant, *Memoirs and Selected Letters*, p. 365.

Sure that rebel reinforcements . . . would soon be upon him: For a concise description of early operations around Vicksburg, including a mention of David Todd, see Shea and Winschel, *Vicksburg Is the Key*, pp. 140–51. Quotation "in the name of humanity," p. 151.

138 "I now determined upon a regular siege": Grant, *Memoirs and Selected Letters*, p. 357.

It was not in Grant's nature . . . to merely sit and wait: On the efforts of federal sappers, see Shea and Winschel, *Vicksburg Is the Key*, pp. 154–58. On Vicksburg's unusual soils, and for quotation "melts like butter," see National Park Service Web site: www.nps.gov/archive/vick/preserve/erosion.htm; accessed December 26, 2006.

139 close enough to share a wall: See James R. Arnold, *Grant Wins the War: Decision at Vicksburg* (New York: John Wiley, 1997), pp. 260–62; 268–71.

"marked courtesy" and "I hope you will get exchanged": Josephine Craven Chandler, "An Episode of the Civil War, A Romance of Coincidence," *Transactions of the Illinois State Historical Society*, 31 (1924): p. 114. The incident occurred on May 14, 1864.

140 "who is going to be the smarter": Quoted in Arnold, *Grant Wins the War*, p. 274.

Grant hoped that if his men could hold the crater long enough: For a description of the engagement and the quotation "My God! They are killing my bravest men," see ibid., pp. 274–76.

141 "I do sincerely hope": Ben Hardin Helm to Emilie Todd Helm, June 26, 1863, Helm Papers, KHS.

"anything but a pleasing personage": Daniel M. Holt to wife, May 15, 1863, in Daniel M. Holt, *A Surgeon's Civil War: The Letters and Diary of Daniel M. Holt*, ed. James M. Greiner, Janet L. Coryell, and James R. Smither (Kent, Ohio: Kent State University Press, 1994), pp. 97–98. Holt did have some positive things to say about George: "This Dr. Todd is anything but a pleasing personage — short, rather inferior looking with an impediment in his speech, the first impression as to intelligence is unfavorable; but subsequent acquaintance reveals quite a different man. He is pleasant when engaged in lively conversation, and much of the hesitation in speech is overcome as he becomes interested in the matter under discussion: I think I should like him very much even though he is thoroughly rebel in every particular: still the gentleman within him prevents all allusion to unpleasant topics such as discussions upon the political questions of the day, and relative merits of Confederate and loyal soldiers."

"arrested ... in his insolence": *Franklin Repository,* July 15, 1863, p. 1.

"took charge of the stealing operations": *Franklin Repository,* July 8, 1863, p. 5.

"no business being there": Diary of William Heyser, June 28, 1863, "Valley of the Shadow: Two Communities in the American Civil War," Virginia Center for Digital History, University of Virginia.

142   seven hundred amputations: On the claim that George performed seven hundred amputations, see *Charlotte Observer,* May 24, 1892, p. 1.

"Scarcely one in a hundred": Quoted in Robert E. Denney, *Civil War Medicine: Care & Comfort of the Wounded* (New York: Sterling, 1994), p. 215.

143   "It was an easy matter": Quoted in Denney, *Civil War Medicine,* p. 218.

"For so many long days": Quoted in Shea and Winschell, *Vicksburg Is the Key,* p. 176.

"excellent indeed," "Forty-eight days," "I have escaped," and "hate[d] to be idle": David Todd to Betsey Todd, July 5, 1863, Helm Papers, KHS.

"Going down I fell in with Capt. D. H. Todd": Diary of Joseph Addison Waddell, September 8, 1863, "Valley of the Shadow." See also Nathaniel Dawson to Elodie Todd Dawson, August 24, 1863, Dawson Papers, SHC: "Your brother David was here on yesterday on his way to Richmond," Nathaniel wrote Elodie from Montgomery. "He was well and left in the evening, and will be back in two weeks. I do not know what his purpose in going there is."

144   "As usual with me": Benjamin Hardin Helm to Emilie Todd Helm, July 22, 1863, Helm Papers, KHS.

"I am very anxious": Benjamin Hardin Helm to Emilie Todd Helm, April 12, 1863, Helm Papers, KHS.

"War. War the sole theme": Emilie's diary has never been found. Her daughter Katherine Helm certainly used it to prepare *Mary, Wife of Lincoln* (1928). The book's subtitle — *"Containing the recollections of Mary Lincoln's sister Emilie (Mrs. Ben Hardin Helm), extracts from her war-time diary, numerous letters and other documents now first published by her niece"* — confused one Thomas Galey into thinking the diary itself was being published. On April 26, 1928, he wrote Emilie that he was "overjoyed to learn from the *Kansas City Star"* that she had "released the precious diary for publication." On the reverse of his letter appears to be Emilie's response: "I am only giving out parts of my diary to my daughter who is writing the life of my sister, Mary Todd Lincoln. My diary will be of no interest to the public so I will destroy it." She later did just that. Nevertheless, in the undated miscellaneous scraps of the Emilie Todd Helm collection, there is a single transcribed page of the diary. The story and quotation about the doll are taken from the surviving manuscript page. For the page, see miscellaneous writings, Helm Papers, KHS. On the letter from Galey to Emilie, see Townsend Papers, UKY. For a more extended discussion of the diary excerpts that appear in *Mary, Wife of Lincoln,* see note in this chapter following the key phrase "Mr. Lincoln and my sister."

145   "Cracking jokes" and "in the finest spirits": Quoted in Peter Cozzens, *This Terrible Sound: The Battle of Chickamauga* (Champaign: University of Illinois Press, 1996), p. 319.

145   "got up and mounted his horse": Quoted in Davis, *Orphan Brigade*, p. 182.
One of the Union soldiers later admitted: R. F. Scribner, *How Soldiers Were Made; or, The War as I Saw It* (New Albany, Ind., 1887), pp. 154–56.
"perfect tornado of bullets": W. W. Herr, "Kentuckians at Chickamauga," *Confederate Veteran*, October 1895, p. 295.

146   "giving & taking death blows": Quoted in Davis, *The Orphan Brigade*, p. 185.
"He had just said" and "Get an ambulance": "Pirtle's Graphic Recital of the Particulars of Gen. Helm's Death," undated news clipping, Helm Papers, KHS.
The Orphans' losses in front of the federal breastwork: Good accounts of the three charges that resulted in Helm's death include the separate reports of James W. Moss and J. C. Wickliffe, *OR*, ser. 1, vol. 30, pt. 2, pp. 208–9, 213–14.
"Is there hope?": Ed Porter Thompson, *History of the First Kentucky Brigade* (Cincinnati: Caxton Publishing House, 1868), p. 385.
"Sick . . . discouraged and out of heart": Undated Civil War reminiscence in Helm Collection, KHS.

147   "We have met with a serious disaster": William S. Rosecrans to Abraham Lincoln, September 20, 1863, *CW*, vol. 6, p. 474.
"We now have a tolerably accurate summing up": Abraham Lincoln to Mary Lincoln, September 24, 1863, *CW*, vol. 6, p. 478.
"I never saw Mr. Lincoln more moved": *Washington Sunday Herald*, December 5, 1886.
"deal gently for my sake" and "Is the young man, Absalom, safe?": 2 Samuel 18:5, 18:32–33 (King James Version).

149   Hardin Helm was buried in a graveyard in Atlanta: Helm's funeral took place at St. Paul's Episcopal Church in Atlanta. His body was prepared at Colonel Dabney's, where Emilie stayed for a week after the funeral. She then removed to the home of E. M. Bruce in Madison, Georgia. Bruce himself attempted to get Emilie a pass to go north to Kentucky, but there is no sure sign that he succeeded. See E. M. Bruce to Abraham Lincoln, October 6, 1863, Lincoln Papers, LOC.
She wanted to be with her mother: See E. M. Bruce to Abraham Lincoln, October 6, 1863, Lincoln Papers, LOC.
"intruded" . . . "hour of deep affliction": E. Haldeman to Emilie Todd Helm, September 25, 1863, Helm Papers, KHS.
"pour some balm": Virginia Page to Emilie Todd Helm, October 11, 1863, Helm Papers, KHS.
"widow of [their] gallant deceased general": Braxton Bragg to Emilie Todd Helm, November 9, 1863, KHS.
"Mrs. Helm, widow" and "I trusted the mention of both relations": Braxton Bragg to Emilie Todd Helm, November 12, 1863, KHS.

150   "Inform[ed] . . . that Mrs. Helm": *Macon Daily Telegraph*, November 4, 1863, p. 2.
"[He was] my son": Lucinda Helm to Emilie Todd Helm, October 21, 1863, Helm Papers, KHS.
"Come home to us Emilie": Lucinda Helm to Emilie Todd Helm, October 21, 1863, Helm Papers, KHS.

"I am totally at a loss": John L. Helm to Elizabeth Todd, October 11, 1863, Helm Papers, KHS.

"[I must] make every exertion": Elizabeth Todd to Elodie Todd Dawson, October 6, 1863, Helm Papers, KHS.

"Mrs. Robert S. Todd": Abraham Lincoln to Lyman B. Todd, October 15, 1863, *CW,* vol. 6, p. 517. Lincoln had sent the pass to Lyman Beecher Todd, a cousin of Mary's and the postmaster of Lexington. Because of the strained relations between Betsey and the White House, and because of his easy access to a telegraph, Lyman operated as a convenient go-between. After waiting more than two weeks for Lincoln's pass of October 15, Lyman telegraphed the president: "Your pass for Mrs. Robert Todd has not reached me." "I sent the pass by Telegraph more than ten days ago," Lincoln responded on the October 31. "Did you not receive it?" Lyman had expected the pass to arrive by mail. On November 2, the pass was found or resent, and Betsey set off immediately. On November 9, Lyman informed the president, "Aunt Betsy Todd left for the South on 3rd Inst. bearing your Kind Passport." Lyman B. Todd to Abraham Lincoln, October 31, 1863, and Lyman B. Todd to Abraham Lincoln, November 2, 1863, Lincoln Papers, LOC.

"the mother of Mrs. Lincoln ... arrived in this city": *Richmond Dispatch,* November 14, 1863. The story was picked up by the *Philadelphia Inquirer,* November 21, 1863, p. 4. See also J. B. Jones, *A Rebel War Clerk's Diary,* vol. 2 (Philadelphia: Lippincott, 1866), p. 99.

permanent residence in the South: Reprinted in the *Staunton Spectator,* November 17, 1863, p. 2.

151   free the woman or leave her in the South: It is not entirely clear, however, that the slave was Emilie's to free. See H. M. Bruce to Emilie Todd Helm, September 30, 1863, Helm Papers, KHS: "By what route do you purpose going [home to Kentucky]? Through this city [Richmond], by flag of truce, would be the safest, if you could get anything from the U.S. Sec'y of War for the purpose which, no doubt, you could obtain by requesting it by letter to Mr. or Mrs. Lincoln, in your doing of which I can see no impropriety if you choose [purposely torn] forward me your letters and I will have it sent to Washington by flag of truce and will come out for you and the dear little children if the arrangement be made. The only objection to your going this way is, I presume, that you could not take Margaret by this route, as you might do should you go by Nashville." The Helms also had another slave, named Phil, in the Deep South. With some of the Helms' things, he returned on his own through Union lines to Kentucky.

she could not take the oath: As more areas of the South had come under federal sway, the issue of the oath had become an increasingly divisive one. See for instance Benjamin Morgan Palmer, *The Oath of Allegiance to the United States, Discussed in Its Moral and Political Bearings* (Richmond, 1863).

"Send her to me": Helm, *Mary, Wife of Lincoln,* p. 221. The telegram itself has never been found. Lincoln undoubtedly invited his sister-in-law to the White House, but he may or may not have used these exact words.

152   "Mr. Lincoln and my sister": The only firsthand account we have of Emilie's stay in the White House is the long passage in *Mary, Wife of Lincoln* that its

author, Katherine Helm, introduces as an excerpt of her mother's diary. The excerpt contains no dated headings, which are typical of diary entries, and no ellipses to suggest where the entries have been cut or cobbled together. The long block quotation is written in the first person throughout but not always in what historians might call "diary tense." Diaries tend to be written in a mix of present tense and immediate past tense; they describe what the self *is* doing or *has just* done. The excerpt in *Mary, Wife of Lincoln* occasionally breaks "diary tense": "the room I *occupied* had been fitted up for the Prince of Wales" or "Mr. Lincoln in the intimate talks we *had* was very much affected over the misfortunes of our family" (italics mine). Sentences like these are retrospective. By the time Emilie wrote them, she was no longer at the White House in the Prince of Wales Room; she was no longer talking to Lincoln about her unfortunate family. This in no way undermines the importance of the excerpt as a historical source or its delightfulness as a text. It is replete with Emilie's voice, words, and experiences. And it contains many diary-like elements: "There is an expedition to the Russian fleet and all the members of Congress have gone to it." "Driving out in the state carriage today, we came suddenly on a street car from which some little boys were jumping." These kind of spontaneous, undigested accounts of Emilie's time at the White House are both authentic and critical to a full portrait of Little Sister's time with the Lincolns. The point, then, is not to throw out the source altogether but to get to the bottom of how it was created.

The most likely scenario is this: Emilie did not want her daughter to have full access to her diary. Instead, she gave her "transcriptions" of the diary, which she had edited and liberally seeded with recollection. This explains the oddity of the long passage in *Mary, Wife of Lincoln*. It also explains the single transcribed diary page that can be found in the Emilie Todd Helm Papers, KHS. Certainly, William Henry Townsend, a historian who knew Emilie in later life, confirms that she would have been unlikely to give anyone unfettered access to the diary: "Mrs. Helm was exceedingly cautious about allowing any examination of this diary. There were some pages in it which she did not mind me seeing, since I was a very old friend of the family, and then there were other sections which she had permitted only her children to see, and there were still others which she had strongly glued together many years ago, which she, of course, permitted no one to see." William Henry Townsend to Philip R. Baker, January 18, 1955, Townsend Papers, ALPL.

152 "We talk of old friends" and "We approach any subject timidly": Helm, *Mary, Wife of Lincoln*, p. 222.
Lincoln had stepped forward to remove her bonnet: "Lincoln and Helm, the President's Confederate Brother-in-Law," unidentified clipping in Helm Papers, KHS.
"What do you think of Mr. Lincoln?": This and all other quotes and events described in the following paragraphs on Emilie's stay are from Helm, *Mary, Wife of Lincoln*. See pp. 222, 225–32.

156 The oath, apparently, he pretended she had taken and set aside: There is no way to know if Emilie actually took the oath. She claimed that she did not and subsequent interactions between herself and Lincoln suggest that she did not.

156   "Mrs. Emily T. Helm": Both oath and pardon, Abraham Lincoln, December
       14, 1863, Lincoln Papers, LOC.
       cotton Emilie claimed to own in the South: Where did Emilie get the cot-
       ton, and why would she expect Lincoln to help her sell it? The first ques-
       tion is a bit of a stumper. Six hundred bales is a lot of cotton, and its market
       value in late 1863 ($118,000) was a lot of money. Emilie and Hardin had
       had no acreage and no field hands, so they did not grow the cotton; they
       must have "acquired" it during the war. There is no reason to believe they
       acquired it illegally. Given the number of distressed planters, Hardin might
       have bought an option on some cotton while he was in the Deep South. Per-
       haps, given his military position, he thought he would be able to protect it
       and get it out of the South. More probably, though, the cotton's owner was
       actually Hardin's brother-in-law and former law partner, Horatio Washing-
       ton Bruce. Bruce had married Lucinda Barbour Helm in 1856 (the same
       year Hardin married Emilie), and the two men had formed a law partner-
       ship in 1859. In 1862, when Hardin was organizing his cavalry, Bruce had
       been elected to the Confederate Congress to represent the "seceded" Ken-
       tucky. While in Congress, Bruce became adept at finding back channels for
       the sale of Confederate cotton, and he bought up a number of options in the
       hope of selling more. Perhaps he was using Emilie as a front and would pay
       her a fee if she could get it out. Perhaps he owed Hardin money or wanted
       Emilie to be financially secure.
           The second question — why Emilie would expect Lincoln to help her — is
       an easier one. On the surface, it seems odd that the North would buy cot-
       ton from the South at all. Why did the North impose a blockade if it was
       only going to circumvent it? Why did Northerners inject capital into a re-
       gion that would only use the money to buy arms to shoot them with? Two
       reasons: First, the trade was just too lucrative. The blockade, the South's
       own embargo, and the steady reduction in cotton crops as planters, to feed
       the Confederate army, shifted more acreage to foodstuffs: all drove cotton
       prices through the roof. With such a margin to be made, Northerners would
       and did engage in it, whatever the government might say. For its part, the
       Lincoln administration, partly hoping to resecure the South through eco-
       nomics, preferred to try to regulate the trade than to suppress it. Thus, they
       required traders to have a license and a permit, to trade with the South on
       reduced terms, to pay not in gold but greenbacks, to never trade contraband
       goods, and so on. They also tried, less successfully, to make the permit pro-
       cess open to all loyal citizens to prevent profiteering or the formation of mo-
       nopolies. But the process was more open to some than others — and Lincoln,
       despite being what his wife called a "monomaniac" on the subject of hon-
       esty, was quite guilty of helping friends to help themselves. For more on this
       subject, see David G. Surdam, "Traders or Traitors: Northern Cotton Trad-
       ing During the Civil War," *Business and Economic History* 28, no. 2 (Win-
       ter 1999): pp. 301–12. For evidence hinting at Bruce's connection to Emilie's
       cotton, see Pauline Benson to Emilie Todd Helm, undated, Helm Papers,
       KHS.
       "You know Little Sister" and "For weal or woe": Helm, *Mary, Wife of Lin-
       coln*, p. 233. The full quotation: "for weal or woe he [Hardin] felt he must
       side with his own people."

6. 1864–65: A Whole People

157   "thin and feeble": Elodie Todd to Nathaniel Dawson, June 16, 1861, Dawson Papers, SHC.

"far from well": Elodie Todd to Nathaniel Dawson, July 3, 1861, Dawson Papers, SHC.

"I fear": Elodie Todd to Nathaniel Dawson, April 1, 1862, Dawson Papers, SHC.

"too delicate": Nathaniel Dawson to Elodie Todd, December 11, 1861, Dawson Papers, SHC.

158   "We are always together," "[We] resemble each other," and "I cannot govern": Elodie Todd to Nathaniel Dawson, July 23, 1861, Dawson Papers, SHC.

"I am one of the most unforgiving": Elodie Todd to Nathaniel Dawson, June 12, 1861, Dawson Papers, SHC.

"I [occasionally feel]": Elodie Todd to Nathaniel Dawson, May 9, 1861, Dawson Papers, SHC.

"great personal charm": Henry Kyd Douglas, *I Rode with Stonewall, being chiefly the war experiences of the youngest member of Jackson's staff from the John Brown Raid to the hanging of Mrs. Surratt* (Chapel Hill: University of North Carolina Press, 1940), p. 270.

"in appearance, mind and manner": Katherine Helm, *Mary, Wife of Lincoln*, p. 181.

"gone through the lines" and "The gold thus brought": "A Premium Uniform," *Richmond Enquirer,* March 2, 1864, p. 1.

"earnest one-term man": Horace Greeley to John G. Nicolay, April 26, 1864, Lincoln Papers, LOC.

159   "It is stated in the best-informed circles": "Aid and Comfort for the Enemy," *New York Tribune,* March 28, 1864, p. 4.

"was a rebel spy," "in substance," "written and signed," and "To-day": *New York World,* April 1, 1864, p. 4. See also *Private and Official Correspondence of General Benjamin F. Butler* (Norwood: Plimpton Press, 1917), vol. 4, pp. 98–99.

160   "Mr President Sir": O. Stewart to Abraham Lincoln, April 27, 1864, Lincoln Papers, LOC.

"Will you please inform me": John G. Nicolay to Benjamin F. Butler, April 19, 1864, Lincoln Papers, LOC.

"I am sorry that you or any body": For this and the other quotations in this paragraph, see Benjamin F. Butler to John G. Nicolay, April 21, 1864, Lincoln Papers, LOC.

"from the first, without truth": John G. Nicolay to Horace Greeley, April 25, 1864, Lincoln Papers, LOC.

"I want to publish all the truth": Horace Greeley to John G. Nicolay, April 26, 1864, Lincoln Papers, LOC.

161   "I took advantage of . . . fortuitous circumstances": This and the other quotations in this paragraph from Martha Todd White to Abraham Lincoln, December 19, 1863, Lincoln Papers, LOC.

162   Lincoln sent her a pass: *Diary of Gideon Welles* (Boston: Houghton Mifflin, 1911), vol. 2, p. 21.

"if Mrs. W. did not leave": Ibid.

"badly treated" and "temper came out": Martha Todd White to Abraham Lincoln, March 14, 1865, Lincoln Papers, LOC.

"mass of luggage": Douglas, *I Rode with Stonewall*, p. 271.

163   to come south and kill him [Butler]: See T.R.R. Cobb to Marian Cobb, June 10, 1862, Thomas Reade Rootes Cobb Papers, UGA.

conversation turned to Martha Todd White: Douglas, *I Rode With Stonewall*, p. 269.

"Discovery" . . . would have involved": Ibid., p. 271.

"General Butler did not wish" and "Mrs. White showed no other": Benjamin F. Butler to John G. Nicolay, April 21, 1864, Lincoln Papers, LOC.

164   That story . . . actually *predated* Matt's return to the South: The original *Richmond Examiner* story, published on March 2, 1864, and picked up by the *Memphis Daily Appeal* on March 5, 1864, predated White's trip by weeks. A mystery remains as to who fabricated the Uniform of the Golden Buttons myth. A hint can be gleaned from an article published later by the *New York Herald*. "From a late personal interview with Major Mulford, commander of our flag of truce boat, I learn that the [*Tribune*] article does not contain one word of truth. Our flag boat has lately been making one trip per week to and from City Point, and the Major brought up a copy of an Atlanta (Ga.) paper, containing the substance of the [White charges] two weeks prior to his carrying Mrs. White through our lines, and the lady herself spoke of having seen the article, before leaving Washington. I certainly think the *Tribune's* correspondence should pay more attention to the truth and less to giving publicity to defamatory articles in regard to our officers, particularly when those articles are stolen by him from rebel newspapers, instead of being 'stated in best informed circles' in Washington." *New York Herald*, April 2, 1864, p. 5.

"most beautiful woman": Douglas, *I Rode with Stonewall*, p. 271.

Her [Hetty Carey's] wedding to General John Pegram: In his letter to Nicolay, Butler also alluded to wedding clothes: "I did understand that there were in Mrs. Whites trunk some bridal presents to a young relative about to become a bride, and as I knew it must have taken so much Southern gold to buy them, as they could not have been bought with their currency and could be of no possible use to the Southern army, I concluded it was a fair exchange or at least one in which we got the better bargain." Benjamin F. Butler to John G. Nicolay, April 21, 1864, Lincoln Papers, LOC.

Another of Matt's trunks contained a keg of brandy: For more on the story of John Hunt Morgan and Matt's brandy, see Douglas, *I Rode with Stonewall*, p. 271; and Henry Kyd Douglas to Emilie Todd Helm, October 4, 1898, quoted in Townsend, *Lincoln and the Bluegrass*, p. 317.

Matt was invited to call upon Mr. And Mrs. Davis: Douglas, *I Rode with Stonewall*, p. 272.

165   "with great vim": Grimsley, "Six Months in the White House," p. 57.

Credulity and decency are easily mistaken for each other: Noah Brooks said something of the same with respect to Lincoln: "A nobler and purer nature than his never animated man. His chiefest errors have been that the heart overruled the head, and a kindness, which has been mistaken for weakness, has too often prevailed when sterner counsels have been heard." Burlingame, *Lincoln Observed*, pp. 67–68.

165   "He gave the details": *Diary of Gideon Welles*, vol. 2, p. 21.

166   "90 by 60 feet" and "Taken together": *Charleston Mercury*, January 14, 1862.
       See also Thomas More Downey, "A Call to Duty: Confederate Hospitals in
       South Carolina," M.A. thesis, University of South Carolina, 1992.
       During the reorganization [of Charleston's hospitals]: See Downey, "A Call
       to Duty."
       he [George] had performed the first successful amputation at the hip joint:
       The claim that George successfully amputated at the hip is made in Evans,
       Mrs. Abraham Lincoln, p. 50: "[George] performed, while surgeon in the
       Confederate Army, the first successful amputation at hip joint, a matter of
       record in the government archives at Washington, D.C." Evans cites a per-
       sonal letter as his source. The letter has not been found nor has any corrob-
       orating evidence been located in government archives.

167   "We had no shelter": *Report on the Treatment of Prisoners of War*, p. 1086.
       "the most horrible place," "A more horrible-looking set," and "come around
       among the men": Ibid., p. 1005.

168   "[Todd was] the most degraded": Ibid., p. 1008.
       "A more rabid secessionist": Samuel H. M. Byers, *With Fire and Sword*
       (New York: Neale Publishing Company, 1911), p. 142.
       "never heard a man more capable": *Report on the Treatment of Prisoners of
       War*, p. 1086.
       "raving fits," "kicked him in the most brutal manner," "I am G—d d——d glad
       of it," and "Soon the screams": Ibid.

169   "You have no right," "did not care a damn," and "For God's sake": Ibid., p.
       1008.
       the Kentucky Emilie returned to: For more on Kentucky's divisions, see
       Lowell H. Harrison, *The Civil War in Kentucky* (Lexington: University
       Press of Kentucky, 1975).

170   "in the 'Great Hog Swindle'": For a more thorough history, see Palmer H.
       Boeger, "The Great Kentucky Hog Swindle of 1864," *Journal of Southern
       History* 28, no. 1 (February, 1962): pp. 59–70.
       "the most convenient place": Burbridge's policies backfired, of course. His
       population became not more quiescent but less so. In September he was
       heartened to hear that John Hunt Morgan had been cornered and killed
       in Greeneville, Tennessee. Morgan's raiders were only replaced by the likes
       of Sue Munday and William Quantrill, however — hardened bushwhackers
       with not even Morgan's sense of restraint. For details, see Louis De Falaise,
       "Gen. Stephen Gano Burbridge's Command in Kentucky" *Register of the
       Kentucky Historical Society* 69 (April 1971): pp. 101–27; quotation, p. 112.

171   "against the mere fact": Abraham Lincoln to Stephen G. Burbridge, August
       8, 1864, *CW*, vol. 7, p. 485.
       "Mr. Lincoln is already beaten": Horace Greeley to George Opdyke, August
       18, 1864, in Harper, *Lincoln and the Press*, p. 309.
       "Do you expect to be elected?": Burlingame, *An Oral History of Abraham
       Lincoln*, p. 58.
       "The springs of [my] life": William O. Stoddard, *Abraham Lincoln: The
       Man and the War President* (New York: Fords, Howard, and Hubert, 1896),
       pp. 408–9.
       "The tired part of me": Quoted in Richard Hofstadter, *The American Po-*

litical Tradition: And the Men Who Made It (New York: Alfred A. Knopf, 1973), p. 173.

"After the war?": Stoddard, *Abraham Lincoln*, pp. 408–9.

"prematurely aged": Burlingame, *Lincoln Observed*, p. 13.

172 "ghoul": Harper, *Lincoln and the Press*, p. 318.

"undertaker": Harold Holzer, ed., *Lincoln as I Knew Him: Gossip, Tributes, and Revelations from His Best Friends and Worst Enemies* (Chapel Hill, N.C.: Algonquin, 1999), p. 107.

"huge skeleton": Donn Piatt in Allen Thorndike Rice, *Reminiscences of Abraham Lincoln by Distinguished Men of His Time* (New York: North American Publishing, 1888), p. 479.

"[His] personal appearance is the subject": Holzer, *Lincoln as I Knew Him*, p. 92.

"His hair is grizzled": Burlingame, *Lincoln Observed, pp.* 13–14.

"hearty, blithesome, genial": Holzer, *Lincoln as I Knew Him*, p. 89.

"idolator . . . adulator": *New York Tribune*, March 17, 1865; quoted in Harper, *Lincoln and the Press*, p. 345.

"I hope I am not intruding": Emilie Todd Helm to Abraham Lincoln, December 20, 1863, Lincoln Papers, LOC.

"Hoping you will pardon": Kitty Todd to Abraham Lincoln, October 18, 1864, Lincoln Papers, LOC.

"Efforts to reach *you*": Margaret Todd Kellogg to Abraham Lincoln, September 5, 1864, Lincoln Papers, LOC.

173 The meeting between Lincoln and Little Sister: See William Henry Townsend to Philip R. Baker, January 18, 1955, Townsend Papers, ALPL: "It is true that correspondence in the Robert Todd Lincoln papers indicated that she made another trip to the White House sometime in the autumn of 1864, but this was a hurried one in an effort to obtain a permit to go South and dispose of some cotton which had been owned by her husband. The President was unable to permit this, since she had refused to take the oath of allegiance and her visit was short and a rather bitter one."

his [Levi's] kids were sent away: After she filed for divorce, Louisa moved in with her widowed mother, Ellen Searles, who also lived in Lexington. Louisa was not in the house long, however, before she died. Ellen could not take care of the children for whatever reason, and two of them — Ella (thirteen) and Louisa (five) — were shipped off to Springfield to live with their aunt and uncle Ann Todd Smith and Clark Moulton Smith. The choice of the Smiths was probably made because they had lost three of their own children. See 1860 census, Fayette County, Kentucky, and Clark M. Smith to Abraham Lincoln, February 7, 1864, Lincoln Papers, LOC.

"means of *substincance*," "from $150 to $200," and "With the kind assistance": Levi O. Todd to Abraham Lincoln, September 12, 1864, Lincoln Papers, LOC.

174 "utter want and destitution," "With such a sad," and "The last money I have": Emilie Todd Helm to Abraham Lincoln, October 30, 1864, Lincoln Papers, LOC.

Lincoln almost didn't know anymore: For an example of Lincoln weighing his personal responsibility for the war, see David R. Locke in Rice, *Reminiscences of Abraham Lincoln*, pp. 450–51: "[Lincoln] was as tender-hearted as a girl. He asked me if the masses of the people of Ohio held him, in any way, personally responsible for the loss of their friends in the army. 'It's a good thing for individuals,' he said, 'that there's a government to shove over their acts upon. No man's shoulders are broad enough to bear what must be.'"

175 "blast of hell": Bell I. Wiley, ed., *This Infernal War: The Confederate Letters of Edwin H. Fay* (Austin: University of Texas Press, 1958), p. 40.

"deadly wind": Quoted in Earl J. Hess, *The Union Soldier in Battle: Enduring the Ordeal of Combat* (Lawrence: University Press of Kansas, 1997), p. 46.

"hurricane of combustibles": John M. Copley, *A Sketch of the Battle of Franklin, Tennessee, with Reminiscences of Camp Douglas* (Austin, 1893), p. 51.

"murderous leaden storm": H. C. Clarke, *Diary of the War of Separation, a Daily Chronicle of the Principal Events and History of the Present Revolution* (Vicksburg, 1862), p. 173.

"loathsome earth-soiled vestiges": David Hunter Strother quoted in Hess, *The Union Soldier*, p. 149.

"kicking like a flock of dead partridges": Quoted in Aaron Sheehan-Dean, ed., *The View from the Ground: Experiences of Civil War Soldiers* (Lexington: University Press of Kentucky, 2006), p. 132.

"Some of my generals": Schuyler Colfax in Rice, *Reminiscences of Abraham Lincoln*, p. 339.

"[Lincoln] did merciful things": Robert G. Ingersoll in ibid., p. 312.

"Men and women were continually coming to him": Stoddard, *Abraham Lincoln*, p. 407.

176 "our Southern brethren": Abraham Lincoln, Speech at Kalamazoo, Michigan, August 27, 1856, *CW*, vol. 2, p. 362.

"national feeling of brotherhood": Abraham Lincoln, Speech at Peoria, Illinois, October 16, 1854, *CW*, vol. 2, p. 272.

"[The United States is the] home of one national family": Abraham Lincoln, Annual Message to Congress, December 1, 1862, *CW*, vol. 5, p. 527.

"We are all of the same family": Abraham Lincoln quoted by Donn Piatt in Rice, *Reminiscences of Abraham Lincoln*, p. 489.

"this unhappy fraternal war": Abraham Lincoln, Reply to Joseph Bertinatti, July 30, 1864 in Basler, *Collected Works*, vol. 7, p. 473.

Southern magazines: See, for example, "The Difference of Race between the Northern and Southern People," *Southern Literary Messenger*, June 1860; and "Manifest Destiny of the World — Its Republic and Its Empire," *Southern Literary Messenger*, September 1859.

"one national family . . . one united people": Abraham Lincoln, Annual Message to Congress, December 1, 1862, *CW*, vol. 5, p. 527. The full quote: "That portion of the earth's surface which is owned and inhabited by the people of the United States, is well adapted to be the home of one national family; and it is not well adapted for two, or more. Its vast extent, and its variety of climate and productions, are of advantage, in this age, for one people, whatever they might have been in former ages. Steam, telegraphs, and intelligence, have brought these, to be an advantageous combination, for one united people."

177 "moral impossibility": Burlingame, *Lincoln Observed*, p. 177.

By 1861, Southern papers reprinted the parts of the speech: For Southern papers that confused Lincoln as the author of the "irrepressible conflict" theory, see: "Irrepressible Conflict Again Proclaimed," *Dallas Weekly Herald,* March 13, 1861, p. 1; "Lincoln is Not a Conservative Republican," *Dallas Weekly Herald,* December 5, 1860, p. 2; "The Black Republican Nominee," *Macon Daily Telegraph,* May 21, 1860, p. 2; "The 'Irrepressible Conflict' Championship," *Macon Daily Telegraph,* May 30, 1860, p. 3; *Houston Weekly Telegraph,* June 5, 1860, p. 2.

178   above all, *Macbeth:* On Lincoln and *Macbeth,* see Michael Knox Beran, "Lincoln, *Macbeth,* and the Moral Imagination."
"contracted in one brow of woe": *Hamlet,* act 1, scene 2.
"hath long been mad": *Richard III,* act 5, scene 5.
"down-fall'n birthdom": *Macbeth,* act 4, scene 3.
"Let us seek out some desolate shade": Ibid.

179   "I tremble for my country": Thomas Jefferson, *Notes on the State of Virginia* (Chapel Hill: University of North Carolina Press, 1996), p. 163.
"The awful calamity of civil war": Abraham Lincoln, Proclamation Appointing a National Fast Day, March 30, 1863, *CW,* vol. 6, p. 156.

180   "villagers and working-men" and "gloomy eyes": John N. Kasson quoted in Rice, *Reminiscences of Abraham Lincoln,* pp. 384–85.

181   "As I dwell on what I myself heard": Walt Whitman in ibid., p. 470.
"indispensable hero of the great drama": Horace Greeley in Holzer, *Lincoln as I Knew Him,* pp. 111–12.
"I have not suffered": Rufus Rockwell Wilson, *Lincoln Among His Friends* (Caldwell, Ind.: Caxton Printers, 1942), pp. 181–82.
"no blood relatives of Mr. Lincoln": George Alfred Townsend, *The Life, Crime, and Capture of John Wilkes Booth* (New York: Dick & Fitzgerald, 1865), p. 18.

Epilogue

182   Congress opened an inquiry into prison abuses: The issue of prisoner abuse was highly politicized in the immediate postwar period — and has been ever since. Not coincidentally, the first issue of the *Journal of Southern History* devoted an article to the subject. See William B. Hesseltine, "The Propaganda Literature of Confederate Prisons," *Journal of Southern History* 1, no. 1 (February 1935): pp. 56–66.
"Had Todd been at Andersonville": *Report on the Treatment of Prisoners of War,* p. 1065.
"killed toward the end": *Flake's Bulletin* (Galveston), November 8, 1867, p. 2.

183   "was wounded": Emilie's statement is technically accurate, though misleading. *HI,* p. 694.
"one at Corinth": This statement, however, is beyond misleading. Unidentifiable issue of the *Confederate Veteran,* Townsend Collection, UKY (series F, box 8, folder 1).
"lay mortally wounded": Helm, *Mary, Wife of Lincoln,* p. 207. Helm's book also includes a quotation, supposedly from Emilie's diary: "I have lost my husband, they have lost their fine little son, Willie, and Mary and I have lost three brothers in the Confederate service" (pp. 221–22). It is impossible to

believe that Emilie miscounted the number of brothers she lost during the war. Either she or her daughter, purposely or otherwise, misremembered the facts. This calls into question the veracity (though not the usefulness) of the diary excerpt itself, a subject more fully discussed in the note beginning "Mr. Lincoln and my sister," chapter 5.

183   he had escaped Vicksburg without a scratch: David Todd to Betsey Todd, July 5, 1863, Helm Papers, KHS.

vomiting up blood like a harpooned whale: Charles Carroll Gray Diary, August 18, 1861, SHC.

short obituary notices ... list David's cause of death as "consumption": *Galveston Tri-Weekly News*, August 2, 1871, p. 1; *Philadelphia Inquirer*, August 1, 1871, pp. 1, 4.

"whore-house brawl": William H. Townsend to Harry E. Pratt, March 22, 1954, in Townsend Papers, ALPL.

"he was not born to die": Charles Carroll Gray Diary, August 30, 1861, SHC.

"peculiar situation": Jas. Gilkeson to Elizabeth Todd, February 7, 1867, Helm Papers, KHS.

until after her death: A notice of Betsey's death appeared in the *New York Times*, February 18, 1874, p. 1: "Mrs. R. S. Todd, the step-mother of Mrs. Abraham Lincoln, died on Saturday morning at the residence of Mrs. Emily T. Helm, in Madison, Ind. The remains will be taken to Lexington, Ky., for interment."

184   "In memory of my boys": Marie Louise Pointe, "Abraham Lincoln's True Love Story," an article from the *New Orleans Picayune* among the clippings in the Helm Papers, KHS.

"drown the troubles": Preston to Elodie Todd Dawson, December 12, 1864, Dawson Papers, SHC.

"I try to console myself": Elodie Todd Dawson to Emilie Todd Helm, September 16, 1877, Townsend Collection, UKY.

By late summer Elodie was bedridden: all details and quotations in this paragraph can be found in unsigned to Emilie Todd Helm, November 15, 1877, Townsend Collection, UKY.

185   Mary lolled inconsolably ... while servants and interlopers looted the downstairs: In *Mary Todd Lincoln*, Jean Baker partly shields Mary from the charge that she looted the White House herself, pointing to a few instances in which objects belonging to the house later showed up elsewhere. There is ample evidence, however, that Mary pillaged her share and more. See Michael Burlingame, ed., *At Lincoln's Side: John Hay's Civil War Correspondence and Selected Writings* (Carbondale: Southern Illinois University, 2000), p. 200–201.

"Mary has had much to bear": *HI*, p. 444.

"monster of mankind": Quoted in Jean Baker, *Mary Todd Lincoln*, p. 349.

186   "I would not care": Mary Lincoln to Mrs. White, December 14, 1866, GLC. On Mary Lincoln's trial and confinement, see Jean Baker, *Mary Todd Lincoln*, pp. 315–50; and Mark E. Neely, Jr., and R. Gerald McMurtry, *The Insanity File: The Case of Mary Todd Lincoln* (Carbondale: Southern Illinois University Press, 1986).

187   "It is the most natural": Quoted in Jean Baker, *Mary Todd Lincoln*, p. 340.

"Aunt Lizzie's interference": Ibid.

"the happy era": Elizabeth Edwards to Emilie Todd Helm, April 29, undated, Helm Papers, KHS.

"We are both unusually feeble": Elizabeth Edwards to Emilie Todd Helm, June 22, undated, Helm Papers, KHS.

"somber years": Elizabeth Edwards to Emilie Todd Helm, April 29, undated, Helm Papers, KHS.

"Insanity appeared": Elizabeth Edwards to Robert Todd Lincoln, August 13, 1875, Robert Todd Lincoln Papers, ALPL. See also Wayne C. Temple, *Abraham Lincoln: From Skeptic to Prophet* (Mahomet, Ill.: Mayhaven Publishing, 1995), p. 384.

"wayward girl": Ada Bailhache to Truman Bartlett, July 4, 1912, Truman Bartlett Papers, Boston University. I am indebted to Michael Burlingame for calling this reference to my attention.

"never recovered from": Ibid.

"The disappointments": Elizabeth Edwards to Emilie Todd Helm, December 3, undated, Helm Papers, KHS.

188   "the most quick-tempered": Evans, *Mrs. Abraham Lincoln*, p. 46.

Ann buried herself: Elizabeth Edwards to Emilie Todd Helm, September 28, undated, Helm Papers, KHS.

"from exposure in the service": *Transactions of the Illinois State Historical Society* 32 (1925): p. 91.

"fistulous openings": Charles Ryan to Edward Wallace, March 4, 1865, Lincoln Papers, LOC.

"sweetly situated": Elizabeth Edwards to Emilie Todd Helm, September 28, undated, Helm Papers, KHS.

"taciturn . . . cold & reserved": Elizabeth L. Norris to Emilie Todd Helm, September 28, 1895, Norris Collection, ALPL.

189   "have some of the money": "The Confederate Treasury," *Charlotte News*, May 10, 1892, p. 3.

"there might be rioting": Ibid.

"magnificent epic": quoted in William C. Davis, *An Honorable Defeat: The Last Days of the Confederate Government* (New York: Harcourt, 2001), p. v.

George had a long and successful medical practice: All quotations in the paragraph can be found in "A South Carolina Sensation," *Charlotte Observer*, May 24, 1892, p. 1; "A Shocking Affair," *The (Columbia) State*, May 25, 1892, p. 3; *Dallas Morning News*, May 29, 1892, p. 2.

190   Martha died in 1889: All details and quotations in this paragraph are taken from W. A. Evans, *Mrs. Abraham Lincoln*, p. 50.

her first cousin Percy Dawson: Lawrence Percy Dawson was himself an interesting character. In 1886, his father, Nathaniel, was appointed commissioner of education and took the seventeen-year-old Percy to Washington as his confidential clerk. Three years later, Percy was arrested for raiding the Bureau of Education's stamp box. Ironically, he later became a Dallas County sheriff and was shot and killed in 1925 while attempting to settle a land dispute. See *Columbus Enquirer-Sun*, November 11, 1886, p. 3; *Washington Post*, October 31, 1889, p. 1; *Washington Post*, November 1, 1889, p. 8; *Macon Weekly Telegraph*, October 31, 1889, p. 2; telegraph, Selma to

Lexington, August 27, 1925: "Father killed this after. in discharge of Duty, Nat Dawson," Townsend Collection, UKY.

190   "a lecturer upon English literature," "So far as I have looked," and "well worthy": Handbill in miscellaneous writings, Helm Papers, KHS.

191   "live as long as . . . [Kentucky's] fair daughters": "A Sketch of General Ben Hardin Helm," originally published in *The Land We Love*, June 1867, pp. 163–67; among the clippings in the Helm Papers, KHS.

This, then, was Emilie's job: Emilie might have escaped the tropes of Confederate widowhood. She had remarkable powers as a raconteur, and while she might not have been able to make a living as an author, she might have used her inventiveness to imagine a different life for herself. One of her unpublished pieces — the story of a honey farmer who tells all his troubles to his bees — is quite sublime. But most of Emilie's fiction serves the Cause she called "not Lost but sleeping." One such tale — "The Spirit of 1860" — concerns a freedwoman named Chloe, an obvious proxy for Emilie's own Mammy Sally. After Emancipation, Chloe not only refuses to leave her widowed mistress but actually supports the white family by taking in laundry. After the mistress dies, Chloe's "white chillen" lovingly repay their debt: "The two survivors of that little family have never allowed Chloe to work. They bought a lot and put her up a little home. Chloe has an old fashioned garden full of pinks and roses that bloom fresh every summer; the best of these are reserved for the graves of her dear 'white people.'"

If "The Spirit of 1860" betrays Emilie's hope for race relations, "How Emily Phillips Changed Her Name" betrays her fears. In this semiautobiographical tale set during Reconstruction, a white woman named Emily *Phillips* is locked in a war of words with a black namesake. As a slave, the black woman had just been "Emily"; now, like most new freedmen, she has taken the surname of her former owners. Black Emily and white Emily live in the same town. The local postman, who is black, delivers all packages marked "Emily Phillips" to black Emily. The local postmaster, just to be insulting, does the same with all of white Emily's letters. Tired of her mail being picked over and broken into, white Emily lectures black Emily "on the subject of her acquired name," but she meets resistance: "With flashing eyes and arms akimbo on her comfortable fat sides she told me that Fore God she had as much right to her name as I had to mine." Finally, in the story's denouement, white Emily outmaneuvers her nemesis and reclaims sole possession of her name.

The story might be called gifted if it had *any* consciousness of how much it reveals. White Emily's very identity is challenged by the sudden appearance of a black version of herself.

"The Spirit of 1860," "How Emily Phillips Changed Her Name," and UDC speech containing the quote, "not lost but sleeping," all in miscellaneous writings, Helm Papers, KHS.

"not think ill [of] a nephew": Robert Todd Lincoln to Emilie Todd Helm, July 4, 1909, Robert Todd Lincoln Papers, CHS.

192   "Mother, why would you": Tom Stephens to author, October 13, 2006, based on his own interviews with Mary Genevieve Townsend Murphy at Helm Place. For more details on the burning of the diary, see William H. Townsend to Philip R. Baker, January 18, 1955, in Townsend Papers, ALPL.

Index